TAIWANESE CULTURE, TAIWANESE SOCIETY

A Critical Review of Social Science Research Done on Taiwan

Stephen O. Murray and Keelung Hong

UNIVERSITY
PRESS OF
AMERICA

JUN   '95

Lanham • New York • London

Copyright © 1994 by
University Press of America,® Inc.

Way
d 20706

reet
England

ved
tes of America
Information Available

Library of Congress Cataloging-in-Publication Data
Murray, Stephen O.
Taiwanese culture, Taiwanese society : a critical review of
social science research done on Taiwan / by Stephen O. Murray
and Keelung Hong.
p.   cm.
Includes bibliographical references and index.
1. Taiwan—Social conditions.   2. Taiwan—Civilization.
I. Hong, Keelung. II. Title.
HN747.M87   1994   306'.095124'9—dc20   93–48342 CIP

ISBN 0–8191–9433–6 (cloth : alk. paper)
ISBN 0–8191–9434–4 (pbk. : alk. paper)

 The paper used in this publication meets the minimum requirements of
American National Standard for Information Sciences—Permanence
of Paper for Printed Library Materials, ANSI Z39.48–1984.

in memory of

洪盛

洪劉仁

and the many other victims
of Chinese domination of Taiwan

Contents

Preface
by Keelung Hong[*]

Like my parents, I was born on a Taiwan that was a part of the Japanese Empire. I was a young child when the Chinese army of Chiang Kai-Shek slaughtered tens of thousands of Taiwanese. We had to compete with privileged invaders for higher education and positions using the language of Beijing imposed by the mainlander dictators, rather than using my mother-tongue, Holo (Hokkien), the language of more than four-fifths of the people on Taiwan. As for Native Americans in reservation schools, my school classmates were turned into spies to make sure that no one used our mother tongue. If we used our native language—even to say each others' names—we were punished. We had been renamed in Beijinghua, just as the names of our cities and villages had, and were required to use those imposed by Chinese tyrants. Rather like the Afrikaners who began as Dutch colonists but were cut off from their ancestral homeland and treated those people who preceded them in South Africa as inferior, those who had lost "the mandate of heaven" to rule China and were cut off from their ancestral homeland treated Taiwanese as subhuman.

My father had struggled most of his life to gain a decent job under the Japanese colonial regime which also had limited the number of Taiwanese in managerial roles. In 1952, three years after the Republic of China armies were crushed on the mainland and Chiang Kai-Shek fled to Taiwan, my father was forced out of his job in one of the state monopolies. I was nine years old and he was 50. He was never employed again, and struggled to support ten children on the small amount of land that he owned. He told us that his job was taken away to give to a mainlander, not because he couldn't or wasn't doing the job well. In short, the reason he lost his job was that he was Taiwanese. Like many Taiwanese officials of the government and the government monopolies, he was punished for "collaborating" with the Japanese. Never mind that a Chinese government gladly gave Taiwan to Japan without consulting anyone living on Taiwan in 1895. Never mind that the KMT had not claimed Taiwan prior to World War II. Everything on the island was

---

* An earlier version entitled "How I Became Taiwanese and Why It Matters" was presented as a plenary address to the 1992 national meetings of the Taiwanese-American Citizen's League held at Mills College in Oakland, California. I would like to acknowwledge the support of Yen Chuang Foundation for the preparation of this book.

treated as spoils of war to the KMT, who claimed that they had won the war. In the first years, they grabbed anything of value on Taiwan that could be moved and shipped it to their homeland. After they lost China, they took jobs from our fathers.

They also commandeered most of the rice. During the time of Japanese rule, Taiwan had been a major exporter of food, but we were not very far from starvation under our new rulers. When I was growing up, there was rarely anything more substantial to eat than rice soup with some soy sauce or a few fermented black beans. I remember very well my mother telling me that she hoped that I would have a good enough future that I would be able to have full bowls of dry rice, instead of rice soup swallowed with the bitterness of knowing that my father no longer had a job because he was regarded as not being sufficiently Chinese.

I did well in school, memorizing whatever was required. We were officially Chinese, but second-class Chinese. I was taught that the language and customs of my people were inferior to the language and culture of the Middle Kingdom as improved upon by Sun Yat-Sen and Chiang Kai-Shek. We were considered barely civilized descendants of pirates and head-hunters. Our language was considered corrupted by what the keepers of the great Chinese tradition treated as Polynesian baby-talk (for being filled with reduplications). In the view of the Chinese who ruled us and tried to suppress our festivals, folk religion, and folk healing, we were addicted to backward, wasteful superstitions instead of being dutiful followers of the wise and virtuous Chiang Kai-Shek.

Even before I left home to go to high school and college, I hardly saw my family. I left early in the day and returned late at night. I rarely spoke Holo, and it became difficult for my parents to understand their son who mixed in so much Beijinghua when he tried to speak Holo. After compulsory military service, I was able to leave Taiwan and to undertake graduate study in the United States. Here I was able to speak Holo with my friends. Expecting that I would be even harder to understand than before I left Taiwan, members of my family were pleasantly surprised that my Holo improved in the United States.

Emigration from Taiwan was one of the few ways in which Taiwanese of my generation could better our lot. Even now, most of the elite positions in the government and the institutions controlled by the government are occupied by mainlanders or by their children. Our best chance to get ahead was to get out. Emigration was the escape valve for the oppressive system of the Chinese oligarchy. Even though most Americans are unable to distinguish Taiwan from Thailand or China, we had a better chance to compete in our third language in North America than we had on Taiwan in our second language. Most of us—my immigrant generation and the following generation born in America—

are here because Taiwanese were discriminated against by a supposed "Republic of China" that exists nowhere else except on Taiwan.

In the United States I was also able to read about the history of Chiang Kai-Shek and the KMT and the 1947 massacres. Reading George Kerr's *Formosa Betrayed,* I understood that the reign of terror in which tens of thousands of Taiwanese were slaughtered frightened my parent's generation into silence. The fear of expressing feelings was the same as what I observed in Prague under communist rule. Criticism of the Chinese dictators on Taiwan remained very dangerous, and it was sedition even to discuss independence for Taiwan (even without advocating it). We knew that claiming that the so-called "Republic of China" was a bulwark of "the Free World" was a malicious joke, but in the Taiwan I left in the late-1960s, it was impossible to say so out loud or in print: freedom of speech definitely was no part of "Free China"!

As I said, in American university libraries I was able to read about Taiwan and the injustices Taiwanese suffered, most spectacularly in the 1947 massacres. I was even able to read about Formosan nationalism, and I also was able to read about and to observe other peoples' sufferings and determination to preserve an identity. I suppose that if the Kuomintang had made Holo and Hakka the official languages in 1945, if they had not discriminated against Taiwanese, if they had not replaced people like my father with Chinese, we might not feel so Taiwanese. But, as I hope I have shown in my own history, the Chinese ruling Taiwan made the difference between mainlanders and Taiwanese crucially important. We were discriminated against in schools and in getting jobs. With rationalizations about language and origin, we were constantly reminded of our differences, all of which were treated as instances of our inferiority to the "real Chinese." The boundaries between the ruling Chinese minority from the mainland and the Taiwanese majority were drawn by those with power who systematically undercut our chances to get ahead. They did not count common traits and stress what was shared by Taiwanese and Chinese. Whatever similarities in language, culture, and genes existed, the Chinese emphasized their distinctness from and superiority to Taiwanese (even while, for external consumption, with the aid of American social scientists, they were minimizing differences, claiming Han unity with Taiwanese "brothers" who had been Ming loyalists through more than three centuries of Manchurian and Japanese interludes). The Chinese rulers made being Taiwanese matter a great deal! And they have also sought to foster internal divisions, to play aboriginal tribes and Hakka-speakers against Holo-speakers in the same way that the ethnic minority ruling South Africa seeks to play those from one tribal background against those from another.

Although I have learned many things about Taiwan from reading what has been written in English, as I read social science studies I had some unpleasant surprises, as well as the occasional pleasures of recognizing facets of Taiwanese culture. The greatest shock, when I began to look at American ethnographies of Taiwanese villages, was to see that the customs and beliefs that the Chinese viewed with such contempt, and actively sought to destroy, were represented as "traditional Chinese culture." A euphoria at not being regarded as inferior quickly wore off. It was very odd to see what are supposed to be native terms not in Holo, the language of the people who use them, but in Beijinghua, the language of the people who dismiss our religion and customs. I know that when anthropologists write in English about groups numbering in the hundreds in Amazonia, they do not present native terms in Portuguese or in Spanish. Similarly, concepts from African tribes embedded in English texts are not translated into French or Afrikaans first. They are represented in the native language, not in the language of the government, even when—unlike Taiwan—the language of the government is the language of the majority of the country's population.

I soon realized that American anthropologists and mainland Chinese on Taiwan were not interested in Taiwanese culture. They seemed to be looking at us, but were really looking through us to try to see some traditional Chinese culture without seeing our historical experiences and what we made of it (Taiwanese culture). Being invisible or transparent constituted only a slight promotion in the valuation of our culture, because this work legitimates robbing us of our language and justifies subordinating our culture to the so-called great tradition of Chinese civilization, just as we are economically and politically subordinated to the ethnic minority dictatorship which still rules Taiwan under the fiction of being the "Republic of China."[1]

It was immediately obvious to me that publication of fieldwork on Taiwan obliterated Taiwanese culture to claim the higher-prestige object of study, Chinese culture. Foreign scholars' use of the language of domination has been ideologically useful to the KMT in legitimating suppression of the majority's language, as well as our aspirations to self-government as Taiwanese rather than Chinese, and for maintaining the pretense of there being a "Republic of China" and keeping unthinkable any "Republic of Taiwan."

---

[1] For those unfamiliar with the Kuomintang's (KMT) need for this fiction it is quite simple. In the territory actually controlled by the KMT, three million mainlanders are a small minority. If, however, the KMT represented a billion Chinese, twenty million Taiwanese would be a minority. Thus, the proportional representation in the government that rules only Taiwan is based on this second calculus.

To try to understand this complicity with the domination of my people I enlisted the help of the sociologist and historian of anthropology Stephen Murray, who has written—in his native language—analyses based on the confrontation of texts produced by American, American-trained, and American-influenced social scientists with my own experience of Taiwan and that of other natives I know. We begin by looking at the writings of the most widely-known work done on Taiwan, proceed to review several other lines of research, and then turn to suggesting some reasons for the curious attempts by American anthropologists to be giraffes looking across water of the Taiwan Straits at China, while ignoring the fact that they are standing on a land mass that has become "developed" and polluted while most of them were dreaming, along with the remnants of a defeated Chinese army, about vanished Chinese dynasties and some timeless Chinese essence.

Irritated by an earlier version of part of this book, Hill Gates told me that "anthropologists are not the enemy." While I agree with her that much so-called "political science" touching on Taiwan shares more "free China" fantasies than do the village and urban neighborhood studies done by anthropologists, the denial of and tacit complicity with derogation and destruction of our language and culture by anthropologists are especially insidious. I wish that it were true, as Gates maintained, that American anthropologists had helped or were helping preserve components of our culture. Unfortunately, they were and are instead co-operating with official ethnocide and linguicide by an army of occupation foisted on Taiwan by the winning side in World War II. As soon as they could get the consent of the set of autocrats ruling mainland China, most of the anthropologists who had done fieldwork on Taiwan moved to their real interest, China, and happily prostituted themselves to another set of oppressive masters who think their illegitimacy can be shored up by foreign research.

This book critically describes what they did before they moved on. It is not intended to be a description or even an outline of what Taiwanese culture is, but, rather, an interpretive review of the representations of Taiwanese realities in social science literature, especially anthropology. (For what we consider the best introduction to various topics in what has been published about Taiwan see the references boldfaced in the index.)

Introduction
by Stephen O. Murray

The "tribe" I studied in my doctoral dissertation research was American anthropologists.[1] I have done both participant observation and historical research on this tribe for nearly two decades, and am quite familiar with its standard operating procedures. If not always accepting them, at least taking native views seriously is fundamental to American anthropology—and has been since before its institutionalization by Franz Boas and his followers (i.e., back in the 19th century field researches of Cushing, Mooney, and others). Similarly, even those anthropologists who do not believe that language determines what a people think generally recognize the importance of people's languages to their identities and cosmologies, and are careful to preserve the terms used by the people they live with and study.[2] Orthography is a perennial problem, but I can think of nowhere other than Taiwan where the solution to writing "native terms" has been to translate them into the language of the colonial government. I was shocked to find not the native Hakka and Holo terms but translations into the alien administrative language (Beijinghua) commonly used in writing up fieldwork done on Taiwan.[3] Aghast to read in the official journal of the American Anthropological Association what I took to be a criticism by one anthropologist who has worked on Taiwan of another for using what

---

[1] *Social Science Networks*, University of Toronto, 1979; published as *Group Formation in Social Science* (Edmonton: Linguistic Research, Inc., 1983).

[2] Native views and terms, indeed, are the raw material extracted from developing countries or from the peripheries of developed countries and then manufactured into books and articles. See Dell H. Hymes, *Rethinking Anthropology* (New York: Random House, 1972), and Talal Asad, *Anthropology and the Colonial Encounter* (London: Ithaca Press, 1975) on scientific colonialism that refines the cultural and linguistic resources of various "others."

[3] Beijinghua is, of course, used in Taiwan, and if anthropologists had studied the ethnic minority oligarchy, it would be normal practice for them to use it. Anthropologists are more likely to do research for elites than to study elites, however, and the research they have done on Taiwan has been mostly of farmers (whom they often call "peasants"), laborers, and indigenous Taiwanese healers and priests.

people said (Holo rather than Beijinghua), I joined Keelung Hong in public criticism of the misrepresentation of Taiwanese terms.[4]

Interested in the social construction of phenomena to study (such as "traditional China"), I looked systematically at what has been written by anthropologists on the basis of research on Taiwan and discussed the claims made in this literature with Keelung Hong. Although the English phrasing of our critique is mine, most of the ideas (except those about the historical contexts of American scholarship) are his.

In the autumn of 1992, after decades of being blacklisted, he was able to return to Taiwan, and was able to show me some of what I had been reading about (through glasses of varying darkness!). In consultation with his family, Taiwanese and Taiwanese-American friends and a steady stream of visitors from Taiwan to the San Francisco Bay area, he not only challenged many particular claims in this literature but clearly saw and strongly reacted to the systematic bias obliterating Taiwanese realities in order to study the venerable and singular Chinese tradition. As has already been obvious in his preface, he did not appreciate anthropologists' complicity with a Chinese oligarchy that made being "Taiwanese" salient by making it a basis for discrimination, while advertising a singular "China" to external supporters, especially in America.

Although the translation of native terms into another language is unprecedented anthropological practice, complicity with various forms of domination is so often-precedented as to qualify as part of standard operating procedure, unfortunately. On Taiwan as elsewhere, "the colonial power structure made the object of anthropological study accessible and safe—because of it sustained physical proximity between the observing Europeans and the living non-Europeans became a practical possibility."[5] There may be limits to what anthropologists will do to

---

[4] It is possible that David Jordan only meant that there should be a list of characters in Robert Weller's *Unities and Diversities in Chinese Religion* (Seattle: University of Washington Press, 1987), not that Weller should have substituted Beijinghua terms for Holo ones, but Jordan did not support this interpretation either in his published reply nor in replying to a letter I wrote him asking him if that is what he meant. Jordan's review was in *American Anthropologist* 89(1987): 995; our critical response and his bland reply were in 90(1988):976-8. That attempting to achieve historical understanding does not preclude judgments I defend in the methodological appendix to my *Theory Groups in the North American Study of Language* (Amsterdam: John Benjamins, 1993).

[5] Asad, *op cit.*, p. 17. The same dynamic operated between Japanese or Chinese ethnographers and the aboriginal Austronesian-speaking tribes (whose members we refer to as "Formosans"). The corpus of research on

gain access to the field, but there do not seem to be any limits to what they will ignore once there, or to the silence those who want to return to "the field" will maintain back home about whatever the rulers do not want discussed.

Anthropologists are less well-funded than other social scientists and one should not mistake them for being part of the elite (at home or in the field). Rather, they depend upon rulers to be able to go into the field and, once there, are eager to avoid offending the official patrons they depend upon. Anthropologists' cultural hero Bronislaw Malinowski is a prototypical case: both in his eagerness to try to lure colonial sponsors and in the lack of buyer interest in the wares he was hawking.[6] The eagerness with which American anthropologists threw themselves into "applied anthropology"/"human engineering" in the World War II concentration camps for Japanese-Americans provides another repellant example.[7] Regimes generally have been little interested in renting anthropologists to apply anthropological "knowledge," although the cover of anthropological "science" is sometimes useful for spies, and, occasionally, information about local lifeways is sought by armies of occupation or other administrators.

these "primitive" Taiwanese cultures are not considered here, because neither author reads Japanese. See the bibliography in Herbert Passin's "A Note on Japanese Research in Formosa," *American Anthropologist* 49 (1947):514-18. For an overview of research on Formosans published in Chinese see the special issue of the *Bulletin of the Institute of Ethnology, Academia Sinica* 40 (1975), entitled *Symposium on Taiwan Aborigines: Retrospect and Prospect.*

6 The prostitution of science varies in consciousness, with Malinowski's being very conscious and open. Current officials of the American Anthropological Association recoil in a horror (that I think is contrived) at what they see as attributing motives to anthropologists or officials. Attributing motives to non-American non-elites does not seem to concern them in quotidian ethnographic practice, but rather than rail at their double standard, I want to make clear that statements about complicity and other interpretations do not claim privileged insight into intents or presume servants' consciousness of whose interests they serve. On the other hand, I do not think most anthropologists are as naive as the genre conventions of the well-intentioned, ignorant and bumbling ethnograper pretend.

7 See Orin Starn, "Engineering Internment: Anthropologists and the War Relocation Authority," *American Ethnologist* 13 (1986):700-20; Peter T. Suzuki, "Anthropologists in the Wartime Camps for Japanese Americans," *Dialectical Anthropology* 6 (1981): 23-60.

Practitioners of other social science disciplines are also for rent (if not at quite so low a rate as anthropologists) to whomever will pay for research. The so-called "Republic of China" has sponsored political "scientists," and also economists and sociologists, all of whom have been more than willing to ignore the Taiwanese majority and the manner of rule by the heavily-armed Chinese oligarchy. In the annotated bibliography we have sampled these other literatures, although we have not covered such work as thoroughly as the anthropological writings. The main focus of our analysis of the social science literature on Taiwan is on culture, the unit claimed by anthropologists. For all the literature on religion and shamanism, some anthropologists looked at land reform, labor force movement and allocation, etc. in history, so American anthropologists have not treated "culture" as wholly idealist or fixed.

We do not endeavor to substitute a more-constrained-in-space-and-time essence "Taiwanese culture" for the essence "Chinese culture" stretching across millennia and a huge space. The salience of a "Taiwanese"/"Chinese" distinction was constructed (initially by Chinese) in history: first the contempt of Ming and then Qing officials for the troublesome island colony which the latter dyansty's officials were eventually happy to unload to Japan; most saliently, after World War II, by the discriminations and derogations by the mainlander oligarchy that the US deposited on Taiwan after defeating Japan in World War II.[8]

The aftermath of Yugoslavia and of the Soviet empire show that resentments for ethnic dominations may smoulder for decades and even centuries. We hope that, once the fiction of "Republic of China" is abandoned, the World United Formosans for Independence platform's

---

[8] See "Class and ethnicity" below. Under Leninist regimes generally, there is a "split between the State, which people feel is not theirs, though it claims to be their owner, and the motherland, of which they are the guardians" (Lezek Kolakowski, *Modernity on Endless Trial*, University of Chicago Press, 1990, p. 59). This split is all the more acute on Taiwan where the fatherland extolled by the regime is overseas (China). The "deep-rooted sense of belonging to a unified civilization that boasts several thousand years of uninterrupted history" David Yen-Ho Wu says is "an important aspect of being Chinese" ("The Construction of Chinese and Non-Chinese Identities," *Dædalus* 120,2 (1990), p. 160) is less-than-fully available to Taiwanese and difficult even for mainlanders on Taiwan to sustain, given the interruption of their tenure and knowledge of events on the Chinese mainland since their flight, or their parents'.

respect for language and cultural differences[9] will prevail and that Taiwanese will neither be victims of new Chinese oppression, nor avengers of the wrongs they have suffered on the remaining post-World War II Chinese colonists and their (born-on-Taiwan) descendants. The US government has been to such a considerable extent responsible for the imposition of Chiang Kai-Shek and his followers on the Taiwanese that no American is in any position to tell Taiwanese that they are "Chinese" (or "brothers" of Chinese or that Taiwanese cultures and languages share so many features with Chinese cultures and languages that they should not claim to be Taiwanese). I believe that there are human rights that should be respected and that one of these is a right to self-determination—for Taiwan and Tibet among others. This right need not depend on the existence of a distinct culture (or language or history or religion).

By no means is the right to self-determination the only basis for recording and celebrating Taiwanese culture(s). Asserting that there is a Taiwanese reality tends to correlate to other politics than the conceptual ethnic-cleansing of positing a single Chinese essence. Either claim has political repercussions (whatever the intent of those categorizing phenomena as "Taiwanese" or as "Chinese").[10] There is no fixed and value-free standard of the amount of cultural difference that justifies a state. Ethnic groups are fuzzily-bounded,[11] as nation states generally

---

[9] Among the goals of WUFI specified in the first convention that could be held in Taiwan (in 1992) are "to respect the mother tongues of all Taiwanese ethnic groups... to found an open and pluralistic society... to safeguard the rights and interests of the indigenous peoples... [and] to ensure completely open access to electronic media."

[10] Some consider using "Taiwanese" as "political" and "Chinese" as neutral. Anthropologists have a great deal of difficulty in seeing that accepting official definitions and labels of situations is as political as using those of oppressed minorities and that to accept (and reproduce) the lexicon of dominators provides them undeserved legitimation. The notion of distinct, homogeneous cultures is deeply entrenched in social theory and in anthropological practice even in fashionably postmodernist mystifications of power differentials. A singular essence "Chinese culture" is far from being the only one assiduously maintained.

[11] See Fredrik Barth, *Ethnic Groups as Boundaries* (Boston: Little Brown, 1969). For examples, see Alma Gottlieb, *Under the Kapok Tree: Identity and Difference in Beng Thought* (Bloomington: Indiana University Press); Lin Poyer, "Maintaining 'Otherness': Sapwuahfik Cultural Identity," *American Ethnologist* 15 (1988):472-485. Even Wu, op. cit. p. 167, acknowledges that "the differences between two Han groups can, in some cases, be more pronounced than that between a Han and a so-

are not (even when territorial claims overlap). The Republic of Taiwan will be multi-ethnic and multilingual and, we can only hope that it will be more tolerant of its diversity than the Republic of China and the Americans who it has permitted or aided to do research on Taiwan have been. "Neither leveled nor levellers be" is my envoi both to Taiwanese and to aliens who study Taiwan.

Place Names

Except in titles or in direct quotations, county (guan) names are Holo. Clockwise from capital (followed by the one inland county and the "Pescadores" islands these are:

Taiwanese (Beijinghua)	Characters
Daiba (Taipei)	台北
Gilan (Ilan)	宜蘭
Hualien (Hualien)	花蓮
Daidan (Taitung)	台東
Bindong (Pingtung)	屏東
Go'hiong (Kaohsiung)	高雄
Dailam (Tainan)	台南
Gayi (Jai'i)	嘉義
Huenlim (Yunlin)	雲林
Jianghua (Changhua)	彰化
Daidiong (Taichung)	台中
Miaoli(n) (Miaoli)	苗栗
Hsindi(t) (Hsinchu)	新竹
To-Hn (Taoyuan)	桃園
Lamdao (Nant'ou)	南投
Pei'o (Penghu)	澎湖

The cities that have the same name as the guan which contains them are also given in Holo. Names of villages and towns are listed as whichever author whose work we are considering wrote them. If an author shifted his or her romanization, the most recent one has been

---

called minority nationality group." On the Sapirian tradition of treating culture as a process of constructing meanings and identities rather than as an inventory of traits, see Dell Hymes, *op. cit.*, pp. 33-35, 46.

superimposed on annotations of earlier publications (but not into titles or direct quotations).

Native Terms

Despite some tendency to work close to the capital, ethnographers have for the most part not studied native speakers of Beijinghua (or other central or northern Chinese languages). Instead, they have studied native speakers of Hakka and Holo (Hokkien). In common with general anthropological practice everywhere but Taiwan, we endeavor either to render concepts in English or to use native terms, not to translate what is presented as "native terms" into a third language. If we were reviewing studies of Mediterranean, or European culture and society, reports of fieldwork in Portugal would present native terms in Portuguese, and reports of fieldwork in Catalonia would present native terms in Catalán rather than in the dominant "world language" from the Iberian peninsula, Spanish, a language to which both are genetically related, one which has many more speakers in the world, and one which is the official national language of a state which includes Catalonia.

Both Holo and Hakka are spoken outside Taiwan—and beyond Taiwan and China. Holo is probably known to more persons of Han descent in southeast Asia than any other Chinese language. Certainly, there are more native speakers of Holo in either China or Taiwan than there are native speakers of all the American Indian languages in the United States, and native terms from languages with only handsful of speakers are presented in anthropology journals without anyone proposing to translate them all into Navajo, the language known to more speakers (and probably to more anthropologists).[12]

Fieldwork done with speakers of other languages (Hakka, the Austronesian aboriginal languages, and also various Chinese languages including Beijinghua used for salvaging informants' memory culture of life in China) should render any native terms analyzed or quoted in the language of the people. Neither in political nor in scholarly practice do we advocate substituting suppression of everything but the majority language (Holo) for the current tyranny of a linguistic minority. We are not able to restore what has been rendered in Beijinghua into the languages of Taiwan other than Holo. If anything that was Hakka was mistaken for Beijinghua and has been rendered in Holo, this has been inadvertent. It

---

12 Representation in the fieldworkers' language is not neutral, either: see Talal Asad, "The Inequality of Languages," pp. 156-60 in J. Clifford & G. Marcus, *Writing Culture* (Berkeley: University of California Press, 1986).

is our strong conviction that in writing about Hakka communities, Hakka terms should be used, not translations into Holo, any more than into Beijinghua.[13]

On occasion, especially for some widely-used Beijinghua terms, English, Holo, and Beijinghua terms are listed. In the glossary, terms are listed alphabetically as romanized in the text, followed by an English gloss, and written Chinese characters. Although it is popularly believed that literate speakers of any Chinese language interprets characters the same way, this is a myth. There are written words which are unintelligible to speakers of some other Chinese languages. As the romanization reflects Holo pronunciation, the Chinese characters are (one, traditional form of) written Holo.

Another widely-diffused myth is that Chinese languages are entirely monosyllabic (that Chinese is the ultimate analytic language). This seems particularly inapt for place-names (placenames? toponyms) and hyphens have fallen by the wayside in many of our renderings.

We have resisted a strong temptation to do the same thing to personal names. However, we have capitalized the "second word," which might seem to move in the opposite direction from compounding syllables. The reason for capitalizing the "second word" is that the convention for names is to capitalize every separate component, and we did not want to provide any occasion for anyone to claim lesser dignity is given to persons with Chinese and Taiwanese names. We have vacillated on aggregating a number of "words" in various terms, so that some are, no doubt, inconsistently combined or differentiated.

The dominant romanization of Holo is laid out by Bodman in 1955.[14] So many consonants in it feel and look wrong to native speakers, that we have romanized *de novo*.[15] Readers familiar with Bodman

---

[13] On the complexity of valuation of languages in multi-ethnic societies see Kathryn A. Woolard, "Language Variation and Cultural Hegemony," *American Ethnologist* 12 (1985):738-48; Susan Gal, "Language and Political Economy," *Annual Review of Anthropology* 18 (1989):345-67; and exemplifcations in these two authors' other work, especially Gal's " Diversity and Contestation in Linguistic Ideologies," *Language in Society* 22:337-59..

[14] Nicholas Cleaveland Bodman et al. *Spoken Amoy Hokkien* (Kuala Lumpar, Malaya: Federation of Malaya Government Officers' Language School).

[15] The warrant for basing orthography on native form feeling is in Edward Sapir's 1933 "La réalité psychologique des phonèmes," *Journal de Psychologie Normale et Pathologique* 30:247-65 (the English original version of which was first published in David G. Mandelbaum (ed.), *Selected Writings of Edward Sapir in Language, Culture, Personality*

romanization (or in some cases with romanizations of closely cognate Beijinghua terms) will find many terminal consonants in parentheses to indicate that they are unvoiced. This may seem to some to introduce phantom terminal consonants. Others will be alarmed at the deletion of the usual profusion of glottal stops after the initial consonant. Some writers indicate glottal stops for every dental consonant. We believe these to be phantoms. Those which we hear are included. Many initial "s"s are indeed glottalized, and there should perhaps have been even more initial "hs" (or "x" as in pinyin) represented.

It is certainly not easy to romanize Holo—with its "swallowed" terminal consonants, possible widespread initial glottalization, and very complex system of tone gradations. Without extraordinarily technically involved representations, the elaborate tonal aspects of Holo cannot be displayed. The same romanization renders distinct words—not only is tone phonemic, but the number of vowels represented is too few. The romanizations do not provide sufficient uniqueness for linguistic analysis, but we are not attempting to provide a linguistic analysis of Holo, only to provide some approximation of terms for persons who cannot speak it. The glossary of characters should make clear to any Holo speakers which terms are involved—as should the English glosses in the text.

Other Bibliographies Concerned with Taiwan

For guidance through government publications dealing with demography, there is an annotated bibliography prepared by Henry Chang (1973). A selection from the massive amount of University of Michi-

---

(Berkeley: University of California Press, 1949). The immediate inspiration for going with romanizations that feel/look right to the native author was H. Russell Bernard, "Preserving Language Diversity," *Human Organization* 51 (1992):82-89, and the exemplar of those principles in H. Russell Bernard and Jesús Salinas Pedraza, *Native Ethnography: A Mexican Indian Describes His Own Culture* (Newbury Park, CA: Sage, 1989). General ones of enduring influence on me are Kenneth Hale's chapter "Some Questions about Anthropological Linguistics: The Role of Native Knowledge" in Hymes, *op. cit.*, pp. 382-97, and both Hymes's and Hale's longstanding advocacy of working with native speakers rather than privileging analysis by "professional" (often seemingly tonedeaf) outsiders. Such pioneers in the institutionalization and professionalization of American cultural and linguistic anthropology as Franz Boas, Alfred Kroeber, and Edward Sapir all fostered analyses by and collaborations with natives, as did Bronislaw Malinoski and A. A. Radcliffe-Brown in the British tradition of social anthropology.

gan research on family planning is contained in Cernada (1970). A synthesis is contained in R. Freedman (1969). Legal and administrative works are covered by Johnson (1988) and Miller and Miller (1988). A comprehensive unannotated bibliography of material published in English through the early 1980s was prepared by Jacobs, Hagner and Sedgley (1984). A general bibliography the selection criteria for inclusion in which are unobvious was prepared by Lee (1990). The annotated bibliography of Lee and Tai (1981) does not cover academic literature and does not cover non-academic literature very well:

Center for Quality of Life Studies (1984)*T'ai-wan ching chi fa chan Ying wen wen hsien mu lu. Ch'u pan* (Economic development in Taiwan: a selected bibliography) (Daiba: Center for Quality of Life Studies 1984).

Cernada, George P. (1970) *Taiwan Family Planning Reader: How a Program Works* (Dai-diong: Chinese Center for International Training in Family Planning).

Chang, Henry C. (1973) *Taiwan Demography: A Selected Annotated Bibliography of Government Documents* (Minneapolis: Center for Population Studies).

Freedman, Ronald (1969) *Family Planning in Taiwan* (Princeton University Press).

Jacobs, J. Bruce, Jean Hagner and Anne Sedgley (1984) *Taiwan: A Comprehensive Bibliography of English Language Publications* (Bundoora, Victoria: La Trobe University Borchardt Library).

Johnson, Constance A. (1988) *The Republic of China on Taiwan: A Selectively Annotated Bibliography of English-Language Legal Materials* (Washington, DC: Library of Congress Law Library).

Lee, Karen S., and Anna C. Tai (1981) *An Annotated Bibliography of Selected Work about the Republic of China* (Daiba: Kwang Hwa).

Lee Wei-Chin (1990) *Taiwan*. (Santa Barbara, CA: ABC-Clio).

Miller, E. Willard, and Ruby M. Miller(1988) *The Third World, Taiwan*. (Monticello, IL: Vance Public Administration Bibliographies).

Looking Through Taiwan To See "Traditional" China*

Taiwan is a small, densely populated, and now highly industrialized island on which the American social science research on "Chinese" culture and society was concentrated from the late 1950s through the late 1970s, at the same as time Taiwan was rapidly industrializing. Japanese and Chinese anthropologists working on Taiwan prior to the 1970s studied the aboriginal enclaves in the mountains of the island. Bernard Gallin and Rita Gallin recalled that they found sociologists at National Taiwan University, not anthropologists, interested in their work during their first trips (during the late 1950s and early 1960s) to do fieldwork in rural Taiwan.[1] Arthur Wolf similarly recalled that, into the 1960s,

> Chinese and foreign anthropologists studying Taiwan practiced a strict division of labor. The Chinese studied the aborigines, and the foreigners studied the Chinese [Taiwanese]. The two groups exchanged reprints and dinner invitations, but when they went to

* Portions of this introduction were presented at the 1989 annual meetings of the American Anthropological Association in Washington, and of the North American Taiwanese Professors' Association at the University of Maryland. We would like to acknowledge the encouragement and comments by the audiences as well as by Roberto Alvarez, Fredrik Barth, Russell Bernard, Regna Darnell, Judith Farquhar, Richard Stamps, William Tang, David Tsai, Amparo Tusón, and Unni Wikan. We are especially deeply indebted to Donald Nonini, whose painstaking reading of an earlier version much enhanced the readability of the text as well as steering us away from some mistakes and dubious interpretations. Earlier versions of various parts of this introduction have been published in *Dialectical Anthropology* 16 (©1991 by Kluwer Academic Publishing), *Typhoon* (courtesy of the Taiwan Forum of the University of California, Berkeley), the *Taiwan Tribune*, the *Northern California Formosan Federation Newsletter*, and as a working paper of El Instituto Obregón.

[1] Bernard and Rita S. Gallin, "The Rural-to-Urban Migration of Anthropologists in Taiwan," pp. 223-248 in G. Foster & R. Kemper (Eds.), *Anthropologists in Cities* (Boston: Little Brown, 1974).

the field they went in different directions to study different problems.[2]

Our interest in this volume is with research on the culture of Hakka- and Holo- (Hokkien-) speakers. Their ancestors left behind the elaborate lineages of southern China, mostly between the 17th and 19th century. Native speakers of Hakka and Hokkien whose ancestors resided on Taiwan prior to Japanese occupation in 1895 generally call themselves "Taiwanese" in contrast to the Polynesians (Formosans) there before them and the influx of "mainlanders" who arrived on Taiwan between the defeat of Japan in World War II and the final defeat and evacuation of surviving remnants of the Kuomintang (henceforth KMT) bureaucracy and army from China in 1949. American anthropological work has focused almost exclusively on rural Hokkien- (Holo-) and Hakka-speakers, although "Taiwanese" includes those of Polynesian descent (which, to some degree, most Taiwanese are) and those of the children of those born in China who arrived during the late 1940s who identify themselves as "Taiwanese." There is a great deal of anthropological literature, if hardly any in English, on aboriginal tribesmen;[3] none on mainlanders' children who identify themselves as Taiwanese. Our review of representations by American social scientists recapitulates the concentration on Holo- and Hakka-speakers, but is not intended as endorsing narrowing "Taiwanese" to exclude anyone born on Taiwan and identifying as "Taiwanese" from the category.

Arthur Wolf and the Unthinkability of "Taiwanese"

Arthur Wolf was one of the first American social scientists to do fieldwork in rural Taiwan. His publications are the most cited anthropological work dealing with Taiwan and have considerable recognition outside East Asian studies. Having found what he was not originally looking for—a predominance of "minor marriages" in the southwestern portion of the Daiba ("Taipei") basin—he related his research on the implications of this phenomenon to a wider audience of social scientists than those interested in East Asia or in Pacific islands such as Taiwan. The high levels of daughters-in-law adopted at early ages (*simbua*) and

---

[2] Arthur P. Wolf, "The Study of Chinese Society on Taiwan" 3-16 in J. Hsieh & Y. Chuang (Eds.), *The Chinese Family and Its Ritual Behavior* (Nankang:Academia Sinica, 1985), p. 3.

[3] See the bibliography in Herbert Passin "A Note on Japanese Research in Formosa," *American Anthropologist* 49(1947):514-518. For an overview of Chinese work, see *Symposium on Taiwan Aborigines: Retrospect and Prospect* (=Bulletin of the Institute of Ethnology, Academica Sinica 40, 1975).

of uxorilocal residence which Wolf and others found to have been very common in northern Taiwan (forty-one and fifteen percent, respectively), do not fit with the norms for the "traditional patriarchal Chinese family" at all.[4] Division of household assets (*huen ge hue*) during the lifetime of the father would seem to constitute another anomaly to "traditional China."[5] Such patterns, though later attenuated, would seem to evidence important cultural differences between "traditional Taiwan" of the first four decades of the twentieth century and mainland "traditional China."[6] That they have been the central focus of Wolf's work makes all the more startling his practice of promoting a view of a single Chinese essence.

Wolf, who continues to find the records of the Japanese Empire the best place to study imperial China, asserts that only historians "still insist on treating China as though it had the internal consistency of rice pudding."[7] Although, in this passage and elsewhere, Wolf seems to acknowledge diversity, it is always within a singular "Chinese society"

---

[4] Arthur P. Wolf and Chieh Shang Huang, *Marriage and Adoption in China* (Stanford: Stanford University Press, 1980), pp. 125, 318. Also see Burton Pasternak, "Age at First Marriage in a Taiwanese Locality 1916-1945," *Journal of Family History* 14(1989): 91-117. The high rate of uxorilocal marriage should not have come as a surprise, since George W. Barclay, *Colonial Development and Population in Taiwan* (Princeton University Press, 1954), pp. 228-9, had reported fifteen to twenty percent of Taiwanese marriages between 1906 and 1930 were uxorilocal, and noted a subsequent decline to six percent by 1943.

[5] Pressures and cultural expectations for early family division are a central concern in his then-wife Margery Wolf's *Women and the Family in Rural Taiwan* (Stanford University Press, 1972). In contrast another pioneer American ethnographer of rural Taiwan, Bernard Gallin, explicitly distinguished Taiwanese and Chinese practices in the first American ethnography of a Taiwanese village, *Hsin Hsing, Taiwan* (Berkeley: University of California Press, 1966).

[6] Although few anthropologists today are as determined to sort out the sources of cultural traits as Boasians and diffusionists were in the first third of the 20th century, there is still an equation of genuine with original, a distaste for historical complexity, and a continuing quest for at least relative "purity" of "tradition." See Hubert Fichte, *Lazarus und die Waschmaschine*. Frankfurt/m: Fischer, p. 285; Stephen O. Murray, "Die ethnoromantische Versuchung," in Hans-Peter Duerr (ed.), *Der Wissenschaftler und das Irrationale,* ed. by , vol. 1, pp. 377-385 (Frankfurt/m: Syndikat, 1981).

[7] Arthur P. Wolf, "The Study of Chinese Society on Taiwan" in J. Hsieh & Y. Chuang (eds.), *The Chinese Family and Its Ritual Behavior* (Nankang:Academia Sinica, 1985), p. 15.

or "Chinese culture." Also, since he and his students deploy a single one of the Chinese languages, Beijinghua, his statement that "most anthropologists are now convinced that Chinese society is as varied in expression as the Chinese language" may concede very little. For that matter, rice pudding is often not homogeneous and does not merely blend together its diverse ingredients, but frequently includes (unassimilated alien) elements like raisins that are distinct from rice. Despite Wolf's nominal recognition of diversity, his practice is one of relentless analysis of "Chinese" society.

Singular nouns modified by "Chinese" and not "Taiwanese" appear in the titles of all Wolf's books, even though there is generally an acknowledgement that the data from Taiwan which are at least the major ingredient, when not the only source of data, may not be representative. For instance, "Considering the source of most of the original data we are presenting, this book might appropriately have been entitled *Marriage and Adoption in Rural Haishan.* We chose *Marriage and Adoption in China* because we believe our argument has implications for the study of Chinese domestic organization generally, not because we view Hai-shan as representative of China."[8]

Considering that Wolf and Huang marshall data from various areas of Taiwan, not just from Haishan, "Marriage and Adoption in Taiwan" or "Marriage and Adoption in Japanese-Ruled Taiwan" might have been considered. Modesty in claiming generalizability somehow just never makes it into Wolf's titles, although his students sometime skip to the local level in theirs.[9] "Taiwanese society", "Taiwanese culture," and "Taiwanese family" are literally unthinkable to Wolf and to some of his students.

In his contribution to *The Anthropology of Taiwanese Society* Wolf covered "domestic organization."[10] He brought himself to use "Taiwanese" six times—in contrast to twenty-five "Chinese" and "Hakka" or "Hokkien" seven times. Even in a volume manifestly about Taiwan, he used the phrase "Chinese family" exclusively. Wolf and other anthropologists writing about religion based on field materials from Taiwan end up with gods, ghosts, and ancestors and/or Buddhism, Confucianism,

---

[8] Wolf and Huang, op. cit., pp. ix-x

[9] E.g., Donald R. De Glopper, "Religion and Ritual in Lukang," in A. Wolf (ed.), *Religion and Ritual in Chinese Society* (Stanford University Press, 1974), pp. 43-69; C[lyde] Stevan Harrell, *Ploughshare Village: Culture and Context in Taiwan.* (Seattle: University of Washington Press, 1982).

[10] Arthur P. Wolf, "Domestic Organization" in E. Ahern and H. Gates (eds.), *The Anthropology of Taiwanese Society* (Stanford: Stanford University Press, 1981), pp. 341-60.

Daoism, animism, and perhaps Christianity as "Chinese religion," which remains and in the singular.[11]

A contrasting treatment by anthropologists of multiple religious realities is provided by Thailand. Even though, unlike Taiwan, Thailand has a state religion which the king has special obligations to protect (Theravada Buddhism), as Phillips noted, there are "four internally consistent and clear, but different belief systems—Buddhism, Brahmanism,[12] a Thai version of traditional Southeast Asian Animism, and simple naturalistic explanations—each of which has certain explanatory functions, but which villagers (often the same individual) also use interchangeably and inconsistently."[13] Even Kirsch, who sees a functional division of labor between religious traditions in Thailand and some systematicness to alternation and syncretism there, distinguishes historical strata and divergent types of religion.[14] No one speaks of an entity, "**the** Thai religion," in the singular. A similar unconcern for theological distinctions typifies syncretic Japanese religious beliefs and practices[15]— and even American "popular religion":

> There is no more reason to expect various Taiwanese customs or beliefs to form a coherent, logically consistent, and uniform system than there is to expect the doctrine of the Trinity, the tooth fairy, and Easter eggs to fit together into a consistent "American popular religion."[16]

---

[11] As in Arthur P. Wolf, *Religion and Ritual in Chinese Society* (Stanford: Stanford University Press, 1974).

[12] The sense of some Taiwanese that their religion is related to Hinduism and the borrowing and transformation of Hindu deities might stimulate research to investigate a "folk brahman complex" carried with Buddhism, as in its diffusion to Thailand—see A. T. Kirsch, "Complexity in the Thai Religious System," *Journal of Asian Studies* 36(1977), p. 252, and Stanley J. Tambiah, *Buddhism and the Spirit Cults in Northeast Thailand* (Cambridge: Cambridge University Press, 1970).

[13] Herbert P. Phillips, "Some Premises of American Scholarship on Thailand," in J. Fischer (ed.), *Western Values and Southeast Asian Scholarship* (Berkeley: Center for South and Southeast Asian Studies, 1973), p. 71.

[14] Kirsch, op. cit., pp. 241-66.

[15] For a very Durkheimian view of the primacy of social accommodation over imaginable doctrinal conflicts, see Edwin O. Reischauer, *The Japanese* (Cambridge, MA: Harvard University Press, 1981), pp. 138-45. Also see Robert J. Smith, *Japanese Society* (Cambridge University Press, 1983) pp. 16, 29, 110-4.

[16] De Glopper, op cit., p. 44.

If four "world religions" and a widespread "folk religion" do not suffice to trigger the plural, "Chinese religions," it is unlikely that "Chinese **societies**" can be conceived, especially by those whose research has been sponsored, facilitated, or merely permitted by the government of "The Republic of China." The government has its own reasons for maintaining a view that there is only "China," and pretending that the government that happens to be located on Taiwan should be recognized as the legitimate singular "China," since it clearly does not give proportional representation to those whom it actually rules. A separate entity called Taiwan is not "good to think" for them. Indeed, "Taiwan" remains a dangerous thought for the KMT.

That a concept "Taiwan" is so unthinkable to the most-cited anthropologist to have done fieldwork on Taiwan makes one wonder what danger it constitutes for him. Fear of losing access to data seems a likely possibility for someone relying heavily on government archives. In the late twentieth century, loss of access to the means of production of data is a salient concern for anthropologists, not just in Taiwan. Fieldworkers unpalatable to the KMT are denied entry to Taiwan, along with native Taiwanese (including the Taiwanese author of this book) who have criticized the government while studying outside Taiwan. American anthropologists familiar with Taiwan cannot be unaware of the KMT's restriction of access. As Hill Gates put it,

> Where we can do fieldwork, our researches are constrained by tight governmental limits on the pursuit of topics that might undermine national policy. Where we can not do fieldwork, we can do anthropology only on the safely dead. Intellectual issues thus come to be defined conservatively, and research topics become studies in the art of the possible."[17]

Arthur Wolf has done both: not only avoided thinking "Taiwanese culture," but concentrating on the safely dead, writing about "traditional China" on the basis of Japanese colonial records.[18] The Japanese popu-

---

[17] Hill Gates, *Chinese Working Class Lives* (Ithaca: Cornell University Press, 1987), p. 240. Presumably, she opted for the former.

[18] Similarly, in using Japanese colonial records in "Seasonality in Vital Processes in a Traditional Chinese Population: Births, deaths and marriages in colonial Taiwan, 1906-1942," *Modern China* 16(1990):190-225, Richard E. Barrett attributed similarity between colonial Japanese and Taiwanese seasonality of birth to climate rather than to culture without considering the possible importance of Japanese culture. Note the title's "**traditional** Chinese."

lation records, covering two generations, have been widely used by American social scientists to examine demographic changes. The massiveness of these archives has been taken for prima facie proof of the validity of the records, as if "because there is so much, it must be accurate." With Wolf's confidence in the homogeneity of "Chinese culture," he does not even consider the possibility that there might be variability among Taiwanese by class or by locale in understanding of *ge* (family), in writing,

> The Japanese settled on the *chia* [*ge*] as the basic unit and wisely left it up to the natives to define the term. All that was required of people was that they register as members of one and only one *chia*. Thus we may be confident that the family preserved in these records is a product of Chinese customs and not an arbitrary creation of the Japanese colonial bureaucracy.[19]

Although he does not consider that Taiwanese may have manipulated definitions and registrations for their own purposes, he at least acknowledges a bias in the records against joint families.[20] Other biases or invalidities Wolf does not discuss. Yet, in the major mid-1950s survey of community studies in Japan itself, Beardsley cautioned against accepting abundant official records as transparent:

> This method, though particularly enticing in Japan where any government office has a wealth of statistics on many different subjects, has very serious limitations, since many statistics touch on matters of taxation and government control, on which the government statistics collector finds it almost impossible to learn the true state of affairs. Careful check of the records against independent surveys of land ownership, occupation, and population in the small communities studied in the Inland Sea has invariably shown discrepancies; sometimes, indeed, the figures bear very slight resemblance to reality.[21]

---

[19] A. Wolf, op. cit. 1985, pp. 31-2; also see A. Wolf and Huang, op. cit., chapter 2.

[20] "They followed Japanese custom in designating the head of the household. When a head died or retired the headship passed to his eldest sons regardless of whether or not the family included the former head's brothers. Since the Japanese must have known that Chinese custom favors brothers over sons, my guess is that primogeniture was introduced as a clerical convenience"—A. Wolf, op. cit., 1985, p. 33.

[21] Richard K. Beardsley, "Community Studies in Japan,"*Far Eastern Quarterly* 14(1954), pp. 44-5.

If the detailed statistics for Japan itself are unreliable, there is little reason to suppose that similar statistics collected in other languages by Japanese officials in a colony are valid or reliable.[22] There has been little (if any) concern about the procedures and motivations of those recording in or reporting to population registries. Studies on the ethnography of official record collection[23] are apparently unknown to those working on the demography of Japanese Taiwan. Wolf once wrote that

> given that the Japanese household registers are the best source of evidence we will ever have for studying family composition in late traditional China, one of our research priorities must be to discover how people interpreted the term "family" when registering with the Japanese police.[24]

However, neither he nor his students have yet published work bearing on this research priority.[25]

In his preface to Huang's and his magnum opus, Wolf alleges that the Japanese "household registers allowed me to determine the precise composition of every family from 1905 through the end of the Japanese occupation in 1945."[26] Who it was in "the family" who bounded "the family," by what criteria, and for what purposes are not problematics addressed within Wolf's work on the colonial Japanese archives. Asking about responses made to Japanese police is "salvage anthropology" that is not being done and soon will be undoable, but researchers could ask

---

[22] Huang Chiehshan, who spent a decade working for Wolf on data from the registries, contended that they were more reliable than records from Japan because of the tighter police control on Taiwan than in the homeland or in Korea—or China of any dynasty (1989 interview). The lack of usable registration data from China is strong evidence that the institution was imperial Japanese, not imperial Chinese.

[23] E.g., John I. Kitsuse and Aaron V. Cicourel, "A Note on the Use of Official Statistics," *Social Problems* 11(1963):131-138

[24] A. Wolf, op. cit. 1985, p. 12.

[25] In the preface to *Marriage and Adoption* (Wolf and Huang, op. cit., p. x), Wolf mentioned that data from land title registers and land tax registers was being culled to collate with the household registry data, so perhaps "yet" should be added, even more than a decade since the publication of this statement. Given the frequency of land transactions, the non-contiguity of holdings, and the variations in grade of land, estimating the value or yield of property owned by families in Japanese Taiwan is not at all an easy task. It will soon be too late to ask Taiwanese about their logics in what they reported to Japanese officials.

[26] Ibid., p. viii.

similar questions about registering with the KMT police now. We know from the Gallins' research on emigrants from the Jianghua village that they call 新興 (Xin Xing) that some long resident in Daiba continue to be registered back in the village.[27] On the basis of censuses of two Daidiong ("Taichung") villages conducted by students from Dunghai University, Thelin found that the KMT household registries overcounted households, and undercounted the number of persons within the households, and suggested motivations relating to taxation for household members to misreport to the official records.[28] Similarly, Tang Mei-Chun reported that in comparing official registrations with a 1969 census of a town that has been engulfed by Daiba, the existence of households and the kinship relationships of those within households were consciously misrepresented. As in the village studied by Thelin, even in the aggregate, Yellow Rock households were overcounted, although there were under-registrations as well as over-registrations. Less socially prestigious kinship relations (*simbua*, matrilocally-resident couples, and illegitimate children) and occupations were systematically under-represented.[29] Other systematic biases in the registers remain to be explored. Given that these registers bear such a weight in the study of "late imperial China" (and, coincidentally, for colonial Taiwan), we can only hope that someone pays attention to the research priority suggested, but ignored in practice by Wolf.

Even within the Japanese colonial data set, if Wolf and Huang's data are disaggregated (by year, as well as by place), we may be able to see that in addition to considerable regional differences within Taiwan, even within the half century of Japanese rule on Taiwan there may have been temporal differences, so that the social structure (viz., marriage patterns)

---

[27] Bernard Gallin and Rita S. Gallin, "The Integration of Village Migrants in Taipei," in M. Elvin and G. Skinner (eds.), *The Chinese City Between Two Worlds* (Stanford University Press, 1974), pp. 344-6. The disparity between actual residence and registration was already noted during his 1958 fieldwork by Bernard Gallin, op. cit., pp. 34-5.

[28] Mark Thelin, *Two Taiwanese Villages* (Daidiong: Dunghai University, 1977). One cannot extrapolate directly from these discrepancies to the Japanese period. Although the KMT took over the institution of household registration and increased police surveillance, short-term and long-term migration to Daiba and to other cities was clearly higher than in the Japanese era, providing increased opportunity for registering absent family members.

[29] Tang, Mei Chun, *Urban Chinese Families: An Anthropological Field Study in Taipei City, Taiwan* (Daiba: National Taiwan University Press, 1978), appendix 3, pp. 179-93.

in even Wolf's microcosm (Haishan) of the timeless essence "China" was changing.[30]

Folk Religion

Over time, the initial focus of anthropological research on Taiwan shifted from kinship and lineage organization to religion, usually with an implicit or explicit assumption that "traditional Chinese religion" has been preserved on Taiwan. Researchers on "world religions" found on Taiwan often have been oblivious to folk religion being a marker of ethnicity in Taiwan. In Taiwan, participation in Taiwanese festivals is scorned by those born in China as "backwards superstition." The ethnic minority government has recurrently attempted to suppress, or at least limit the frequency, duration, and expenditure on festivals derogated by mainlanders with the label "paipai."[31] Reduplication, a common gram-

---

[30] Pasternak, op. cit., pp. 105-6. A. Wolf (in Wolf and Huang, op. cit., p. viii) acknowledged that "changes initiated by the Japanese occupation began to have significant effects" about 1930. Wolf's co-author (Huang 1989 interview) stressed that increased literacy undercut paternal authority, making it possible for sons to refuse to marry girls who had been adopted for future marriage. B. Gallin, op. cit., p. 165, also mentioned "increasingly open opposition of young people," but stressed that an increasing ratio of females to males and improved financial conditions made brides "both easier to find and easier to afford." In arguing for the essential unity of a singular China, (despite linguistic differences between southeastern provinces, and the non-acceptance of footbinding among the Hakka whom he studied in Taiwan), Myron L. Cohen ("Being Chinese: The peripheralization of traditional identity." *Dædalus* 120,2(1990), p. 123) adduces the use of Qing dynastic dates in account books in southern Taiwan for five years after the transfer of Taiwan to Japan as evidence of the hegemony of the (dubiously-Chinese) Celestial Emperors. Five years to change something so fundamental to business practice and everyday thinking as dating seems rapid to us and a better argument for Japanese imperial hegemony as early as 1900. (Cohen appears not to understand "hegemony," since he can write that "hegemony in modern China received no commonly accepted legitimization through culture" (p. 130), aside from having a different standard for communist hegemony in China and Chinese hegemony in Taiwan.)

[31] In China, the KMT actively sought to eliminate temples and wasteful customs in the "Superstition Destruction movement" of 1928-9 (see Hung Chang-Tai, *Going to the People, 1918-1937*, Cambridge, MA: Council on East Asian Studies, 1985, pp. 158-60), foreshadowing the epic rampage of destruction of everything related to "feudal superstitions" of the infamous "Cultural Revolution" of 1966-76. This is but

matical device in Polynesian languages, is regarded by many native speakers of Chinese languages as childish and as evidence of the inferiority and primitiveness of the population of Taiwan—not just the aboriginal Austronesian population, but those whose ancestors "abandoned the Middle Kingdom" to live among the "barbarians." The mainlander's pseudo-Polynesian term "paipai" parodies the imagined primitiveness of aboriginal languages and is a contemptuous denigration of what mainlanders regard as noisy, wasteful festivals of backwards, superstitious Taiwanese, and helps to confirm the belief that they are only one step removed from barbarian headhunters.[32]

The pantheon of a "Chinese religion" held in contempt by those actually raised in China and by their Beijinghua-speaking offspring is supposed by some specialist researchers to mirror a real political structure.[33] In the Durkheimian tradition, cognitive structures in general and religion in particular, are reflections of society. Indeed, it is society that is worshiped in Durkheim's view. As Wolf put it, "it is clear that the peasant's conception of the supernatural world was molded by his vision of society."[34] In the anthropology of religion on Taiwan, however, it is an earthly power that never exercised effective control on Taiwan and which surrendered responsibility for Taiwan nearly a century ago—that is, a political order which is beyond the recall of anyone actively involved in contemporary Taiwanese worship. Not just Taiwan, but the areas of southeast China from which settlers derived

> were largely on their own for a significant part of the later Ching [Qing] dynasty.... It is paradoxical that the [current] iconography derives from an otiose and powerless dynasty several generations

---

one of the commonalities of communist and "Nationalist" regimes. Indeed, on the mainland, as on Japanese Taiwan, village temples were destroyed or converted to other uses by modernizing zealots late in the Qing dynasty: Prasenjit Duara, *Culture, Power, and the State: Rural North China, 1900-1942* (Stanford University Press), pp. 148-55; Robert P. Weller, *Unities and Diversities in Chinese Religion* (Seattle: University of Washington Press, 1987), pp. 52-6, 129-47.

[32] In the view of the Qing official who gladly arranged to give the island to the Japanese, Li Hongzhang (Li Hung Chang, *Memoirs,* Boston: Houghton-Mifflin, 1913), the non-aboriginal Taiwanese were even more degraded than the aboriginal "wild beasts" headhunting in the hills. In reporting the mainlander derogation of Taiwanese, we do not intend to denigrate the aboriginal population, and do not accept the equation of "Chinese" with "superior."

[33] Wolf, op. cit. 1974, among others.

[34] Ibid., p. 8.

past, while the authoritarian and all-pervading present governments are rarely alluded to in its symbolism.[35]

To say, as Wolf does that "the supernatural world is never a simple projection of the contemporary world"[36] is to put it mildly. It is no doubt salutary to "begin the study of Chinese[37] religion with the social and economic history of particular communities," but will careful local history explain the relevance of an extinct social order never particularly salient in the region (northern Taiwan) about which Wolf and others are writing? "To understand the beliefs held at any point in time, one must examine the history of the community as well as the contemporary situation,"[38] Wolf continues, but, just as his demographic work is focused on the Japanese period, what he and his associates have written about religion tends to ignore contemporary situations in general, and ethnic domination in Taiwan in particular. As Rohsenow wrote,

> The struggles of the present are brushed over very lightly.... What events of contemporary life keep century-old animosities alive? .... An analysis which attempts to show the relationship between religious symbols and social organization should make clear the nature of the social relations the ritual sphere is purported to express.[39]

Some others do see religion as a potential expression of rural ethnic protest, although even they too put "Chinese" rather than "Taiwanese" in the titles of works dealing with data from Taiwanese history and contemporary culture.[40] As Bernard Gallin suggested,

> The proliferation of religious activity in Taiwan and increased importance of the supernatural might be viewed as a nativistic movement to mark and enhance Taiwanese identity—as opposed to

---

[35] Hill Gates Rohsenow, "Review of *Religion in Chinese Society*, edited by Arthur P. Wolf," *Journal of Asian Studies* 34(1975), p. 488.

[36] Wolf, op. cit. 1974, p. 8.

[37] Or Taiwanese—a level of analysis between the village and China which never seems to occur to Wolf as a possible one!

[38] Ibid., p. 9.

[39] Hill Gates Rohsenow, "Review of *Gods, Ghosts and Ancestors* by David Jordan," *Journal of Asian Studies* 32(1973), p. 479.

[40] Ahern, op. cit.; Robert P. Weller, op. cit. 1987.

the mainlanders... [who] are openly disdainful of what they refer to as Taiwanese superstition.[41]

Even Cohen is explicit lately that what he calls

> traditional Chinese culture on Taiwan became very much transformed into a modern assertion of national identity, but in this case the identity was Taiwanese and the nationalism was linked to the movement for Taiwan's independence.[42]

Class and Ethnicity

The Taiwanese/mainlander dichotomy is a salient emic distinction, inconvenient though it may be both to anthropologists who want to get on with the study of "traditional China" with whatever materials are available, as well as to traditional Marxists who are committed to regarding ethnicity as epiphenomenal. Such a view is congenial to the rulers of the so-called "Republic of China" and rationalizing ignoring Taiwanese seeing themselves as sufficiently distinctive from the Chinese rulers in either Beijing or Daiba to govern themselves. Their conception of their situation as an oppressed majority population has real social consequences despite academic observers' distaste for ethnic movements or for recognizing ethnic distinctions. Aside from the mutual unintelligibility of languages, the ethnic division between Taiwanese and mainlanders was solidified by the massacre of ten to fifty thousand Taiwanese in the spring of 1947,[43] by a mainlander monopoly into the 1980s of the highest positions in state enterprises (including a large army allegedly poised to regain China and the also elephantine government), by widespread discrimination in allocation of life chances, and by recurrent attempts to extirpate Taiwanese languages, religions, and customs. Origins from different parts of China at different times and variation in cultural items are part of the self-understanding of ethnic differences on Taiwan, but, as Barth noted, ethnic groups have salience "not only by a once-and-for-all recruitment but by continual expression and validation"—or by invalidation through exclusion and perceived discrimina-

---

[41] B. Gallin, op. cit. 1985, pp. 55-56. A resurgence of long-suppressed popular religion (along with a renaissance of elaborate funerals) appears to be part of southern resistance to the northern and iconoclastic communist régime in China: see Luo Zhufeng, *Religion Under Socialism in China* (Armonk, NY: M. E. Sharpe, 1991) and Edward Friedman, "A Failed Chinese Modernity," *Dædalus* 122,2(1993):1-17.

[42] Cohen, op. cit. 1990, p. 132. He sees common roots in the May 4th movement for both communist and KMT iconoclasm.

[43] This history is discussed in a later section.

tion by an ethnically homogeneous ruling elite.[44] Since 1945, "a strong sense of ethnic separateness, felt by both groups, has been created where it formerly did not exist and strengthened where it did."[45] Not all mainlanders are part of the military/technocratic caste.[46] But until recently, practically all of the elite positions in the government have been occupied by mainlanders and their children.

In 1949, the defeated mainlanders transported from China the prestige of government positions and low prestige of businessmen and farmers. Because of the maintenance of "representatives" and bureaucrats in what claims to be the government of China in the latest of a series of provisional KMT capitals,[47] and the imposition of a "national lan-

---

[44] Fredrik Barth, *Ethnic Groups and Boundaries: The Social Organization of Cultural Differences* (Boston: Little Brown, 1969), p. 15; Hill Gates, "Ethnicity and Social Class," in Ahern and Gates (eds.) op. cit. 1981, p. 246. Our conception of reactive ethnicity is akin to that of Michael Hechter, *Internal Colonialism* (Berkeley: University of California Press, 1975) and "Group Formation and the Cultural Division of Labor," *American Journal of Sociology* 84(1978):293-318; though more directly influenced by work on Asian-Americans, viz., Stephen S. Fugita and David J. O'Brien, *Japanese American Ethncity* (Seattle: University of Washington Press, 1991); Shotaro Frank Miyamoto, *Social Solidarity Among the Japanese of Seattle* (Seattle: University of Washington Press, 1939, 1984); Victor G. Nee and Barry Nee, *Longtime Californ'* (Stanford: Stanford University Press, 1973).

[45] Gates, op. cit. 1981, p. 252. Cf. Richard Handler, "On Sociocultural Discontinuity: Nationalism and cultural objectification in Québec," *Current Anthropology* 25(1984): 55-71; and Jocelyn S. Linnekin, "Defining Tradition: Variations on the Hawaiian identity," *American Ethnologist* 10(1983):241-252.

[46] The ascription "working-class" seems dubious in many of the cases included in Hill Gates's *Chinese Working Class Lives*, but some soldiers demobilized from the KMT army and not provided government sinecures were and are poor, and have never been part of the elite caste. In her "Dependency and the Part-time Proletariat in Taiwan," *Modern China* 5(1979), p. 388, Gates argues that a caste of soldiers are encouraged to identify themselves as mainlanders superior to Taiwanese peasants and workers to forestall any class consciousness or revolutionary solidarity. She is more certain that she knows what are the objective class interests of whom and what is false consciousness than we are. From our own close connections with those labelled "subversive" by the KMT, we would certainly challenge her location of "dissidents and 'subversive'" in the lumpenproletariat (p. 389).

[47] Although imposing the language of Beijing on Taiwanese, the Kuomintang never ruled from Beijing.

guage" (Beijinghua, nostalgically called "Mandarin" by some) of which there were no native speakers on Taiwan in 1945, Taiwanese had limited opportunities within the government.[48] Under a minority ethnic oligarchy ruling through martial law and a large secret police force, opposition politics was a route to early death and presented no possibility of upward mobility. Less-prestigious commercial enterprise was more open to Taiwanese than government positions, and other than the safety valve of emigration through foreign study, was the only niche for Taiwanese aspiring to better their lot. Business may be a "crooked path,"[49] in contrast to the royal road of official examinations in the Confucian view maintained by the KMT. There are/were relatively fewer roadblocks of overt discrimination and the subtler consequences of lesser cultural capital in an alien language for Taiwanese businessmen than for Taiwanese seeking a place in the government. Of course,

> even if the KMT had not been committed to a northern China language identified with the traditional capital, the maintenance of Mandarin [Beijinghua] as the official tongue would still have provided a rationale for excluding or demoting Taiwanese from responsibility. It placed the burden of effort, of awkwardness, and of linguistic ineptitude"

on the subordinate Taiwanese.[50] In addition to the cultural capital of language, mainlander nuclear families were better suited to focusing on education of their children than were extended Taiwanese families. In

---

[48] Moreover, "the substitution of Taiwanese for mainlander cadres in a Leninist party and authoritarian government—a substitution that has not gone very far or very fast in any case—is not equivalent to the concession of power to popular sovereignty." Edwin A. Winckler, "National, Regional, and Local politics," in Ahern and Gates (eds.) op. cit., p. 21. Also see Tun-Jan Cheng, "Democratizing the Quasi-Leninist Regime in Taiwan," *World Politics* 41(1989):471-99.

[49] Gates, op. cit., 1979, p. 394; op. cit. 1981, p. 277.

[50] Gates, op. cit. 1981, p. 263. Just as "correctness" and "accent" and interpretation of "talking funny" are used elsewhere to rationalize the maintenance (reproduction) of inequality: see Dell Hymes, "Quantitative/Qualitative Research Methods in Education." *Anthropology and Education Quarterly* 8(1977), p. 169; Susan Gal, "Language and Political Economy," *Annual Review of Anthropology* 18(1989):345-367; John J. Gumperz, *Language and Social Identity* and *Discourse Processes*, both published by Cambridge University Press in 1982; Stephen O. Murray, "Ethnic Differences in Interpretive Conventions and the Reproduction of Inequality in Everyday Life," *Symbolic Interaction* 14(1991): 187-204.

contrast, large Taiwanese families could better mobilize family labor and networks useful to doing business.[51]

To the Taiwanese, business is a hard road, but not the dishonorable one of the Confucian ethos. Supplying the rice and taxes to maintain mainlanders whom they term *lao tzat* (old thieves) in lifetime legislative and administrative sinecures, Taiwanese find it hard to believe "public service" is service to anything other than the incumbents' well-being.[52] Although some of the largest enterprises are owned by mainlanders, a Taiwanese upper class has developed with the success of (generally less large-scale) Taiwanese enterprises, even as some mainlander enlisted men sank into poverty. There is, thus, no one-to-one relationship between class and ethnicity in Taiwan today.

Nonetheless, the Taiwanese/mainlander dichotomy is a salient emic distinction inconvenient both to anthropologists who want to get on with the study of "traditional China" with whatever materials are available, as well as to traditional Marxists who are committed to regarding ethnicity as quaint or epiphenomenal. The faith of the former in a timeless Chinese essence that was carried by those who chose to leave China (and their families), survived Dutch and Japanese colonialism and general Q'ing neglect is matched by the faith of the latter in class as the only possible analytical tool despite the history of ethnic conflict and working class non-solidarity throughout the world in the 20th century and renewed explosions where communist regimes have collapsed. Generally, anthropologists who purport to being engaged in studying "China" have simply ignored ethnic differences, ethnic self-understanding, and ethnic conflict on Taiwan. Those who have focused on rural revolts remain reluctant to see ethnicity as a basis for protest, preferring to attribute all movements of oppressed people to class, and to discount the native's own conception of ethnic oppression and ethnic identity as "false consciousness."

At this late date in the twentieth century, it should be obvious that ethnic identification and mobilization do not disappear even with increasingly capitalist production. Ethnic movements are rampant, toppling regimes that purported to represent "the universal class" across the Soviet empire, blowing apart the former Yugoslavia, and stirring in France and Germany. Groups based on characteristics which classical social theory regarded as already anachronistic a century ago have not

---

[51] See Norma Diamond, "Women under Kuomintang Rule," *Modern China* 1(1975):3-45; idem., "The Status of Women in Taiwan," in M. Young (ed.) *Women in China* (Ann Arbor: Center for Chinese Studies, 1973), pp. 211-42.

[52] See Winckler, op. cit., p. 22; B. Gallin, op. cit., 1966, pp. 75-9.

merely "assumed political functions comparable to those of a subordinate class; they have in important respects become more effective than
social classes in mobilizing their forces in pursuit of collective
ends."[53] If this be "rebellion" rather than "revolution," then "rebellion"
is what recent history discloses, not the incipient fulfilling of the mes-
sianic expectations still pinned on the class that was supposed to be
"universal", the proletariat. It is certainly legitimate to look for class
bases in ethnic conflicts, but insofar as social scientists aim to analyze
actual history rather than to explain the tarrying of the messiah, they
must explain the continued strength and/or emergence of social movements based on consciousness of shared ascribed characteristics. As
Parkin noted, "Whereas the modern proletariat appears to have a purely
theoretical capacity to reconstitute the social order in its own image,
ethnic groups have frequently displayed a more than abstract commitment to dissolving the boundaries of the nation state and redrawing
them anew"[54]—even more spectacularly since he wrote this. The
regime ruling Taiwan has fostered cleavages between Holo and Hakka
and aboriginal peoples while claiming to be the legitimate government
of China, so that the majority of people under his rule are a peripheral
minority of a populous empire extending from Mongolia to Burma.
The persistence of a mainlander Chinese vs. Taiwanese islander distinction to a third generation bears observation, as does the movement by
the Taiwanese majority for a representative democracy.

   Given the family base of many smaller enterprises, a distinction between a proletariat and owners of the means of production is not always
clear. Gates distinguishes a mostly Taiwanese "traditional middle class"/
"petty bourgeoisie" from the mostly mainlander managerial "new
class," and both from an upper class owning major means of production.[55] By considering land the means of agricultural production without recognizing the necessity of fertilizer and irrigation water, she in-

---

[53] David Parkin, "Social Stratification," in R. Nisbet & T. Bottomore
(eds.), *History of Sociological Analysis* (New York: Basic Books, 1978)
p. 622.

[54] Ibid., p. 626. The commitment of communist states to universalism was
not invariant. See Katherine Verdery, *National Ideology Under Socialism: Identity and Cultural Politics in Ceausescu's Romania* (Berkeley:
University of California Press, 1991).

[55] Gates, op. cit. 1981, pp. 273-81. Gates, op. cit. 1979, p. 391 suggests
employment of more than twenty workers as the division between petty
bourgeois family enterprises and the grand bourgeoisie. Eighty-two percent of the firms in the 1973 Industrial and Commercial Census had fewer
than twenty employees (Ibid., p. 390).

cludes farmers who own some land (a third of the total population of Taiwan) in the "traditional middle class."[56] Taiwanese farmers have not exactly been proletarianized, but were knowingly and systematically marginalized beneath the (income and status) level of proletarians.[57] Government control of prices and of essential means of production have made prosperity through growing rice impossible. Similarly, "the fact that rural sugar growers own and operate their own farms tends to obscure the nature of the sugar economy—a highly centralized economy that is controlled through price setting, fertilizer supply, production loans, and irrigation procedures."[58]

Both the mainlander and the Taiwanese families constituting the little-studied upper class tend to have ties with large Japanese enterprises predating the beginning of the Second World War.[59] That "traditional peasants" rather than this elite stratum have been the objects for anthropological fieldwork will probably surprise few anthropologists.[60] Hill Gates was notably frank that "our relative prestige permitted me, at times, to inflict myself on some people, but not on others," of higher class.[61] The failure to address whether the managers of large enterprises in state capitalism constitute a class has not even been raised by the few

---

[56] Gates, op. cit, 1979. p. 390, op. cit. 1981, pp. 275, 279. That her fieldwork has been done in the capital city may account for this naiveté about the status of peasants and the general prosperity of Taiwanese, as well as for some distortions of the contents of Taiwanese "tradition."

[57] See below.

[58] Hill Gates and Emily M. Ahern, op. cit., p. 3, drawing on the work of Chung Min Chen, "Government Enterprise and Village Politics," pp. 38-49 in that volume, and his *Upper Camp, Academia Sinica Monograph* 7(1977). Also see Jack F. Williams, "Sugar: The sweetener in Taiwan's development," pp. 219-255 in R. Knapp (ed.), *China's Island Frontier: Studies in the Historical Geography of Taiwan* (Honolulu: University of Hawaii Press, 1980.)

[59] Ichiro Numazaki, "Networks of Taiwanese Big Businessmen," *Modern China* 12(1986):487-534. Also see Thomas B. Gold, *State and Society in the Taiwan Miracle* (Armonk, NY: Sharpe, 1986).

[60] Given that Taiwan was populated with Han farmers producing for the Dutch, a subsistence peasantry was never characteristic of Taiwan. Having moved on to studying mainland China, Myron L. Cohen has come to reject the applicability of the notion "peasant" in either place: "Cultural and Political Inventions in Modern China: The case of the Chinese 'peasant,'" *Dædalus* 122,2(1993):151-170; inspired by and building on Charles W. Hayford, *To the People: James Yen and Village China* (New York: Columbia University Press, 1990).

[61] Gates, op. cit. 1987, p. 19.

anthropologists who have tried to analyze class within Taiwan—not that the question has been answered convincingly for any other part of the world!

Historical Sources of Taiwanese Invisibility in American Anthropological Discourse

Some American academics have studied movements for Taiwanese independence,[62] but not anthropologists. Despite the well-known exemplary studies of nativist resurgence by Anthony F. C. Wallace,[63] American anthropologists have largely avoided investigation of the resurgence of Taiwanese religion and its connection to Taiwanese struggles for self-determination. Given that American social scientists are generally liberal, and that anthropologists dote on cultural differences, one would expect most of them to be sympathetic to self-determination and cultural maintenance anywhere—in Taiwan as much as in Poland, in Tibet as much as in Afghanistan. American social scientists marching in lockstep with a right-wing dictatorship legitimating, rather than treating skeptically an ideological construct so shaky as "Taiwan is **the** most traditional part of China" is a puzzle.[64] Although such a representation is over-determined, we can suggest several partial explanations of how this status quo came about.

[62] George H. Kerr, *Formosa: Licensed Revolution and the Home Rule Movement, 1895-1945,* (Honolulu: University Press, 1974); Douglas Mendel, *The Politics of Formosan Nationalism* (Berkeley: University of California Press, 1970).

[63] Anthony F. C. Wallace, "Revitalization Movements," *American Anthropologist* 58(1956): 274-81; idem., *The Death and Rebirth of the Seneca* (New York: Knopf, 1970). An excellent exemplar of more recently fashionable social construction of "tradition" analysis is provided by Richard Handler, *Nationalism and the Politics of Culture in Québec* (Madison: University of Wisconsin Press, 1988). For cautions that "authenticity is not a function of antiquity and recency is not evidence of triviality" in cultural patterning see Robert J. Smith, "Something Old, Something New: Tradition and culture in the study of Japan," *Journal of Asian Studies* 48(1989), p. 722. Native concerns with such analyses are sensitively considered by Jean Jackson in "Is There a Way to Talk About Making Culture Without Making Enemies?" *Dialectical Anthropology* 14(1989):127-143.

[64] See Stephen O. Murray, and Keelung Hong, "Taiwan, China, and the 'Objectivity' of Dictatorial Elites," *American Anthropologist* 90 (1988):976-78; Keelung Hong and Stephen O. Murray, "Complicity with Domination," *American Anthropologist* 91(1989):1028-30.

First, the triumph of the "People's Army of Liberation" on main-land China was traumatic for American China experts—not as traumatic as for the KMT, but still traumatic. First General Patrick Hurley, and then right-wing congressmen blamed the "loss of China" to commu-nism on the China experts who had warned of the popular hatred of the KMT in China, as if observers were responsible for the reality they observed.[65] Shooting the messenger carrying bad news is a venerable reaction to frustration about military and political outcomes.

A second component to the acquiescence of American social scien-tists with the representation of Taiwan as typically Chinese is that Maoists made research inside China impossible—just at the time when anthropologists were beginning serious study of peasants and post-pea-sants,[66] just when there were some Americans with the linguistic

---

[65] A concise account is contained in Benjamin Lee Grayson's introduction to *The American Image of China* (New York: Ungar, 1979), pp. 34-47.

[66] Into the 1940s, anthropologists studying "primitive" cultures or engag-ed in "salvage" of aboriginal Amerindian "memory cultures" considered the study of peasants—and even more any study of "postpeasants" who had migrated to towns or cities in search of economic opportunity—to be sociology rather than anthropology. An interest in a type of society between self-contained "primitive" ones and modern, industrial mass societies was central in the work of Robert Redfield, who was well-known but marginal to American anthropology of the time. Having spatialized urbanization into a synchronic rural-urban continuum (*The Folk Culture of the Yucatán* (Chicago: University of Chicago Press, 1940), Redfield found influences of US culture and economy as well as the national Mexican culture and economy in the hinterlands of the Yucatán. In addition to the Yucatán/ Guatemala research project he direct-ed, Redfield also supervised some pioneer ethnographies of peasant communities, including John F. Embree, *Suye Mura* (University of Chicago Press, 1939), Horace Miner, *St. Denis* (University of Chicago Press, 1939), and Edward H. Spicer, *Pascua* (University of Chicago Press, 1940). During the 1950s, he was involved in interdisciplinary seminars on communities making local adaptations of "great tradi-tions," writing reviews of community studies in China and Japan (Robert Redfield, "Community Studies in Japan and China," *Far Eastern Quarterly* 14(1954):3-10) and an introduction to Arthur F. Wright, *Studies in Chinese Thought* (*American Anthropological Association Memoir* 7,1953), en route to his final syntheses, *The Little Community* (University of Chicago Press, 1955), and *Peasant Society and Culture* (University of Chicago Press, 1960). Even apart from the students of Redfield and of Julian Steward, there was "ever-increasing understanding that so-called primitive or non-Western enclaves within large complex polities have been neither so primitive nor so insulated as they have often been represented in anthropological studies to be " (Sidney M.

means to do ethnography in Beijinghua, and just when some studies of communities on mainland China by Chinese natives were becoming available.[67]

Morton Fried did fieldwork in China after the war in an area still controlled by the KMT, though not where the Beijinghua he had studied was spoken. Having had to leave Sichuan without his fieldnotes in 1950, G. William Skinner did fieldwork among Chinese in Thailand for his Ph.D. thesis.[68] In the 1950s no one had yet noticed Taiwan was the place where Chinese culture was best preserved. **Taiwan had not yet become the most traditional part of China.** In the 1953 American Anthropological Association Memoir dealing with China,[69] there is no mention of Taiwan (or Formosa). Similarly, what would soon be represented as the most traditional part of China was unmentioned in Wittfogel's (1957) *Oriental Despotism*.[70] Those who wanted to study Chinese culture where Mao hadn't blocked them during the early and mid-1950s went to Southeast Asia, not to long-colonized Taiwan or Hong Kong.

Along with the first generation of researchers who began fieldwork in Taiwan in the late 1950s and early 1960s (Myron Cohen, Norma Diamond, Bernard and Rita Gallin, Burton Pasternak, Arthur and Margery Wolf), Skinner and Fried taught many of those who later did fieldwork in Taiwan. When their students began fieldwork in Taiwan, they were preoccupied with finding continuities with what their teachers

---

Mintz "Afterword" to Ahern and Gates, op. cit., p. 428). This approach became paradigmatic in the 1980s in American anthropology, although a pre-Redfieldian view continues to be espoused by some anthropologists who see a singular Chinese civilization, e.g., Cohen, op. cit. 1990, p. 119.

[67] Fei Hsiao Tung, *Peasant Life in China* (London: Kegan Paul, 1939); Fei Hsiao Tung and Chang Chih-I, *Earthbound China* (University of Chicago Press, 1945); Francis L. K. Hsu, *Under the Ancestors' Shadow* (New York: Columbia University Press, 1948); Lin Yueh Hwa, *The Golden Wing* (London: Kegan Paul, 1948); Martin M. C. Yang, *A Chinese Village: Taitou, Shangtung Province* (New York: Columbia University Press, 1945).

[68] George William Skinner, *A Study of Chinese Community Leadership in Bangkok Together with an Historical Survey of Chinese Society in Thailand*, Ph.D. dissertation, Cornell University.

[69] Wright, op. cit.

[70] Karl A. Wittfogel, *Oriental Despotism* (New Haven: Yale University Press, 1957) included far less populous places such as Bali and southwestern United States Pueblos.

thought of as Chinese, and had studied in China.[71] Researchers who wanted to study China were welcomed by a government pretending to be China. Moreover, being open to foreigners—whether social scientists or businessmen—at the time that KMT state capitalism was changing to encourage foreign investors—helped demonstrate that there was a "free China," in contrast to the larger, but closed Maoist China. Writing in English about an imaginary Chinese culture and society in Taiwan was the safest kind of free speech for a régime which still restricts other kinds of discourse—especially any discourse about ethnic differences and Taiwanese autonomy. In return, social scientists were grateful for a chance to study at least something they could call "China."

The KMT was eager to facilitate research legitimating its view of reality, arranging access to archives, forcing cooperation from villages officials, providing assistants, and even some financing of research by Americans. Gates noted that

> the Nationalist [KMT] need for legitimacy caused them to emphasize cultural continuities with China.... Often writing in English, and clearly for an American audience, Nationalist supporters in Taiwan and the United States based many of their arguments on the premise that Taiwan was an integral part of China, and its people were wholly and essentially Chinese.[72]

Wishful thinking on the part of those who wanted to study China dovetailed with the need of a government claiming to represent all China, but not sufficiently secure of its legitimacy as a minority in the only territory it controlled, to drop martial law for four decades. Social scientists who sought the legitimacy of being experts on "the world's oldest continuous civilization" or the world's most populous country shared the KMT interest in claiming that "traditional China" had been preserved by caretakers of the Japanese colonial régime for half a century on Taiwan to provide foreign observers a sort of Ming theme park.[73]

---

[71] Gates, op. cit. 1987, p. 237. A later series of conferences which led to Stanford University Press collections during the 1960s and 70s, viewed as "provid[ing] the very substance upon which Sinological anthropology depends for its corporate identity" by James L. Watson ("Anthropological Analyses of Chinese Religion," *China Quarterly* 66 (1976), p. 364) as "foster[ing] a generally conservative tendency to assume Chinese continuities over time and space" by Gates, op. cit. 1987, p. 238).

[72] Gates, op. cit. 1987, p. 232.

[73] Although in one place Wolfram Eberhard, *Settlement and Change in Asia* (Hong Kong University Press, 1967, p.194) noted, "We realize that Tai-

For instance, Taiwan is a particularly good setting for comparative work, according to Baity, because, "the Chinese live there as an overwhelming majority of the population, govern themselves according to more or less traditional Chinese principles and are relatively free of the influences of a present or former colonial power."[74] The fantasy that the Japanese were caretakers of "traditional Chinese society" is explicit in the introduction to *The Anthropology of Taiwanese Society:*

> Taiwan is the only province of China that has not undergone the sweeping changes of a socialist revolution: Chinese life has greater continuity with the past there, it can be argued, than anywhere else. During fifty years of rule, the Japanese did not intentionally alter Chinese customs and social relations; subsequently, the Kuomintang [KMT] government actively promoted adherence to Confucian ideals of social order. Anthropologists have therefore gone to Taiwan to study what they could no longer study in other provinces. It was Taiwan's representativeness, not its special qualities, that first attracted their interest.[75]

---

wan is not an ideal place; it was under Japanese rule" when the document was produced that he was using to limn the status of small Chinese merchants; elsewhere (*Studies in Chinese Folklore and Related Essays, Indiana University Folklore Institute Monograph* 23 (1970), p. 204), he contended that although

> the objection could be raised that Taiwanese are not a good example, because the island has been under Japanese rule for a long time and this would have had an influence, in many questions of religious practices, the Taiwanese even now are more conservative than Mainland Chinese were before 1948.

[74] Philip C. Baity, *Religion in a Chinese Town,* (Daiba: Orient Culture Service, 1975), p. 2.

[75] Gates and Ahern, op. cit., p. 8. Gates, op. cit. 1987, p. 232. later acknowledged that the Japanese wished to "Japanize the Taiwanese," that the impact of Japanese control has been underestimated, and stressed that "we must demonstrate continuities [with the Chinese past] not assume them." She had earlier faulted Pasternak for naiveté in dismissing the importance of Japanese influences on Taiwanese social structure (Hill Gates Rohsenow, "Review of *Kinship and Community in Two Chinese Villages* by Burton Pasternak," *Journal of Asian Studies* 32(1973), p. 78). On Japanese education on Taiwan and the effort to promote the Japanese language through education in Japanese, see T. Sugimoto "Japanese in Taiwan," *Current Trends in Linguistics* 8(1971):969-95.

Just to call Taiwan a "province of China" is to take a stand with the KMT and against the right of self-determination of the people on Taiwan. "Province of China" has little historical warrant. Until 1886 Taiwan was a territory of Fujien. Nine years later it was ceded to the Japanese Empire. While Chen Yi was looting the island after World War II and while the KMT controlled some territory on the mainland, Taiwan was not considered a province. Within the fantasy state of "the Republic of China" Taiwan contains three provinces. Thus, in the three-plus millennia of Chinese civilization, Taiwan was considered a "province of China" only for a few years before the Qing dynasty unloaded what its chief negotiator with the Japanese (Li Hongzhang) regarded as a bleeding ulcer on the motherland. Before the Chinese government transferred its claim to sovereignty over Taiwan to Japan, it was certainly not considered typically "Chinese."[76]

In combing the literature on Taiwan, we have not encountered **any** nineteenth-century claims that Taiwan was the most representative part of China, or the best place to understand Chinese culture and society. It is hard to imagine anyone seriously believing that Japanese imperialism made Taiwan more Chinese instead of more Japanese. If half a century of Japanese rule is "a bridge to the past,"[77] it is quite an unusual assumption that colonial rule preserves the preexisting "traditional culture," especially a colonial rule that introduced universal education— conducted in Japanese, not in any Chinese language—"pacified" the

---

[76] Li, op. cit. Interestingly, the title of the first sustained discourse on Taiwan in English, the entirely fraudulent George Psalmanazar's 1704 *An Historical and Geographical Description of Formosa, an Island Subject to the Emperor of Japan*, shows how little-established in European views was the subordination of the island to Qing Emperors. In *Exemplars* (Berkeley: University of California Press, 1985, p. 90) Rodney Needham notes that there was an 1896 reprinting (by Kegan Paul in London) of that curious piece of ethnographic fiction with no indication that it was fictitious and had even been retracted in a posthumous publication by its author. Chuang, Ying-Chang "Ching dynasty Chinese immigration to Taiwan," *Bulletin of the Institute of Ethnology, Academia Sinica* 64(1987):179-203 estimates that in the last years before giving Taiwan to Japan, Qing forces controlled ony one-third of the island's territory. On the independence of Taiwanese economic development from Qing policy, see idem., "Settlement Patterns of the Hakka Migration to Taiwan," *Bulletin of the Institute of Ethnology, Academia Sinica* 34(1988):85-98.

[77] Gates and Ahern, op. cit. 1981, p. 9. See the similar claim of Chen Ci Lu, "The Taiwanese Family," *Journal of the China Society* 7 (1971), p. 64.

aboriginal Austronesian population of Taiwan so that peasants could concentrate on agriculture and forget about defense, presided over the demographic transformation from an island with the death rate equivalent to the birth rate to one with the birthrate double the death rate,[78] and also built a network of roads and railroads which markedly increased the access of the countryside to production for export.[79]

Generally, production for export is considered an indication of "modernization." As a Japanese colony, Taiwan was integrated into the world economy more than any part of mainland China. An early "green revolution" made it far more productive than any part of mainland China was (or is). Nowhere else in the world is integration into the world economy taken as an indication of preserving tradition. Yet those who want to study "traditional Chinese culture" have only to cross this Japanese bridge to the past—and, once on the other side, to ignore the influence of Dutch East Indies Company recruiting, sponsoring, and supervising the Hakka- and Hokkien-speaking men leaving their lineages behind in southeastern China to clear land and grow crops for export. Of course, in the view of those who wish to find "traditional Chinese culture," neither the European supervisors nor the aboriginal Formosan tribes they fought and with whom the migrants intermarried were of any cultural importance. Having gladly given Taiwan to Japan, Li Hongzhang wrote,

> Formosans are neither of us nor with us, and we praise all the ancestors that this is so! In all Asia, in all the world, I believe there are no tribes of animals called men more degraded and filthy than these people of Taiwan. And have we not enough of criminals and low creatures to deal with on the mainland? These people are not farmers, they are no hill-men, nor hunters of wild beasts whose skins bring in money and keep men's bodies warm in the cold winters. No, they are not even fit to be soldiers in trained armies, for they have no discipline, nor could they be taught. Neither would they make good sailors on regular ships though many of the coastmen are good enough as wild pirates and buccaneers of the sea. They are cut-throats, all of them, along the coasts and back into the jungles. And so they have been from the days of Chia-Ch'ing to the present time. No, they are

---

[78] Irene B. Taeuber, "Migrants and Cities in Japan, Taiwan, and Northeastern China," in Elvin and. Skinner, op. cit., p. 362.

[79] See Barclay, op. cit.; Richard E. Barrett and Martin K. Why "Dependency Theory and Taiwan: A deviant case analysis," *American Journal of Sociology* 87(1982):1064-1089; Andrew J. Grajdanzev, *Formosa Today* (New York: Institute of Pacific Research, 1942); Samuel P. S. Ho, *The Economic Development of Taiwan*, 1860-1970 (New Haven: Yale University Press, 1978).

not all even of so good a class as that! For what are opium smokers, head-hunters, and filthy lepers... A very large number of these people are opium users of the lowest kind, and those who do not use this hellish concoction only abstain from it because it is not within their power or means to obtain that dirtiest of evil drugs.[80]

This late Qing official did not anticipate that in far less than a century anyone would claim that Ming culture was transported wholesale to Taiwan in the final years of the Ming dynasty, and there alone lives on. In 1895 the island was viewed as unimportant to China and as quite abhorrently **un-Chinese.**

If, rather than efforts of seventeenth century European or twentieth century Japanese curators of "Chinese culture," it was the retreat of the remnants of the KMT army to Taiwan that made Taiwan the most representative or traditional part of China, one might expect that anthropologists would have studied the mainlanders, using their memories to reconstruct what Chinese life was like before 1931 (when Japan invaded Manchuria), much as Native Americans told the first generation of professional American anthropologists about pre-reservation life. Although the KMT supporters who fled to Taiwan constitute a quite unrepresentative sample of the population of China, at least they grew up in China and had not been socialized within the Japanese Empire. However, insofar as there has been "salvage anthropology" on Taiwan, it has concerned either the aboriginal Formosans, or research in the Japanese archives. Studies of the "memory culture" of China, akin to the classic works of Yang and Lin, have not been encouraged or elicited from mainlanders resident on Taiwan by American social scientists (or by their Chinese and Taiwanese students). American social scientists beginning in the late 1920s preferred studying functioning cultures to eliciting recollections and sorting through them to compare "culture elements." The functioning culture of units small enough to be studied in a year or so of fieldwork were Taiwanese villages, not the urban enclaves of exiled mainlanders,[81] despite the urban focus of Fried's and Skinner's work.[82]

---

[80] Li, op. cit., p. 268.

[81] One particularly striking failure of anthropologists on Taiwan is to look at what mainlanders did about forming lineages when they were separated from their natal lineages and dwelling in a hostile frontier area dominating, but outnumbered by natives. A great deal of early work, especially by Columbia-trained anthropologists, dealt with the conditions of lineage formation in the 18th and 19th century on Taiwan, but this interest did not extend to seeking to observe this feature of "Chinese culture" among contemporary mainlanders in protracted exile on Taiwan. It is

Although there has been some painstakingly systematic work on Japanese archives and other government records, another characteristic of an early age of faith in cultural homogeneity and easy access to it continues. As Fried noted in his review of community studies done on mainland China,

> since the subjects of anthropological research in the past were almost invariably [treated as/ conceived to be?] of a simple homogeneous nature, there was little need for the field worker to concern himself with the source of his information, other than to be reasonably certain that he was not relying too heavily on the reports of people who were recognized within their own culture as being markedly deviant.[83]

Anyone, in any place—Indonesia, Malaysia, Singapore, Thailand—would do to elicit "Chinese culture." Who needed sampling if communities and individuals were interchangeable? Sampling is not one of the strengths of American anthropology, and was even less so in the 1950s, and intracultural variance was grappled with then by only a few anthropologists.[84]

---

also odd that the "sojourner" conceptualization—developed by "Chicago school" sociologists to account for Chinese in North America who planned to return to China (see Paul Chan Pang Siu, "The Sojourner," *American Journal of Sociology* 58 (1972):34-44; idem., *The Chinese Laundryman*, New York: New York University Press, 1987)—has not been applied to mainlanders on Taiwan.

[82] Donald Nonini (1990 personal communication) reminded us of this, and suggested that the initial decision to study Taiwanese rather than mainlanders rather than a predilection for studying non-urbanites was crucial in melting down Taiwanese materials to sculpt "traditional China."

[83] Morton H. Fried, "Community Studies in China," *Far Eastern Quarterly* 14(1954), p. 24. See Stephen O. Murray, "The Creation of Linguistic Structure," *American Anthropologist* 85(1983):356-62; the critique by Julian Steward in *Area Research, Social Science Research Council Bulletin* 63(1950) to the application of simplistic anthropological assumptions about cultural homogeneity; and the critical discourse of that era reviewed by Stephen O. Murray in "The Reception of Anthropological Work in American Sociology, 1921-1951," *Journal of the History of the Behavioral Sciences* 24 (1988):135-51.

[84] E.g., Anthony F. C. Wallace, "Individual Differences and Cultural Uniformities," *American Sociological Review* 17(1952):747-750; C. W. M. Hart, "The Sons of Turimpi," *American Anthropologist* 56 (1954):242-261. Cf. the more mainstream homogeneity of each of the five cultures in longtime contact that were contrasted in Clyde Kluckhohn's study of

Gates suggested a third, related basis for studying Taiwan as a surrogate for rural China—not Ming or Qing China, but the China in which a communist peasant revolution had just triumphed—in order to try to understand conditions leading to that revolution, and to look for possible ways to prevent other, similar revolutions:

> By the late 1950s it was clear that American anthropological field-workers would not be welcome in the People's Republic of China for the foreseeable future. It was beginning to appear too that the McCarthyist destruction of China scholarship in the United State was hampering the American ability to understand events in China proper. Support [from foundations] emerged for anthropological investigation of everyday Chinese life in Taiwan, where, it was assumed, traditional Chinese culture had been preserved from the changes set in motion by the Communist revolution... The anthropological literature... contains a marked bias toward seeing Taiwan as a sample of an essentially homogeneous Chinese whole.[85]

It would have to be admitted that Taiwan is an excellent place to study the KMT officials and army who "lost China," as well as its tactics after retreating there to ensure that they were not pushed further east—that is, into the sea. Following the massive wartime effort to develop expertise on the areas in which American troops were fighting or in which the government anticipated military action and/or post-war occupation, and preceding the counter-insurgency research such as Project Camelot, the 1950s, was a boom time for area studies. The "Truman doctrine," and its enthusiastic extension by Eisenhower's Secretary of State John Foster Dulles, made the entire world America's beat with a responsibility to save that world from communism, which seemed seductively attractive to peasants. Whether land reform and rural reconstruction might halt the "Red Tide" was an important policy question even before the escalation of American military presence in Southeast Asia led to grasping for "the hearts and minds" of peasants suffering through a guerilla war there. Although land reform would seem patently "un-American," given the importance of land speculation and large landholdings in American history and current agricultural production, it does

---

values: Evan Z. Vogt, and Ethel M. Albert (eds.) *People of Rimrock* (Cambridge, MA: Harvard University Press, 1966).

[85] Gates, op. cit 1987, pp. 236, 232.

seem to have been approved and even prescribed for other parts of the world, in particular during the military occupation of Japan.[86]

A fourth factor in explaining why American social scientists looked through Taiwanese culture without seeing it is a general problem of "Orientalism." Edward Said, who is a member of another group that was politically invisible until very recently to Americans, fifteen years ago wrote a comprehensive critique of Western research on the Middle East.[87] He noted that in the study of Arabic, Indian, Chinese, and even Japanese culture, Western scholars were preoccupied with a glorious, classical past as preserved in old texts, rather than in making sense of the messy, living present. He noted a general flight from the disorientation of direct encounters with living carriers of a culture to the safety and manageability of documents. One does not expect to encounter this pattern among anthropologists, but it does seem to occur among some who work on civilizations with long written traditions. Reading American sinologists, one feels that they want to skip over not only the Japanese occupation of Taiwan and of northeastern China, but the whole Manchu period and reach back to Ming China.[88] Said shows that the

---

[86] See Robert J. Smith and John B. Cornell, *Two Japanese Villages* (Ann Arbor: Center for Japanese Studies, 1956), and the account in Herbert Passin, *Encounter with Japan*, (Tokyo:Kodansha, 1982).

[87] Edward Said, *Orientalism* (New York: Vintage, 1978). As he wrote, the "Orient" has

> a kind of extrareal, phenomenologically reduced status that puts it out of reach of everyone except the Western expert. From the beginning of Western speculation about the Orient, the one thing the Orient could not do was to represent itself. Evidence of the Orient was credible only after it had passed through and been made firm by the refining fire of the Orientalist's fire (p. 283)

> The Orient is eternal, uniform, and incapable of defining itself; therefore it is assumed that a highly generalized and systematic vocabulary for describing the Orient from a Western standpoint is inevitable and even scientifically "objective." (p. 301).

With the substitution of "China" and "sinologist" for "Orient" and "Orientalist" these (and much else of his critique) applies directly to the fabrication of a singular "Chinese culture."

[88] Or beyond: see Mitsuo Suzuki, "The Shamanistic Element in Taiwanese Folk Religion," in A. Bharati, *The Realm of the Extra-Human: Agents and Audiences* (The Hague: Mouton, 1976), p. 259 relating twentieth century Taiwanese *dang-gi* directly back to the epoch of the Warring States.

positing of timeless entities such as "Chinese society" is a recurring habit.[89] The most distinguished comparativist sociologists interested in China—Wolfram Eberhard, Max Weber, and Karl Wittfogel—often treated materials from different millennia as part of a single "Chinese society." For Taiwan, Japanese and KMT household registration records rather than ancient literature and court records provide the escape of preference from complicated contemporary realities to documents. Murphy provided two apt analogies to the standard operating procedures of Sinology: this literature is like what Asians might write about Europeans "if they felt obliged to avoid the confusion of referring to Germans, French, and Italians as different peoples... [and] as if Asian scholars were explaining current European attitudes by reference to material from the early Roman Empire."[90]

Into the 1960s, if "primitives" were not available for study (and after half a century of Japanese rule, the Formosan aboriginal cultures could not be so classified even by those eager to ignore any changes in Hakka and Holo cultures on Taiwan), then anthropologists studied peasants. In either case, the

> classical manner in ethnography may be summarised thus: It is assumed that within a somewhat arbitrary geographical area a social system exists; the population involved in this social system is one culture; the social system is uniform. Hence the anthropologist can choose for himself [/herself] a locality of any convenient size and examine in detail what goes on in this particular locality. He then generalises from these conclusions and writes a book about the organisation of the society considered as a whole.[91]

---

[89] On the widespread marketing of primordialized representations see Arjun Appadurai, "Disjuncture and Difference in the Global Cultural Economy," *Public Culture* 2(1990):1-24 and the example in Wendy Griswold, "The Writing on the Mud Wall: Nigerian novels and the imaginary village," *American Sociological Review* 57(1992):709-724. That "traditions" are constructions of varying historical plausibility is widely accepted in contemporary anthropology (Wendy Leeds-Hurwitz, *Semiotics and Communication*, Hillsdale, NJ: Erlbaum, 1993, pp. 161-70; Linnekin, op. cit.; Handler op. cit.).

[90] H. B. M. Murphy, reviewing A. Kleinman and T. Y Lin, *Normal and Abnormal Behavior in Chinese Culture* (Dordrecht: Reidel, 1981) in *Transcultural Psychiatric Research* 14(1982):37-40.

[91] Edmund Leach, *Political Systems of Highland Burma* (Boston: Beacon Press, 1954), p. 60. For critiques of "village" as a "natural unit" of analysis for peasant societies, see Clifford Geertz, "Form and Variation in Balinese Village Structure," *American Anthropologist* 61 (1959):991-1012; G. William Skinner, "Marketing and Social Structure in Rural Chi-

Although the "whole" for work on Taiwan is often "China," this was not the case of ethnography done in China prior to the victory of the "People's Liberation Army" in 1949. In the community studies done in China before any Western community studies in Taiwan—with the telling exception of Hsu's study of non-Han villagers in the Chinese periphery of Yunnan[92]—there was

> little tendency to overstate the significance of the results in terms of the area to which they applied. Indeed, most of the authors lean the other way, inserting a prominent caveat that the community described is not China but an aspect of a huge and diversified society.[93]

In trying to understand why some American anthropologists writing about Taiwan have followed Hsu rather than the other early writers of Chinese community studies in claiming "the typicality of his population and equat[ing] it without major reservation to a generalized traditional Chinese norm,"[94] perhaps the key is precisely that Taiwan and

---

na," *Journal of Asian Studies* 24(1964):3-23; and Fredrik Barth, *Balinese Worlds* (Chicago: Uniersity of Chicago Press, 1993), pp. 171-3. Bernard Gallin's *Hsin Hsing* was exemplary in stressing that "Hsin Hsing and the other villages of the immediate area are far from being small, isolated units" (p. 45). This pioneer study of a Taiwanese village aimed to describe change, not an incarnation of that timeless essence, "the traditional Chinese village." Although change was not the problematic of her community study, Norma Diamond was also careful to point out that the Dailam fishing village she studied in the early 1960s had been "subjected to modernizing influences for some 60 years [and so] it should not be mistaken for a picture of traditional China" (*K' un Shen, A Taiwan Village,* New York: Holt, Rinehart & Winston, 1969, p. 2; cf. p. 100).

[92] Hsu, op. cit. On the complicated partial sinification and (post-communist-takeover) retribalization of those Hsu studied, see David Yen-Ho Wu, "Chinese Minority Policy and the Meaning of Minority Culture: The example of the Bai in Yunnan, China," *Human Organization* 49 (1990):1-13. Some traits considered outside China as typical of "traditional China" have become part of the self-identification as non-Chinese in Yunnan (as in Taiwan in opposition to another modernizing regime opposed to "feudal superstitions").

[93] Fried, op. cit., p. 22.

[94] Ibid., p. 22, also see pp. 19-20.

Yunnan are peripheral areas with strong historical non-Chinese influences.[95]

Nonetheless, there are also works closer to the Taiwanese ground. In effect, there is intracultural variation within American anthropology. The Taiwanese basis of research is more readily visible in the titles of books and articles by anthropologists not trained at Berkeley and Columbia, as can be seen in Table One.

There is no diminution over time of Taiwanese invisibility in American anthropological work done on Taiwan. Indeed, there is a slight (though statistically non-significant) increase in Taiwanese invisibility in the titles. Early booklength American ethnographies of Taiwan, e.g., Bernard Gallin *Hsin Hsing, Taiwan*, and Norma Diamond's *K'un Shen, A Taiwan Village*, included "Taiwan" in their titles—in English, at least.[96] Before producing the string of titles with "Chinese," even Arthur Wolf entitled his (1964) dissertation *Marriage and Adoption in a Hokkien Village.*

There are (statistically significant) differences by topic of research, however. As shown in Table Two, research on kinship and religion especially evidences participation of American anthropologists in the imposition of "traditional China" on Taiwan. Work on ethnomedicine and working women is by no means unconcerned with the "great tradition" of Chinese civilization, but has generally contained closer attention to Taiwanese distinctiveness. In addition to professional socialization, that is, a Berkeley/Columbia tradition of keeping the Taiwanese location out of titles, significant variation can be accounted for by whether research was done in Daiba Guan, or further from the capital.

Using stepwise regression of a dichotomous dependent variable of whether "Taiwan" or "Taiwanese" occurred in the titles of 223 books and articles based on fieldwork in Taiwan by American-trained anthropologists, we found training at Columbia University, the University of Washington or the University of California at Berkeley in contrast to training at institutions other than these three to be the best explanatory variable. Rsearch topics involving kinship, medicine, religion vs. other topics, and research in Daiba Guan vs. elsewhere also had statistically significant effects. Betas were .37, .23, and .20, respectively. The same three variables were the only ones accounting for significant variance in

---

[95] Even the southeast China from which Taiwanese ancestors emigrated is dubiously "traditional China": see Helen F. Siu, "Cultural Identity and the Politics of Difference in South China," *Dædalus* 122,2 (1993):19-43

[96] Aside from the un-Taiwaneseness of "Hsin Hsing" as a placename, the Chinese on the cover of the book skips from "Hsin Hsing" to the subtitle without including the characters for Taiwan.

Table One
*Country(ies) Listed in Titles of Books and Articles Reporting Research
on Taiwan by American-trained Anthropologists by Institution of
Ph.D.-Training*

University where trained	Percentage of Publications with			(N)
	Only China[*]	China Primary[+]	Taiwan Primary[**]	
Berkeley	78%	0	22	(9)
Washington	67%	0	33	(6)
Columbia	64%	14	22	(36)
Stanford	55%	4	41	(22)
Harvard	50%	0	50	(8)
Cornell	40%	9	51	(53)
Others[++]	19%	9	72	(68)
Johns Hopkins & Michigan	18%	9	73	(11)
Michigan State	0%	20	80	(10)
Total	39%	9	52	(223)

[*] "China" or "Chinese" in title without "Taiwan" or "Taiwanese" in title or subtitle.

[+] "China" or "Chinese" in title, with "Taiwan" or "Taiwanese" in title or subtitle.

[**] "Taiwan" or "Taiwanese" in title, "China" or "Chinese" in subtitle or in neither title nor subtitle.

[++] Universities whose alumni published fewer than five publications based on research in Taiwan are combined as "Other." $X^2 = 53.2$, 18 d.f., $p < .0001$.

China/Chinese receiving primacy in the title (whether or not Taiwan was also visible there), with betas of .37, .24 and .14, respectively. The multiple Rs were .46 and .43, respectively. In addition to interaction effects of the variables with statistically significant correlations to the two specifications of the dependent variable, year of publication, book vs. article, and alternate combinations of topic were included in the analysis, but did not have statistically significant effects. Still, the positive effect for year of publication (indicating increasing Taiwanese invisibility) makes dubious the claims that there is a widening sensitivity to essentializing a monolithic "Chinese culture."

Table Two
*Taiwanese Visibility in Publications by Topic of American-Trained Anthropologists**

| Topic | Percentage of Publications with | | | |
	Only China+	China Primary	Taiwan Primary	(N)
Medicine	62	0	38	(13)
Family/ Kinship	51	9	40	(23)
Religion	54	0	46	(85)
Women	18	6	76	(17)
Other	28	8	64	(85)
Total	39	9	52	(223)

+ Includes four titles with "Taiwan" or "Taiwanese" and "China" or "Chinese" in subtitle.
* Publications without "Chinese", "China", "Taiwanese", or "Taiwan" in the title. X^2=29.2 with 8 d.f. p=.001.

Gates and Ahern claim that anthropologists "develop an instinct for telling if a book with 'China' in its title deals with Taiwan, Hong Kong, the PRC, or the T'ang dynasty."[97] Other than by recognizing the authors on the basis of their earlier work, we doubt that this supposed "instinct" develops. In our experience it is necessary to look at the book or article. Even then, especially in Ahern's work, it is sometimes difficult to tell apart assertions which are generalized from Taiwan to China from those based on mainland Chinese sources. Moreover, it was not always necessary to depend upon a developing such an "instinct" to know whether a publication described Taiwan.

Ethnomedicine
The study of folk medicine blossomed on Taiwan during the 1970s. Although more likely than research on other topics to have "Chinese"

---

[97] Op cit., p. 7.

rather than "Taiwanese" in titles, unlike the more or less contemporaneous work on "Chinese religion," the medical anthropology literature based on fieldwork in Taiwan were more likely to record native terms in whichever language was used by healers and their clients. Most of the illustrative material in Arthur Kleinman's very influential 1980 book *Patients and Healers in the Context of Culture* is from Taiwan.[98] In addition to establishing explanatory models of illness rather than of disease as the proper focus of medical anthropology, that book made Taiwan the exemplary case of medical pluralism. The families of sick Taiwanese do not merely "doctor shop," but (often in succession) try healers from different medical traditions. These include Western medicine with its focus on micro-organisms (viruses and bacteria) and its often-high-tech remedies, Chinese medicine (*diong-I*) with its humoral aetiological theory and herbal remedies, geomancy (*hong-sui*) providing insights into problems resulting from improper alignment of houses or tombs, and Taiwanese spirit mediums (*dang-gi*) exploring illnesses caused by ancestors and other spirits, who must be palliated in order for the ill person to recover. Each kind of practitioner offers explanations of what went wrong to bring about illness, as well as attempting to provide cures. Some of the cures work in some cases, and some of the explanations are accepted. However, there is considerable variance in attribution of which treatment was efficacious,[99] and in confirming the validity of diagnosis.

In contrast to analyses of "Chinese religion" in the singular on Taiwan, the pragmatic diversity in medical behavior and intracultural variation in the salience and content of medical beliefs were stressed in medical anthropological work done on Taiwan during the 1970s.[100] Bernard Gallin cautioned against inferring commitment to a medical tradition (i. e., salience): "Utilization of the traditional systems does not necessarily imply belief in these forms of medicine. Many people 'go through the

---

98 Arthur Kleinman, *Patients and Healers in the Context of Culture* (Berkeley: University of California Press, 1980). There are also examples from his later paradigm's exemplar: *The Illness Narratives* (New York: Basic Books, 1988).

99 Not even temporal contiguity, i.e., the remedy closest in time to recovery, is an adequate predictor of which medical belief system will be substantiated by the illness trajectory.

100 On dangers of essentializing "Chinese medicine" and "patient," see Judith Farquhar, "Problems of Knowledge in Contemporary Chinese Medical Discourse," *Social Science and Medicine* 24(1987):1013-21.

motions'"[101]—just as they do in the realm of religious rituals. As he had described "Hsin Hsing" villagers earlier, "not even the most skeptical are entirely convinced that the rituals are ineffectual."[102] Gallin also cautioned,

> we must be more careful not to attribute the same knowledge, perceptions, and behavior to all member of Chinese society[ies]. For too long, we took for granted the universality of the knowledge and even the behavioral manifestations of the tenets of the great Confucian tradition among the Chinese population[s].[103]

De Glopper puts it even more bluntly:

> There is no single, pristine Great Tradition of Chinese medicine. There are several distinct schools, and when you look at what actual practitioners are doing, the variety is even greater... Since people commonly utilize several therapies at the same time, it seems hard to assume that they are strongly motivated by a desire for conceptual consistency or a single language with which to experience their illness... They do not place their entire confidence in any single practitioner, whether M.D., traditional doctor, diviner, or spirit medium. In my experience on Taiwan a tendency to keep one's options open and to prefer multi-causal explanations is common among ordinary people, as is an appreciation of the unique qualities of very particular case or event. What cured one may not cure another, or what cured someone at a particular time may not work later, because the circumstances are different.[104]

In contrast to the situation in other research specialties, Taiwanese culture is visible and recognized in medical anthropology work.[105]

---

[101] Bernard Gallin, "Comments on contemporary sociocultural studies of medicine in Chinese societies," p. 277 in A. Kleinman et al., *Medicine in Chinese Cultures* (Washington: U. S. Government Printing Office, 1975).

[102] B. Gallin, op. cit. 1966, p. 264.

[103] B. Gallin, op. cit., 1975, p. 278.

[104] Donald R. De Glopper, "Old Medicine in a New Bottle," *Reviews in Anthropology* 4(1977), p. 356. He also rejected a single system "Chinese religion" typifying Lukang, the Jianghua town where he did fieldwork: Donald R. De Glopper, op. cit. 1974.

[105] We have not found any Kleinman publication with "Taiwan" or "Taiwanese" in the title, including the chapter titles in Kleinman. op. cit. 1980, but within his work and that of other medical anthropologists it

This does not mean that the anthropologists had any particular interest in Taiwanese culture. As in other specialties, fieldwork shifted from Taiwan to China when researchers could go there at the end of the decade (with Kleinman again in the lead). Nevertheless, they did not posit a consistent, overarching entity, "Chinese medicine," for comparison with "Western medicine."[106] The data on local and individual diversity in medical belief systems in retrospect might seem unmistakable, but anthropologists have demonstrated a considerable capacity for ignoring intracultural variation in presenting models of this or that culture, and, during the same period, "Chinese religion" remained an authoritative construct despite data of similar diversity from Taiwan.

One partial explanation for the difference between these research specialities is that the typically Orientalist fascination with texts was markedly lower in the work on medicine on Taiwan than in the work on religion, despite the corpus of Chinese texts in various medical tradi-

---

is much easier to tell when data from Taiwan is being discussed than in the literature on "Chinese religion" based on fieldwork on Taiwan.

[106] However,Taiwanese data are fit into dubious etic domain of "medicine." We found it hard to believe the claim by Kleinman (op. cit., p. 219) that Taiwanese *dang-gi* "use the term 'client,' *k'e-jen*, literally, 'guest.'" Aside from *k'e-jen* being a Beijinghua term (rather than the Hokkien *lang-kheh*), it is too mercantile and not sufficiently reverent. Inquiries to devotees of a Dailam *dang-gi* from across Taiwan in 1992 confirmed that our skepticism was justified, that *k'e-jen*, is irreverent, and that the proper term is *xin do* (follower). Bruce Holbrook ("Ethnoscience and Chinese Medicine, Genuine and Spurious," *Bulletin of the Institute of Ethnology, Academia Sinica* 43[1977]:129-180) challenged *dang-gi* being considered part of the same domain as *se-i-sien(g)* (Western-style doctor) and *diong-i-sien(g)* (Chinese-style doctor). He also rejected Kleinman's folk/professional dichotomy, arguing that "there are no native terms for these mystically cognized categories" (Holbrook, op. cit., 151; criticizing Arthur Kleinman "Medical and Psychiatric Anthropology and the Study of Traditional Forms of Medicine in Modern Chinese culture," *Bulletin of the Institute of Ethnology, Academia Sinica*.39(1975):107-123; and op. cit., pp. 50-70; on the problematic conceptual status of "professional" see Julius Roth, "Professionalism: The Sociologist' Decoy," *Sociology of Work and Occupations* 1(1974):6-23). However, it does not seem to us that Holbrook established the emic salience of his own domain "Chinese medicine" including "real" and "fake" Chinese and Western doctors, either. Just as, despite the preoccupation of anthropologists with kinship, the full set of Taiwanese kinship terms has not been published, there is no emically-warranted typology of whatever the emic domain closest to the etic domain "medicine" may be, despite the volume of work on Taiwanese healers and clients.

tions. Another reason for the difference in visibility of Taiwanese materials is that medical anthropologists were much more concerned with ethnosemantics than anthropologists writing about "Chinese religion,"[107] and therefore more leery about translating native terms into Beijinghua.[108]

Furthermore, although medical specialists were certainly a focus of attention for medical anthropologists, religious specialists, particularly Daoist priests, were more central in the anthropological discourse about religion in research done in Taiwan. That is, the behavior and beliefs of those mixing or successively using divergent medical technologies received more attention than the behavior and beliefs of those mixing or successively using divergent religious technologies. Medical anthropology was and is more concerned with messy, varying practices; the anthropology of religion tends to construct cleancut, neat cosmologies.[109]

---

[107] Nonetheless, with an emphasis on intracultural diversity, Kleinman and his followers rejected the quest for formal native taxonomies of mutually exclusive, tightly-integrated, hierarchically-arranged categories and uniquely derivable native diagnoses in the ethnoscience tradition exemplified by Charles O. Frake, "Diagnosis of Disease among the Subanun of Mindanao." *American Anthropologist* 63 (1961):113-32; and, most fully, in Kenneth W. Payne, *The Sulphur Eaters,* Ph.D. dissertation, University of California, 1987. Kleinman (op. cit. 1975) launched an all-out attack on one attempt at ethnoscientific analysis of healers on Taiwan (Bruce Holbrook, "Chinese Psycho-social Medicine: Doctor and tang-ki, an inter-cultural analysis," *Bulletin of the Institute of Ethnology, Academia Sinica* 37(1974):85-112), but blandly absorbed some ethnoscientific work in the background to his synthesis (e.g., see Kleinman op. cit. 1980, p. 30) of clinical and cultural analysis. In general, as Stephen O. Murray, "The Dissolution of Classical Ethnoscience," *Journal of the History of the Behavioral Sciences* 18(1982):163-175, suggested, ethnoscience dissolved into various cognitive anthropologies rather than being destroyed by criticism.

[108] As Judith Farquhar (1990 personal communication) pointed out, the heavy repetition of some Taiwanese terms, notably *tang-ki (dang-gi),* give the appearance that Kleinman used more native terms than he did in writing about the research he did on Taiwan. For instance, on p. 218 of Kleinman, op. cit. 1980, the six underlined "tang-ki" jump out at the reader, but he used (more discreetly italicized) Beijinghua terms for the symptoms of "depressed" and "anxious" rather than what the Taiwanese consulting the *dang-gi* used.

[109] As in Marcel Griaule's *Conversations with Ogotemmêli* (London: International African Institute, 1965).

One "messy" Taiwanese practice in particular, viewed with considerable distaste by Chinese mainlanders on Taiwan, spirit possession, was a central concern of anthropology during the 1970s, although for research locales other than Taiwan it tended to be considered in the domain "religion" rather than the domain "medicine."[110] The lack of shamanistic healing in central and northern China has led to other problematics emerging from fieldwork there, and a lack of comparison to what was studied on Taiwan during the 1970s. Nonetheless, due to the centrality of Kleinman's 1980 book to a paradigm shift within medical anthropology, the diversity and complexity of Taiwanese reality remains unusually visible in that research specialty, and not just the specifically East Asian/West Pacific work within it.

Working Women: The Exception to the Pattern of Finding "Traditional China" on Taiwan

The wide distribution of industrial enterprises to the countryside of Taiwan attracted the interest of many social science observers. Elsewhere, industrialization was an urban phenomenon. Landless workers from the countryside migrated to urban centers. During the first Industrial Revolution in Europe, only mines and lumber mills—both processing raw materials where they were—blighted the countryside. Otherwise, the "dark satanic mills" were located in cities. Noting the rising standard of living in Taiwan, many observers were euphoric, considering Taiwan as a model for rural industrialization without urban social problems. The widespread pollution of the environment went all but unrecorded in the enthusiasm for an example of "spatially equitable" economic development.[111]

---

[110] E.g., I. M. Lewis, *Ecstatic Religion: An Anthropological Study of Spirit Possession and Shamanism* (Baltimore: Penguin, 1971); Erika Bourguignon, *Possession* (San Francisco: Chandler & Sharp, 1976); Peter Fry, *Spirits of Protest* (Cambridge: Cambridge University Press, 1976).

[111] E. g., Jack F. Williams, "Urban and Regional Planning in Taiwan: The quest for balanced regional development," *Tijdschrift voor economische en sociale geografie* 79(1988):175-181; Eva Mueller, "The Impact of Demographic Factors on Economic Development in Taiwan." *Population and Development Review* 3(1977):1- 23; John C. H. Fei, Gustav Ranis and Shirley W. Y. Kuo, *Growth with Equity: The Taiwan Case* (Washington, D.C.: World Bank, 1979); Shirley W. Y. Kuo, Gustav Ranis and John C. Fei, *The Taiwan Success Story* (Boulder: Westview, 1981); Richard E. Barrett and Martin K. Whyte, op. cit.; Gold, op. cit. There is one mention of Daiba pollution in the generally laudatory account of urbanization of Alden Speare Jr., Paul Liu and

The exception to this euphoria was some feminists (Linda Arrigo, Norma Diamond, Rita Gallin, Hill Gates, Lydia Kung) who studied women working in urban and rural factories, and saw that small family enterprises were practically unregulated in terms of worker safety and treatment. They also noted that Taiwanese women constituted a reserve labor army, by postponing marriage and childbirth, much as had the poor families who sold their labor in 19th century British factories. Taiwanese women constituted

> a submissive, docile, and transient labor force, willing to accept low pay and unlikely to remain in one job long enough to agitate for wage increases or improved working conditions. With their minimal training, they are also prepared to accept the lackluster and poorly paid jobs available in labor-intensive industries... To ensure sustained production at low cost during periods of economic growth and political stability during periods of economic recession, the Taiwanese [sic.[112]] government encourages an ideological environment that relegates women to menial labor and household tasks. The marriage of patriarchal ideology and contemporary capitalism allows the family, the nation, and the international market economy to take advantage of women's unpaid domestic and underpaid public labor without altering cultural definitions of male and female roles or

---

Ching Lung Tsay, *Urbanization and Development: The Rural-Urban Transition in Taiwan* (Boulder, CO: Westview, 1988, p. 192). Ho, op. cit., p. 230, noted that air pollution doubled in residential areas of Daiba between 1959 and 1965, commenting "For those living in Taipei and its vicinity the quality of life has been adversely affected by this development—a change not taken into account by the per capita consumption indicator" (or other conventional indicators of development). Cheng, op. cit., p. 499, noted the increasing salience of environmental concerns in Taiwan. Water pollution problems are discussed in 池宗憲, 台灣的血脈 (Daiba: 聯合月刊雜誌社). Also see Jack F. Williams, "Paying the Price of Economic Development in Taiwan: Environmental degradation," *Journal of Oriental Studies* 27(1989):58-78; Walden Bello and Stephanie Rosenfeld, *Dragons in Distress: Asia's Miracle Economies in Crisis* (San Francisco: Institute for Food and Development Policy, 1990), and the massive steering committee's report Taiwan *2000: Balancing Economic Growth and Environmental Protection* (Nankang: Academia Sinica, 1989).

[112] The government of the Republic of China is anything but "Taiwanese"! Although we advocate clear distinction of "Taiwanese" from "Chinese," the government on Taiwan is a Chinese oligarchy.

transforming the structure of male status and authority within the family.[113]

Most of their earnings were turned over to parents, who often invested this income in the education of sons. Diamond reported that women factory workers who lived with their natal families gave seventy to eighty percent of their earnings to their parents. Those moving further away and living in factory dormitories also remitted nearly half of their earnings. Diamond and other anthropologists and sociologists who did fieldwork among women factory workers in Taiwan during its industrialization did not find substantial increases in the independence of these women from decisions made by men.[114]

At least through the 1970s, factory work was a station at which many young women repaid parents the cost of raising them prior to marriage. The median age of females leaving employment (c. 1972) was twenty-nine.[115] With no prospects for advancement within the workplace and with widespread discrimination against the employment of married women, factory discipline is succeeded by subordination to a husband for women working until marriage. The relatively short-term involvement in the labor force, in turn, has been used to justify not promoting women who are viewed as "fickle" and/or "will just get married and leave anyway"—a rationalization not unknown in the USA. The criticism of the exploitation of women factory workers as a reserve of labor to be used or let go with fluctuations in business cycles, and to be routinely exposed to toxic materials in unsafe working conditions, is

---

[113] Rita S. Gallin, "The Entry of Chinese women into the Rural Labor Force: A case study from Taiwan," *Signs* 9(1984), pp. 397-8.

[114] For the most part, the young women maintained traditional views about the appropriateness of female subordination (see Ibid., p. 396; and Norma Diamond, "Women in Industry in Taiwan," *Modern China* 5(1979):317-340), although attitudinal surveys reported Taiwanese men and women stating that women have increasing or equal say in decisions about expenditures (see Martin M. C. Yang, *Socio-Economic Results of Land Reform in Taiwan*, Honolulu: East-West Center Press, 1970, p. 449). Recent work in Shandong by Ellen R. Judd, "Niangjia," *Journal of Asian Studies* 48(1989):525-44 shows that a similar increase in the economic importance of daughters on mainland China has correlated with marriage postponement and with more enduring relations between women and their natal families. This appears to be the case on contemporary, more fully-industrialized Taiwan. See Charles Stafford, "Good Sons and Virtuous Mothers: Kinship and Chinese nationalism in Taiwan," *Man* 27(1992):363-378.

[115] Speare et al., op. cit., p. 103.

the exception to widespread celebration by American social scientists of "the Taiwan miracle."[116] It is also an important exception to subsuming "Taiwanese" under the rubric "Chinese."

With shortages of labor, the pattern has been changing recently, and, according to official statistics, "in 1986 52% of Taiwan's female employees were 30 years of age and older; 42% were married."[117] These statistics raise questions about the continued application of analyses of working Taiwanese women during the early 1970s. The "reserve" may have been "called to active duty," and/or that the demands for more skilled labor have made workers less interchangeable, as also in South Korea.[118]

Although also enamored with the notion of a singular "traditional Chinese culture," political economists have had to examine what happened in the ROC distinct from both colonial Japan and the PRC. In the following two sections we will examine research on two phenomena: the systematic state terror of 1947 and the (not unrelated in attempting to suppress potential Taiwanese bases of opposition) land reform that followed.

A Case Study of Psuedo-Objectivity: The Hoover Institution Analysis of 1947 Resistance and Repression

Research on Taiwanese working women remains an exception to the conception of shared, traditional, Confucian Chinese worship of whomever has power that is advocated by the ROC government and is exemplified by researchers whom it supports and is supported by. A recent, particularly egregious example of complicity with domination (indeed, complicity with large-scale violence) is offered by what allegedly is a value-free political science analysis of a 1947 revolt and its suppression emanating from that bastion of conservative policy, Stanford's Hoover

---

[116] For instance, Kuo et al.; op. cit., Gold, op. cit.; Clark op. cit. This insulting-to-Taiwanese locution is embedded in discourse on political economy arguing against "dependency theory," and as Judith Farquhar and Hill Gates (1990 personal communications) noted, this is a discourse to which anthropologists have not been prominent contributors. See, however, Edwin A. Winckler and Susan M. Greenhalgh, (eds.) *Contending Approaches to the Political Economy of Taiwan* (Armonk, NY: M. E. Sharpe) and Gates, op. cit. 1987, pp. 50-67.

[117] Rita S. Gallin, "Women and Work in Rural Taiwan," *Journal of Health and Social Behavior* 30(1989), p. 374.

[118] Sungnam Cho, "The Emergence of a Health Insurance System in a Developing Country," *Journal of Health and Social Behavior* 30 (1989), p. 469.

Institution. "Given the powerful political passions that still envelop the 1947 tragedy," Lai Tse-Han, Ramon H. Myers, and Wei Wou claimed in their book *A Tragic Beginning: The Taiwan Uprising of February 28, 1947.*[119] "a differentiation of moral and factual issues could be a major step forward in the quest for a just historical judgment" (p. 11). Whether the authors deluded themselves that "justice" is anything other than a moral issue or are attempting to confuse readers is not altogether clear, but the book obviously aimed to exculpate the highest Kuomintang officials, President Chiang Kai-Shek and Governor General Ch'en Yi from responsibility for knowing what KMT troops were going to do when they landed in Taiwan (indiscriminate violence) and for the subsequent (more discriminate) searching out and murder of Taiwanese judged as opponents of the regime.

The political "science" to which the authors aspired is taxonomy rather than analysis. They were particularly eager to classify the events of March 1947, closing their introduction with the admonition from Yin Hai-Kuang, "Whatever something is, that is what you say it is (Shih shen-mo, chiu shuo shen-mo)" (p. 12), and writing that "to call the episode an 'incident' is to place a veil over its actual nature" (p. 8).

"Tragedy" is also veil, one in which they wrapped Chiang Kai-Shek and Ch'en Yi. "Tragedy" is quite an unusual analytical concept in political science,[120] but may be apt for a number of different interpretations of Taiwanese and Chinese history. For many Taiwanese, the first tragedy was that the US Navy transported troops of the Republic of China to Taiwan rather than occupying Taiwan with US or multi-national Allied troops. The armies of occupations of the islands to the north of Taiwan (the Ryukus and of Japan) did not loot the conquered territory, did not dismantle the surviving infrastructure, and withdrew after supervising free elections. Their record stands in marked contrast to the four decades of martial law and continuing para-military rule of Taiwan. An earlier tragedy is that, to keep what Lai et al. (apparently without irony) refer to as "the central government" of Chiang Kai-Shek in the war with Japan, US President Franklin Roosevelt and British Prime Minister Winston Churchill allocated Manchuria and Formosa to be "restored to the Republic of China" in the Cairo Declaration of 1

---

[119] Stanford University Press, 1991. Subsequent pages references are in the text.

[120] "Tragedy" is also the category used by the communist leaders of the People's Republic of China for the "Cultural Revolution" to avoid assessing the responsibility to anyone, especially a party still holding power. See Jonathan Mirsky, "Literature of the Wounded," *New York Review* 39,5 (5 March 1992): 6-10.

December 1943.[121] Following upon Roosevelt's and Churchill's un-concern for Taiwanese self-determination, the depredations of ROC offi-cials and troops were predictable. A number of US military and diplo-matic observers of "the central government" in Chungking filed reports on the corruption and incompetence that characterized a dependent ally which played no active part in defeating Japan.[122] US officials also ob-served and reported upon the plunder and misrule of the island. One of them, George Kerr, later wrote a book, *Formosa Betrayed* [123] based on what he observed.

Unlike Kerr, the tragedy with which Lai et al. concerned themselves was not the jettisoning of the principle of self-determination supposedly maintained by the US, but the failure of Taiwanese to appreciate the frustrations and travails of the army of occupation allocated to them and Taiwanese utter alienation by ROC corruption, incompetence and bru-tality of those supposedly "liberating" them from Japanese colonialism. "The tragedy was a reflection of China's struggles in the 1940s to turn itself from a traditional society into a modern one, with an efficient democratic government," according to Lai et al. (p. 11). It is difficult to know what this statement means. Who is the "China" that was struggl-ing and seeking democracy? Is a "reflection" an epiphenomenon? Are Taiwanese people and their reactions a epiphenomenal and determined solely by events and patterns on mainland China? That Lai et al. wrote of Taiwan as "one small part of China" in the same paragraph (and else-where) supports this last interpretation. Such a characterization is any-thing but neutral, either in the context of 1947 or in that of 1990s de-mands for the independence of Taiwan.

"One small part of China" is a telltale sign that the authors adopted the perspective of the Kuomintang as the legitimate government of Tai-wan. From this perspective—and only from this non-factual perspec-tive—"whether the dissidents' acts in February and March amounted to

---

[121] The "Republic of China" proclaimed on 1 January 1912 had never governed Formosa before 1945. We are not aware of any ROC claims of Formosa prior to the Japanese invasion of mainland Asia in 1937. Both Sun Yat-Sen and Mao Zhedong advocated independence for Formosa before Japan invaded the mainland. In 1945 Japan surrendered unconditionally. It did not "retrocede" Formosa to the ROC or to any other specific government. It was US military forces that provided ROC forces transport to both Manchuria and Formosa, where very similar looting and treatment of the native population as a conquered people followed.

[122] See Barbara Tuchman's *Stillwell and the American Experience in China,1911-1945* (New York: Macmillan, 1971).

[123] Boston: Houghton-Mifflin, 1965.

sedition is a factual question that lacks a moral dimension" (p. 10). To this day, the ROC government treats advocacy of independence for Taiwan as sedition. Whether the only army of occupation from World War II still holding power should be able to define sedition (or, indeed, to define law in general) is a question with a moral dimension that the authors ignore. There can only be "sedition" against a legitimate government, and the legitimacy of KMT rule of Taiwan is not a question Lai et al. raised.

There are many instances of uncritical adoption by Lai et al. of KMT historical perspectives. One of the most egregious is the interpretation of the 1895 declaration of Formosan independence as evidence of Taiwanese "patriotic attachment to China" (p. 44). The "patria" was Formosa, not China. There was a declaration of independence, not a declaration of continued loyalty to China. It is understandable that the KMT would obfuscate this, but when ostensible "scientists" follow this party line, their lack of neutrality is starkly visible.

The authors participated in (rather than analyzed) a number of KMT definitions of a number of past and present situations. We have already mentioned the "restoration" or "recovery" by a government (or party) of a territory it had never previously ruled. By the conclusion of the book, the authors have Mainlanders "returning" where they'd never been. An even more peculiar view is that the ROC defeated Japan (p. 50, p. 169). Neutral observers might wonder what battles the ROC won, how the "central government" happened to be in so peripheral a location as Chungking, and even after Japan surrendered could not get to Taiwan (, Manchuria, etc.) on its own (p. 62). Taiwanese most certainly had not seen ROC troops defeat Japanese troops. No one had! The ROC military continued to demonstrate the same prowess and tactical genius in Manchuria and elsewhere during the late 1940s that it had demonstrated during the war with Japan. To claim that in 1945 the KMT was moving from the stage of "tutelage" to that of "constitutional rule" (p. 51) is almost as peculiar, since security laws continue to make even advocacy of a constitutional convention "sedition" into the 1990s.

Full of sympathy for the difficulties of governing China, the authors bewailed that in the late 1940s "knowing little about what had happened on the Mainland during Word War II, many Taiwanese never appreciated the seriousness of the problems confronting the Nationalist government in 1945" (p. 50). Lai et al. did not explain why Taiwanese should have been grateful or loyal to a government they had neither elected nor sought.[124] The authors seem to have been unable to conceive that any-

---

[124] Lai et al. admitted that before Japanese invasion, "China remained afflicted by warlordism, even in the KMT's base area of Chekiang and

one (in the 1940s or the 1990s) could question the KMT right to rule Taiwan as a part of China. They did not see anything wrong with the KMT view of Taiwan

> as primarily a source of resources with which to fight important bat-
> tles on the Mainland. In fact, Mainlanders felt that because Taiwan
> enjoyed greater wealth and higher living standards than the Main-
> land, Taiwanese should carry a heavier burden than other Chinese in
> the struggle to defeat the Communists and modernize (p. 169).

> The KMT worldview was not unreasonable. The KMT was trying to
> save China from Communism, seeking values in the Confucian tradi-
> tion of indigenous civilization, and pursuing unification and moder-
> nization of China according to Sun Yat-sen's vision (p. 179).

Although they think that it would have been wise for the army of occupation not to alienate the populace, they do not consider the consent of
the governed a moral necessity. They recognized that "people like the
P'engs [P'eng Ming-Min] saw the KMT as an institution that would
drag Taiwan down to the level of Chinese backwardness" (p. 21), but
could only conceive the problem with ROC critics of P'eng's generation as deriving from a lack of "conceptual access to the evocation of
Confucian ideals that was to become central to the ideology and culture
of Taiwan under the KMT" on the part of those exposed to (or in the
KMT view, contaminated by) liberal Western and Japanese ideas (p.
22). Such Taiwanese intellectuals were also offensively (in the view of
the KMT and of Lai et al.) aware of Chinese isolation and backwardness
in contrast to Taiwan's longtime participation in the world economy.
"Nothing was more offensive to the Mainlanders than the idea of looking up to the Taiwanese elite as Japanese-trained experts on modernization when Chinese had just fought and defeated the Japanese," Lai et al.
explained (p. 50).[125]

Governor General Ch'en Yi refused to speak Japanese, although he
appears to have been more fluent in it than he was in Beijinghua, the

---

> Kiangsu," and that, on the mainland, "the KMT was never able to ex-
> pand its membership beyond 600,000, which constituted only about
> 0.003% of the country's total population (p. 52). Aside from the fact
> that these numbers do not make sense together (requiring twenty
> billion Chinese, whereas the 1953 census enumerated 583 million and
> the usual KMT estimate for the population on the eve of the Japanese
> invasion was 450 million), it is difficult to imagine anyone seeking so
> unpopular a party to provide tutelage in democracy.

[125] It is difficult to interpret World War II or even a single battle as having
been won by the modernity of the KMT army.

official language imposed by the KMT, and although practically no Taiwanese understood Beijinghua.[126] Ch'en Yi's government used the fact that "most former Taiwanese officials could not speak *kuo-yü* and were not trained to work in a Chinese administration" to justify replacing those who had "collaborated" with the Japanese "enemy" (to which an earlier Chinese regime had ceded Formosa) with Ch'en Yi's mainlander cronies and followers (p. 67).[127] Officials, from Ch'en Yi down, did not speak the languages (Holo, Hakka, and Japanese) that Taiwanese understood. This language policy guaranteed that Taiwanese perceived the government as alien. It indicated unmistakably the view of the Taiwanese as a conquered people without rights that underlay the conduct of Ch'en Yi's government of Taiwan. Lai et al. found Ch'en Yi's refusal to use Japanese "understandable," although they saw his language policy as contributing to the his and his followers' isolation from Taiwanese realities that led to revolt.

Another of Ch'en Yi's tactical mistakes, in the view of Lai et al., was permitting relative freedom of the press. Apparently, they were shocked (in the 1990s) that an article in the *Ho-p'ing jih-pao* published on 8 August 1946 "emphasized how the Taiwanese sincerely wanted democracy, and gave readers the impression that the administration was not sincerely trying to fulfill those hopes" (p. 77). They were similarly astounded that "reports often depicted complex events in a way that made the administration seem inept... Given the freedom to criticize the government, the press often did not provide balance" (p. 77). Lai et al. provided plenty of evidence of the ineptness of the administration, although the authors are imbued with compassion for the sufferings and loss of face of the backward KMT officials. Immediately after noting a

---

[126] Those who did, had difficulty understanding either Ch'en Yi or Chiang Kai-Shek when they spoke Beijinghua.

[127] Lai et al. acknowledged that

> instead of being co-opted, the Taiwanese elite in the bureaucracy had been dispossessed and grossly insulted.... Under the Japanese, the bureaucracy of 84,559 had included 46,955 Taiwanese, but under the ROC, the bureaucracy of 44,451 included only 9,951. In 1946, therefore, some 36,000 former Taiwanese officials had lost their jobs. If the average household size of these officials numbered around seven persons (the average household size for that period), then about a quarter of a million people were affected by the staff reduction" (pp. 65-7) —

about 4% of the population. The replacement of Taiwanese by mainlanders in government monopoly businesses continued in the 1950s.

lack of balance in the press before March 1947, Lai et al. wrote, "After the spring of 1947, when the press became more strictly controlled, it blamed the Uprising on the 'poisonous' influence of Japanese colonial rule, underworld elements, and riffraff" (pp. 77-78), leaving this official view as an apparent example of the balance so sadly lacking before March 1947.[128] Probably not coincidentally, their example of balance corresponds to the explanation for the revolt offered by Ch'en Yi:

> Ch'en began by arguing that the Taiwanese had lost their understanding of Chinese culture and their spirit of nationalism because of 51 years of Japanese rule. He then blamed the press for criticizing his administration and for sowing seeds of dissension between Taiwanese and Mainlanders. He blamed the Japanese wartime mobilization programs for the anti-Chinese attitude of many urban young people,[129] especially those who had returned form places overseas, like Hainan Island. He also blamed Taiwanese business people for not recognizing how publicly owned enterprises had contributed to the island's recovery (pp. 150-1).

Lai et al. join the Taiwanese of the 1940s in not recognizing economic recovery attributable to state monopolies. They also recognized at least the corruption and incompetence of the Ch'en Yi's government, although they went to considerable lengths to exculpate him personally. For instance, they asserted that "no one could criticize the Governor-General for corrupt behavior" (p. 78). Even if Ch'en Yi did not enrich himself, he presided over looting by his subordinates and bought support by retaining these subordinates.[130] "He took no action against them, even if they turned out to be corrupt or incompetent" (p. 79), as they say. Complicity with corruption is corrupt, and we will falsify Lai et al.'s statement by saying that **we** criticize Ch'en Yi for corrupt behavior, even if he was as frugal as they claim. It was his policy to give control to his subordinates of what had been Japanese private as well as public enterprises. If he didn't know what they were doing, he was in-

---

[128] It is difficult not to see such blaming the press for fomenting dissatisfaction through lack of respect of the government in the rightwing American discourse, particularly in a book coming from the Hoover Institution, a place that it is hard to conceive of as a home of objectivity.

[129] Those involved in advocating independence for Taiwan now (1993) were almost all educated under KMT rather than Japanese rule.

[130] Given the KMT/Hoover Institution view that Taiwan is intrinsically a part of China, it is curious that Ch'en Yi's subordinates had "less understanding of local conditions" (p. 87) than Japanese colonialists had had.

competent. If he did know, he was a partner in corruption, however low a share he took for himself. More than a "development strategy" of "statism" was involved!

Besides minimizing Ch'en Yi's responsibility for undermining the economy and social order, Lai et al. waxed lyrical about the hardships of "mainland officials who had arrived on the island with the sincere intention of reuniting the two societies [but] became frustrated and bitter" at Taiwanese lack of sympathy for the rigors of "public service": "Life in a semi-tropical environment required adjustment, and officials, most of whom could not bring their families, experienced loneliness and frustration" (p. 95). Of course, being posted to someplace distant from one's family was an essential feature of traditional Chinese governance. Moreover, Japanese officials seem to have adjusted to the semi-tropical environment, although Japan is north of the birthplaces of most of the KMT officials who fled to Taiwan during the 1940s.

Despite having acknowledged the substantial mismanagement of the economy, the rampant corruption and misrule that were undermining the rule of law that had characterized the Japanese era, Lai et al. at no point questioned the legitimacy of KMT rule of Taiwan. They judgeed Ch'en Yi and many of his officials as "honest" and "sincere" and as unjustly maligned by Taiwanese (in the 1940s and since). Ch'en Yi and his government would have been wiser to have proceeded differently in the authors' view, but Taiwanese should have been willing to be expropriated for the struggle against communism on the mainland by some residual Chinese patriotism and Confucian sense of duty to accommodate armed aliens. (Presumably, Lai et al. consider this another factual rather than moral judgment.) Lai et al. seem to believe that the population of Taiwan owed the KMT obedience and should have ignored the mismanagement of economy and society Taiwanese experienced in 1945-7, but they nowhere have explained **why** they believe this. Nor have they identified any point at which they think that revolt is justified.

Only within the framework of a legitimate government can "sedition" be a "factual question" (p. 10). Lai et al. counterfeited objectivity within a circumscribed realm of legitimacy to argue that during the first days of March 1947 "demands escalated and took on a revolutionary character is indisputable" (p. 99). Again on p. 102, the objective social scientists note that because some of the "demands would have in effect ended the sovereign authority of the ROC in Taiwan, they can be called 'revolutionary.'" Their own chronology shows that the 32 Demands of the Taipei Resolution Committee made on 7 March (two days **after** Chiang Kai-Shek had dispatched troops to crush the rebellion) were withdrawn on 8 March (before the troops arrived) and belies their conclusion (on p. 177) that the the first trajectory (increasing radicalization of dissident demands) caused the second trajectory (the central govern-ments' shift from conciliation to repression).[131]

Although Lai et al. took great pains to invoke "revolutionary" in re-gard to some Resolution Committee proposals, they adamantly refused to characterize what happened as a "revolution." They do not want to veil what happened between 28 Feb. and 8 March 1947 as merely an "incident," but they also do not want to accede that there could have been a Taiwanese revolution.

Although they do not approve of the amount (and, especially) indis-criminateness of the terror that followed the arrival of reinforcements for the garrison army, Lai et al. maximized estimates of the Chinese casu-alties in the first days of March and minimized estimates of the Taiwan-ese casualties beginning in the early hours of 9 March 1947.[132] Note their use of the passive in the following: "Killings occurred, trials were conducted, people involved in the recent Uprising were imprisoned and in some cases innocent people were persecuted" (p. 151).[133] Just as Lai et al. do not hold Ch'en Yi responsible for the conduct of his govern-ment in 1945-7, they exculpate Chiang Kai-Shek and his commanders for the massacres beginning with the landing of troops in Keelung 9

---

[131] They plausibly argued (pp. 176-7) that Ch'en Yi did not want to have to request the diversion of troops from the mainland civil war. However, this does not make clear when it was that he began to buy time with the expectation of later repression. The authors were quick to credit Ch'en Yi with sincerity in this, as in other matters.

[132] Lai et al. considered the judge's mention of "several thousand" casu-alties rather than "more than 10,000" in the trial of Monopoly Bureau officials charged with instigating a riot as evidence that the number was less than 10,000 on p. 159. One can think of many reasons for a ROC judge not to mention the number of casualties even had he known their number. Lai et al. did not discuss allegations that some Taiwanese corpses were dressed in army uniforms or the attempts to use the official registries to estimate the number of Taiwanese who were killed in 1947. Provincial Councilwoman Chang Wen-Yin contrasted the 1948 death rate with the 1947 data to estimate that 19,146 were killed. To the horror of the official inquiry contracting it, Chen Kuan-Zheng's modeling of fatalities based on disappearances of names from household registries and expected deaths from natural causes raised esti-mates of fatalities to 100,000 (*Taiwan Tribune*, 20 Jan. 1992) and included a figure of 18-28,000.

[133] An exception to the lack of agents is "Gen. P'eng Meng-chi, comman-der of the Go'hyiong Fortress HQ... ordered the massacres in Kaohsiung and Tainan" (p. 161).

March, "spray[ing] the wharfs and street with gunfire, shooting anybody on sight" (p. 156).

No more than the corruption of ROC officials on Taiwan could the conduct of ROC troops have been a surprise to Chiang Kai-Shek or to Ch'en Yi, for "the tactic of shooting indiscriminately at people and houses had long been used by KMT troops and warlord armies on the Mainland when putting down opposition" (p. 156). Lai et al. repeated without questioning Ch'en Yi's claim that "he had not anticipated the vindictive behavior of the troops" (p. 178), and wrote that "Chiang Kai-shek and Ch'en Yi could not have been expected to control those divisions and regimental commanders and officers who rounded up and shot unarmed citizens, secretly disposed of their bodies, and strafed residences and shops" (p. 161).

Considering that Ch'en Yi requested the troops and that Chiang Kai-Shek dispatched them, this is one of the most peculiar statements in the entire book. The Governor General and the President/Generalisimo may not have issued specific orders to gun down unarmed civilians upon landing, but both have to have known that this was more than likely and to have expected it. Someone issued specific orders to seize "revolutionaries" in subsequent days. Lai et al. did not trace the origins of these lists, however, and guidance of this systematic roundup of purportedly "disloyal" intellectuals cannot be attributed to rowdy troops that had just landed.[134]

Chiang Kai-Shek and Ch'en Yi were in command and responsible for what occurred. It is a matter of fact that they did not issue orders against the conduct that Lai et al. acknowledge was standard operating procedure for ROC troops—conduct that would constitute war crimes in international conflict.

Although they are fully aware that Ch'en Yi requested reinforcements and Chiang Kai-Shek decided to send the 21st Division on 5 March (pp. 142, 144), Lai et al. repeated Chiang's disingenuous rationale of 10 March 1947: "Last Friday, March 7, the so-called Feb. 28th Incident Resolution Committee unexpectedly made some irrational de-

---

[134] "Our sources are silent about who provided the lists of people for Nationalist troops to arrest, imprison, and even shoot" (p.164). There is no indication that Lai et al. made serious attempts to find out. With similar(ly motivated) lack of diligence, they were only able to find one account by a military participant, and do not mention asking about it in the "around 60" interviews they conducted. They mentioned being granted permission to examine the records of the Garrison Command in Taipei without ever being able to gain actual access to them (p. 12), but it seems they did not try very hard to find out who supplied lists of Taiwanese to roundup or of accounts of officially-sanctioned violence.

mands..." (p. 147). Demands made on 7 March were irrelevant to what had been decided two days earlier. Such a public statement provides dubious "pinpointing" of what was significant in Chiang's decision on (or before) 5 March. Taking after-the-fact public pronouncements as adequate analyses of motives is a dangerous methodology for political science. To claim that demonstrably anachronistic accounts "pinpoint" motivation is to participate in rather than to analyze an ideology and shows yet again that Lai et al. (and Thomas Metzger, who "provided the framework for this study"—p. viii) are apologists for the KMT rather than the objective scientists they claim to be.

The authors revealed their involvement in KMT ideology of the 1990s (again) in their trivialization of advocacy for independence by some Democratic Progressive Party leaders "because they lacked any other significant issue... to woo voters from the KMT" (p. 184). Metzger, Lai et al. remain unwilling to take seriously that any Taiwanese (now or in 1947) seeks independence for Taiwan. Since the end of World War II, most places that were colonies before the war have achieved independence. Peoples suppressed for decades by Leninist regimes from the Baltic to the Balkans have struggled to establish independent states. Yet the purportedly objective social scientists who planned and wrote this book were unable to conceive that anyone but gangsters and terrorists would challenge the legitimacy of the Leninist regime foisted on Taiwanese by the victors of World War II. To them, nationalism, "common in our century," is reasonable if it is Chinese, but unreasonable if it is Taiwanese (p. 179). What could be more objective?

If the authors were sincerely concerned with making a contribution to social science rather than with minimizing the culpability of the KMT/ROC for the massacre of many thousands of Taiwanese civilians, one might expect comparison to other revolutions, successful or failed, or at least to comparison to other occurrences of urban revolts in Chinese societies.[135]

---

[135] The only comparison they made was to coastal provinces after the Japanese surrender, where the reaction to KMT misrule "never crystallized into any widespread uprising involving the seizure of government facilities, demands that the ROC forces disarm, and call for immediate democratization" (p. 173).

Lai et al. recurrently contrasted the number of ROC troops on Taiwan in early 1947 to the higher number of Japanese troops earlier as some sort of explanation of the revolt of 1947. The number of police was roughly the same, and the authors seem to forget that Taiwan was a wartime base for the Japanese empire. Japanese troops were not used to

A *Tragic Beginning* is **not** a contribution to a comparative science of politics. Although it marks an advance from absurd traditional KMT "explanation" of communist agitation as the cause of dissatisfaction in Taiwan in 1947 by acknowledging the incompetence and corruption of Ch'en Yi's administration, the book is still an attempt to defend Ch'en Yi and Chiang Kai-Shek. Despite claims to being "factual" and "objective" and not making moral judgments, Lai et al.'s underlying assumption that the KMT government is legitimate and that advocacy of independence is illegitimate is not a factual judgment nor a matter of science. The authors are either incapable of differentiating fact and value or misrepresenting what they are doing in the book that is based upon and filled with anti-democratic values. Whether one judges their neo-conservative, neo-Confucian values as moral or as immoral, their pretense of objectivity was fraudulent. Directly and indirectly,[136] they are paid apologists for the Kuomintang and its continued fantasy state, the "Republic of China."

Studies of Land Reform

Albeit more subtly than the attempt by Lai et al. to explain away ROC violence in suppressing resistance in early March of 1947, research on a major process of subsequent history also identified with the Chinese overlords on Taiwan rather than examining how Taiwanese felt and were affected by the Chinese government. Evaluating the impacts of KMT land reform was a central problematic of early research on Taiwan.[137] These scholars did not prescribe it as a model, probably realizing that such a policy can only be carried out by an alien régime with-

---

control Taiwanese after the initial pacification in the first decade of Japanese colonial rule.

[136] That is, as employees of the ROC and of the Hoover Institution, to which the ROC has given considerable sums of money, whether or not any ROC funds were allocated specifically to financing the research and writing of this book.

[137] Frank B. Bessac, "Some Social Effects of Land Reform in a Village on the Taichung Plain," *Journal of the China Society* 4(1964):15-28; Idem., "An Example of Social Change in Taiwan Related to Land Reform," *University of Montana Contributions to Anthropology* 1 (1967):1-31; Bernard Gallin, "Land Reform in Taiwan: Its effect on rural social organization and leadership." *Human Organization* 22 (1963):109-22; Idem., "Rural Development in Taiwan: The role of the government," *Rural Sociology* 29(1964):313-23 and op. cit. 1968; Anthony Y. Koo, *The Role of Land Reform in Economic Development: A Case Study of Taiwan* (New York: Praeger, 1968); Martin M. C. Yang, op. cit., 1970.

out local ties. As Amsden noted in analyzing Taiwan as an exceptional case,

> Taiwan's land reform was engineered exogenously, by the Kuomintang, in alliance with the Americans. The Taiwanese landed aristocracy could be expropriated because the Americans and mainlanders were under no obligation to it. This was a most unusual situation, and unlikely to be repeated.[138]

Anthropologists are more reluctant than political scientists to praise military conquest as the royal route to progress, whether or not they appreciate the impact and extent of the KMT slaughter of Taiwanese in 1947.[139] Moreover, they appear to realize that not just rural landowners but agriculture was sacrificed to promote industrialization of Taiwan in a series of government policies made without any popular input.

Another obstacle to explaining the process and the outcomes is that there were no anthropologists observing the decision-making of the central government, nor rural aspirations in the late 1940s and early 1950s, nor even the implementation of various land-to-the-tiller laws between 1948 and 1953. Anthropologists arrived in Taiwanese village **after** the fact and tried to estimate the effects of land reform on rural social structure.

Martin Yang, the author of one of the pioneer community studies from China,[140] reported the results of a 1964 survey by 30 interviewers of 1250 ex-tenant farmers, 250 current tenant farmers, 250 ex-landlords, and 100 non-farmers from five regions in his 1970 book, *Socio-Economic Results of Land Reform in Taiwan*. Those who were still tenant farmers after land reforms provide a control group for comparison of direct effects of land reform. Yang found relatively equivalent rates of adopting various "modern" characteristics by tenant farmers and by former tenant farmers suggest that land reform was not an important cause of other changes viewed as "modernization,"but a concomitant variation. For instance, an increase in voting for village head by ex-tenants of 84% was matched by an increase among tenants of 83%; a 75% in-

---

138 Alice Amsden, "Taiwan's Economic History: A cast of étatisme and a challenge to dependency theory," *Modern China* 5(1979), p. 373.

139 The continued terror at the time of land reform, when no American ethnographers were yet in the field in Taiwan, as well as the bitterness of those who had acquired land, is shown in Vern Sneider's novel, *A Pail of Oysters* (New York: G. P. Putnam's Sons, 1953). The best American account of the 1947 massacres is George H. Kerr's *Formosa Betrayed*, op. cit.

140 *A Chinese Village*, op. cit.

crease in consulting Western-style physicians by ex-tenants was surpassed by a 113% increase by tenants, and so on through family roles and acceptance of agricultural innovations. Although the data are not always presented in ways permitting comparison,[141] and although the questions about approval of land reform were quite general and framed about what most people thought rather than what the individual men questioned thought, most ex-tenants considered land reform positively, and so did Yang. He was concerned that fragmentation of landholdings would make further agricultural development difficult. He warned,

> The land problem in Taiwan is far from being resolved... Redistribution of landownership might later become a hindrance to the development of a modernized agriculture... The smallness of the farms [after land reform] is such a serious deterrent to modernization and mechanization that significant advances can hardly be hoped for.[142]

Gallin also noted the small and fragmented holdings of farmers in the village he studied in the late 1950s. He reported that less than half the farmers did not realize any cash from their crops. He also reported a slight decrease in land cultivated in contrast to 1949-51,[143] and noted that when the tax burden was added to the mortgage payments, farmers who had been tenants on public lands (primarily holdings of the Taiwan

---

[141] For instance, 38% of former tenants built new houses, 39% percent repaired houses, and 61% of current tenants rebuilt or repaired their houses. Not knowing how many ex-tenants both repaired and built houses, it is not even clear which group did more home improvement. Depending on how many former tenants both repaired and built houses, 61% compares to some percentage between 39 and 77.

[142] Yang, *Results* , pp. 258-9. Chen, Hsi-Huang "Economic Analysis of Small Farms," pp. 378-9 in T. Yu & Y. Yu, *Essays on Taiwan's Agricultural Development* (Daiba: Lien Ching, 1975) challenged the contention that small farms are less efficient by showing that the value of output per hectare of farms of less than half a hectare was NT$40,900 in contrast to NT$26,700 for larger farms. However, the output per man was $20,000 in contrast to $25,000 for larger farms. Hwang Chi-Lien *Wages and Income of Agricultural Workers in Taiwan.*(Daiba: National Taiwan University Research Institute of Rural Socio-Economics. 1968) reported that 1963 yields per family for tenant farmers was NT$29,877, in contrast to $34,653 for owners, and $39,095 for part-owners. These data suggest that owners produce more than tenants, and part-owners/part-tenants produce still more (per person rates were $30K, $40K, $43K, respectively).

[143] B. Gallin, *Hsin Hsing,* Table 13.

Sugar Corporation) were paying more of their crops than before the sale of the land.[144] He concluded that the Land-to-the-Tiller Act

> in itself had not brought any noteworthy increase in the standard of living... Villagers who work outside of Hsin Hsing have done more to raise the standard of living than has the decrease in tenancy. The increased use of cash has also led to an apparent rise in living standards. In Japanese times, villagers tended to save their money toward future land purchases. Today, people no longer save money for fear of inflation.[145]

Gallin also noted that a result of the static land market was "an ossification of socioeconomic mobility within the rural area,"[146] pushing aspirations into business and out of agriculture, if not out of the countryside.

In contrast to Gallin's and Yang's careful consideration of land reform in the context of various social changes with varying unanticipated effects, Koo compiled data on increased agricultural productivity and income on Taiwan after 1948. Since he did not disaggregate data by size of landholding, nor by change in ownership, his attribution of all changes in the agricultural sector to land reform was more an act of faith or an instance of the post hoc ergo proper hoc fallacy, than it was an analysis of differential effects of various changes in agriculture on Taiwan in the 1950s and 60s.[147] It was hardly the case that everything except land tenure remained constant in rural Taiwan in the 1950s and 60s, so that effects could clearly be attributed to land reform. Chen Hsiang-Shui argued that there is only an indirect relationship between land reform and increased productivity, that trends in the latter preceded land reform, and that they depended on the acceptance of technological changes such as hybrid seeds, fertilizers, and insecticides.[148]

Longer term trends in agricultural development on Taiwan fit Chen's view better than Koo's. Within the long history of non-subsistence agriculture in Taiwan, Myers and Ching questioned whether equality in land tenure is a prerequisite of agricultural development, since

---

[144] Ibid., pp. 96-7.

[145] Ibid., 108-9.

[146] Ibid., p. 120.

[147] Cf. the argument for the technological basis of increased productivity proposed by Chen Hsiang-Shui, "Land Reform in Green-Tree Village," *Bulletin of the Institute of Ethnology, Academia Sinica* 43(1977):65-84.

[148] H-H Chen, op. cit.

Taiwan under Japanese colonial rule achieved rapid and sustained agricultural growth despite widespread tenancy and very unequal land distribution. The Japanese successfully repeated the institutional organizational and reforms, tested during the early Meiji period, of working through the landlords and wealthy farmer class to encourage the introduction of innovations into agriculture.[149]

They singled out improved seeds as the most important change leading to increased productivity during the Japanese era. While concurring on the importance of technological improvements, especially

successful adaptation to Taiwan of seeds with high yields, greater resistance to disease and high wind, and more receptivity to fertilizer and intensive care," Ho stressed that "science alone cannot transform agriculture without certain rural institutions being created first or at least concomitantly,"[150]

and credited district agriculture improvement stations applying the findings of the Taiwan Agricultural Research Institute, both established by the colonial government. In the following decades many national and international incentives to change were offered to rural Taiwanese. Increasing the number of landholders and decreasing the size of landholdings were only one change among many. Between 1951 and 1960 ten percent of the growth in agricultural output resulted from increases in crop areas.[151]

For the subsequent decades Fei, Ranis and Kuo considered "land reform, followed by increases in multicropping and cultivation of new crops by the poorer (smaller) farmers, caused agricultural income to become significantly more equally distributed over time,"but not the primary cause of greater family income equity in rural Taiwan:

Because nonagricultural income was more equally distributed than agricultural income, the growth of rural industries and services made a substantial contribution to FID [family income distribution equity]... The steady increase of opportunities in rural by-employment available to members of rural families, especially the poorer

---

149 Ramon H. Myers and Adrienne Ching, "Agricultural Development in Taiwan under Japanese Colonialism," *Journal of Asian Studies* 23 (1964) , p. 555.

150 Samuel P. S. Ho, *The Economic Development of Taiwan, 1860-1970* (New Haven: Yale University Press, 1978),pp. 58-9.

151 Ibid., p. 155.

ones, greatly contributed to the complementarity of growth and FID.[152]

Hidden taxes, in particular the government's fertilizer monopoly, and the official undervaluation of the price of rice in contrast to the market price, transfer agricultural surpluses to other economic sectors. Landholders raising other crops had to purchase rice at market prices to pay land taxes, to provide the additional rice required to be sold at the official price rate, and to buy fertilizer, and determination of how much rice had to be bartered for fertilizer to the Food Bureau (the fertilizer monopoly).[153] These systematic government extractions of rice at valuations below market values significantly hampered the possibility of families improving their standard of living by agricultural production, especially during the 1960s, and "effectively transferred part of the increase out of agriculture"to industry.[154] Ho notes that

---

[152] Fei, et al., op. cit., pp. 314-5.The same authors (Kuo et al., op. cit., p. 50) later wrote that "land reform was the primary ingredient of sustained increase of agricultural productivity in the early 1950s." Ho (*Economic Development*, p. 161) showed that the increases in productivity and income in the late 1950s was nearly as much as in the early 50s. Moreover, although the the annual rate of growth in agricultural production was 4.6% during the 1950s, it was 4.1% during the 1960s and had been 4% under the Japanese between 1923-1937 (Ho, *Economic Development,* p. 155). This long-term trend argues against the importance of a causal relationship between land reform and the putative effect of increased productivity.

[153] An additional turn of the screw on farmers not mentioned in the literature, but familiar to rural natives is that farmer association officials, popularly known as "rice worms," after requiring the rice accepted to be of exceptional dryness, add water, and then sell the "surplus" between the quota and the rehydrated weight for their own profit. B. Gallin (*Hsin Hsing*, p. 77) noted the concern about rice being rejected for being too wet, but did not mention that the standard of dryness is considerably less than universalistic or constant.

[154] Chi-Ming Hou, "Institutional Innovations, Technological Change and Agricultural Growth in Taiwan, p. 132 in Y. Wu & K. Yeh, *Growth, Distribution and Social Change, Reprint Series in Contemporary Asian Studies* 11(1978). Also see B. Gallin, *Hsin Hsing,* pp. 76-9; Hsin-Huang Michael Hsiao, *Government Agricultural Strategies in Taiwan and South Korea: A Macrosociological Assessment; Institute of Ethnology, Academia Sinica Monograph* 9(1981); idem., "The Farmers' Movement in Taiwan in the 1980s," *Bulletin of the Institute of Ethnology, Academica Sinica* 70(1990):67-94; Shu-Min Huang, *Agri-*

productivity growth was negative in the 1960s,"when land ceased to be added to that already cultivated. Overall, he attributes "the principal source of agricultural growth since 1951 [to] the more intensive use of nonfarm current inputs, especially chemicals and imported feeds.[155]

The longer-term (1900-60, interrupted by the chaos of KMT occupation) trend of increased agricultural productivity does not appear to have been affected by the land reforms of 1949 and 1953. Implementation of these policies clearly reduced rural inequality. Ho estimates that the price set for compensating expropriated landlords (2.5 annual yields) was less than half the market value prior to these policies. Moreover,

> by forcing landlords to accept bonds as payment, there was an additional redistribution effect, because they were in effect being forced to lend to the government a sizable sum of money at a real rate of interest [4%] substantially below the real current market rate [between 30 and 50 percent per annum]... Most landowners who received stocks of government enterprises regarded them as an inferior form of asset. Consequently, many of them quickly liquidated part or all of the shares paid to them at substantial losses. Koo (1968:44-48, 156-7) estimates that landowners retained only between 4.5 and 9.3 percent of the shared of the Taiwan Cement Company (the most preferred of the government enterprises).... Depending on the stock the sale price was between 36 and 106 percent of par value.[156]

That land—the most valued possession in Taiwan in 1953, or in "traditional Chinese culture"—was surrendered by large and small landlords with no significant opposition needs to be put in the context of the massacres of 1947 and the continued activities of the secret police before drawing any conclusions about "the consent of the governed."

Barred from accumulating land de jure, and de facto barred from all but the lowliest government positions, Taiwanese aspiring to improve their standard of living had to emigrate or become entrepreneurs. Tenant farmers acquired land at a very good price and were able to increase their income faster than if they had continued to pay rent. However, non-agricultural work yielded higher returns. Seeing the disincentives of growing rice and the incentives for industrialization, "the majority of young adults entering the labor force [since the mid-1960s] have gone into

---

cultural Degradation: Changing Community Systems in Rural Taiwan (Lanham, MD: University Press of America, 1981).

[155] Ho, *Economic Development,* p.155.

[156] Ibid., pp. 166-7.

manufacturing or other nonfarm jobs."[157] After lagging farther and farther behind other sectors of the economy, during the late 1980s, farmers organized to protest the many policies that extract agricultural wealth to support industry, the huge army and bureaucracy of "the Republic of China." Brutal police attacks on farmer demonstrations occurred in Daiba in 1988. Taiwanese anthropologists have documented both the movement and attempts to suppress it.

Conclusion
Social scientists have too often supported—in their words, in their presences, and in their deeds—the paternalistic claims of rulers suppressing the very cultures they want to study. Social science work dealing with Taiwan routinely legitimates substitution of the language of Beijing for the majority languages, and justifies ignoring Taiwanese culture by subordinating consideration of its specific features to writing about Chinese civilization, just as Taiwanese are economically and politically subordinated to the fictitious "Republic of China." The "China" that Arthur Wolf and others serve in return for support of their research on what purports to be "China" is an egregious, but unfortunately not unique, example.[158]

---

[157] Alden Speare, Jr., Paul Liu, and Ching-Lung Tsay *Urbanization and Development: The Rural-Urban Transition in Taiwan* (Boulder, CO: Westview, 1988), p. 83.

[158] See Robin W. Winks, *Cloak and Gown: Scholars in the Secret War: Scholars in the Secret War* (New York: Morrow, 1987, pp. 43-51); and Lenora Foerstel and Angela Gilliam (eds.),*Confronting the Margaret Mead Legacy: Scholarship, Empire, and the South Pacific* (Philadelphia: Temple University Press, 1992)

Annotated Bilbiography

Ahern, Emily M. (1973) *The Cult of the Dead in a Chinese Village* (Stanford University Press). On the basis of 1969-70 fieldwork in Q'inan (in Daiba guan), where unusually great agnatic unity cuts off women more than elsewhere in Taiwan, A describes the rituals of four lineage There are no ancestral tablets in homes, and even the kitchen god is worshipped in the lineage hall. The book contains very detailed description of the organization of ancestral halls, preservation and storage of ancestral tablets, competition between lineages in the grandeur of lineage halls, geomancical concerns, and the worship of ancestors from whom inheritances were received. A emphasizes that such ancestors are not conceived of as being especially benign. Indeed, they may be quite capricious and are frequently unwilling to relinquish authority (based on the property they acquired) to their descendants. A argues that "if X inherits property from Y, he must worship Y" (p. 149), although acknowledging some importance in early childhood experience of elders for explaining later ancestor worship behavior and conception of the nature of the ancestors worshipped. Descent is not a sufficient cause of ancestor worship in the Taiwanese view: inheritance is necessary. "In every other situation, there is room for interpretation, contention, and debate" (p. 155). One major example is that uxorilocally-married sons do not necessarily worship their own ancestors (uxorilocal marriage being conceived of as deserting the family and abandoning the parents). Yu (1986) severely criticized many of A's claims.

Ahern, Emily M. (1974) "Affines and the rituals of kinship," pp. 279-308 in A. Wolf, *Religion and Ritual in Chinese Society* (Stanford University Press), proposes that wife-givers are both socially and ritually superior to wife-receivers in Q'inan, regardless of the previous relative economic and social positions of the two families, and suggests that women marry down in family status more frequently than they marry up.

Ahern, Emily M. (1975a) "Sacred and secular medicine in a Taiwan village: a study of cosmological disorders," pp. 91-113 in A. Kleinman et al., *Medicine in Chinese Cultures.* (Washington: U. S. Government

Printing Office), describes hot and cold / yin and yang understandings of health and sickness in Q'inan "to show how a seemingly abstract cosmology as in fact a powerful tool that allows those stricken by distressing sickness to understand what afflicts them, cope with it and ultimately to prevail over it" (p. 99). A stresses the central concern with ascertaining the cause of an illness. Illnesses viewed as caused within the body (*hua-bei*) are taken to Western- or Chinese-style doctors. Illness believed to be caused by a spirit striking a person (*chiong-diuq*) requires assistance from the gods (via their dang-gimediums) who can handle ghosts and demons, "We only go to see a *dang-gi* who can enlist the aid of a god if a doctor's medicine or shot has been tried and failed," (p. 102), is how one informant described the order of making decisions. However, the gods may report that an illness is internal and, in effect, send the patient to a Chinese or western doctor.

Ahern, Emily M. (1975b) "Chinese-style and Western-style doctors in northern Taiwan," pp. 209-218 in A. Kleinman et al., *Medicine in Chinese Cultures* (Washington: U. S. Government Printing Office), differentiates the two kinds of professionals on the basis of transcripts of consultations during at least one working day in the offices of seven Western-style and two Chinese-style doctors in Samgia(p), along with a 1972 questionnaire about preferences in Q'inan. A found that "(1) Many people, especially women and those in older age groups, say that they find Chinese-style doctors and medicine more satisfactory than Western-style doctors and medicine. (2) Chinese-style doctors provide more support for laymen's notions about disease than Western-style doctors. (3) People generally, including those strongly pro-Chinese medicine, at least sometimes make use of Western-style doctors" (p. 215), showing that attitudes are not a sufficient predictor of behavior.

Ahern, Emily M. (1975c) "The power and pollution of Chinese women," pp. 193-214 in M. Wolf & R. Withe, *Women in Chinese Culture* (Stanford University Press) and pp. 269-290 in A. Wolf, *Studies in Chinese Society* (Stanford University Press, 1978), discusses three explanations of Q'inan cultural models of the pollutingness of Chinese women: production of unclean substances (*la-sa(p)*), tinferior social position of women, and the proclivity for breaching order within families. The dangerous "power women have is their capacity to alter a family's form by adding members to it, dividing it, and disturbing male authority" (1978:276). Post-menopausal women, especially rural ones who gather together, continue to present at least the latter two dangers. In general, "polluting events are events that intrude new people or remove old ones in a male-oriented kinship system" (p. 289). Mourning and contact with corpses pollutes men as much as women. Women are removed from their natal family and intruded into the husband's family, and produce new members of the family (temporary ones in the form of daughters, permanent ones in the form of sons), and it is in their involvement with such events that women symbolize dangerous disorder. A attributes the view of women as polluting to implication with the boundaries of the family rather than the lower status of women in Chinese society[ies].

Ahern, Emily M. (1976) "Segmentation in Chinese lineages: a view through written genealogies," *American Ethnologist* 3:1-16. Using written genealogies from the four Chi'nan lineages, A argues that common residence rather than corporate property is the essence of "Chinese lineage," and that residence in the same locale limits the extent of reckoning of shared descent: "documents generally assumed to be principally concerned with kinship ties convey a great deal of information about how kinsmen are organized in territorial communities.... Only if unilineally related kinsmen continue to reside in the same community do they continue to constitute one group within the idiom of the genealogy" (p. 13).

Ahern, Emily M. (1979a) "Domestic architecture in Taiwan: continuity and change," pp. 155-70 in R. Wilson, A. Wilson & S. Greenblatt, *Value Change in Chinese Society* (New York: Praeger). Based on data from Q'inan and Samgia(p) (and using Beijinghua terms), A discusses the orientation (*hong sui*) and structure of village houses.

Ahern, Emily M. (1979b) "The problem of efficacy: strong and weak illocutionary acts," *Man* 14: 1-11, does not present any data on what her Q'inan informants expect or believe that they derive from requests to supernaturals in Tai Di Gong festivals or *dang-gi* -ummons. "In the Chinese act of paying respect to the gods, *pai-pai*, words spoken are addressed to particular, named gods, and requests are made." A concludes that they intend a ritual to produce changes in the world. Rather than ask natives, A opines that "it is probable that the success rate of petitions to the gods are perceived as no less high than the success rate of petitions to officials.... Given the assumption that spirits exist and that they act the way officials of various ranks do, it is only reasonable to petition them. For a Chinese peasant, evidence that high spirits do or do not act is as removed from direct observation as evidence that high officials do or do not act" (p. 7).

Ahern, Emily M. (1981a) *Chinese Rituals and Politics* (Cambridge University Press), provides a synoptic analysis of worship of gods in northern Taiwan (based on her own fieldwork in Q'inan and Samgia(p)) and historical records from Qing Fujien. A argues that religion provides practice in placating powerful but unpredictable authorities (in particular by employing a go-between). Moreover, she argues that even if ritual and religion serve the ends of political authorities, they serve the ends of the powerless in other ways. "If rituals in Taiwan continue to 'talk about' politics, and in particular about structural features of the political system, then it should be no surprise that far-reaching changes have not been observed in the ritual system" from a change of personnel in a hierarchical and centralized bureaucracy (p. 107).

Ahern, Emily M. (1981b) "The Thai Ti Kong festival," pp. 397-425 in E. Ahern and H. Gates, *The Anthropology of Taiwanese Society* (Stanford University Press), describes the annual "slaughter of the honorable pig" festival in Samgia(p), emphasizing the symbolization of "a cleavage between central rulers and local populace" (p. 398) as one of the few forms of protest at collective ethnic oppression allowed under long-running martial law in KMT Taiwan. "The ritual helps them see that the Taiwanese form a single group whose interests may not be identical with those of the mainlander-dominated government" (p. 425). Despite recurrent efforts, the state has not been able to control expenses on ritual.

Ahern, Emily M. and Hill Gates (1981) *The Anthropology of Taiwanese Society* (Stanford University Press). This collection of essays (based on a 1976 conference) on anthropological topics, includes sustained attention to linkages of village to national and international economies.

Aijmer, Goran (1976) *The Religion of Taiwan Chinese in an Anthropological Perspective* (University of Gothenburg Press. This 58-page pamphlet has been unavailable to the authors.

Amsden, Alice (1979) "Taiwan's economic history: a cast of *étatisme* and a challenge to dependency theory," *Modern China* 5:341-379, argues that, contrary to dependency theory, the economic development of Taiwan shows that "class and productive relations within the periphery [of the world economy] are decisive as to how foreign trade and investment affect development" (p. 372). Taiwan is something of a special case, because of Japanese colonialism and exogenous (to the Taiwanese elite) decision to undertake land reform.

Anderson, E. N. (1970) "Lineage atrophy in Chinese society," *American Anthropologist* 72:363-365, contrasts observations of Hong Kong with publications by Pasternak, et al. on the waning importance of lineages in Taiwan.

Appleton, Sheldon L. (1970a) "Silent students and the future of Taiwan," *Pacific Affairs* 43:227-239. discusses the quietism of students competing to escape the oppression and discrimination of Kuomintang Taiwan of the late-1960s, predicting that increases in "both the absolute numbers of students on Taiwan's campuses and the length of time many of them are kept in the special role of students" that more activism would emerge (p. 237), although "their acceptance of the status system is too complete, and their own high status too dearly won" in competitive entrance exams (as well as in competition for foreign study) for there to be widespread support for egalitarian movements (p. 238). Also see A's (1970b) "Surveying the values of Chinese college students," *Asian Forum* 2:75-88, and A's (1970) survey of Rokeach ultimate value rankings discussed in his (1979) article "Sex, values and change on Taiwan," pp. 185-203 in R. Wilson, A. Wilson & S. Greenblatt, *Value Change in Chinese Society* (New York: Praeger). In none of these articles did he differentiate Mainlanders from Taiwanese respondents.

Appleton, Sheldon L. (1970c) "Taiwanese and mainlanders on Taiwan: a survey of student attitudes," *China Quarterly* 44:38-65, reports similar responses of the children of mainlanders and Taiwanese senior high school (p. 150) and college students (700) in 1967 in ranking abstract (Rokeach) values, in reporting following public affairs, and in "conservatism." Whether the questions used as indicators of the latter, in particular, have any validity in responses of aspirants for upward mobility in a state under martial law is dubious (see Bennett 1970, and A's admission [p. 357] that he avoided asking politically sensitive questions in trying to make generalizations about political attitudes).

Appleton, Sheldon L. (1976) "The social and political impact of education on Taiwan," *Asian Survey* 16:703-720, "found that the effects of education on Taiwan seem (1) not to have diminished the high degree of social insularity between Mainlanders and Taiwanese; (2) not to have markedly reduced the educational, occupational and economic advantages held by Mainlanders over Taiwanese; (3) to have encouraged a gradual shift toward self-oriented and individualistic rather than group-oriented and materialistic values; and (4), partly because of this, to have led to high levels of discontent with the social changes accompanying economic growth, and possibly also with political institutions, on the part of the island's best-educated residents" (p. 718) and suggested the difficulty the KMT would have in constructing an ideology salient to a more economically-developed garrison state.

Arrigo, Linda G. (1984) "Taiwan electronics workers," pp. 123-145 in M. Sheridan & J. Salaff, *Lives: Chinese Working Women* (Bloomington: Indiana University Press) presents life histories of a divorcée from Dailam and a *simbua* from Sanchungp'u. A discussion of her involvement with the women among whom she was a participant observer in 1973 and 1975 is contained in pages 100-105 in the same volume.

Arrigo, Linda G. (1985) "Control of women workers in Taiwan," *Contemporary Marxism* 11:77-95, reports the family pressures to remit earnings and the desire of the women with whom A lived in a factory dormitory during the mid-1970s to attain education that would permit them autonomy from families (natal or future) and less dead-end labor-intensive jobs. (See discussion of fieldwork in Arrigo 1984 and also A's "The industrial work force of young women in Taiwan," *Bulletin of Concerned Asian Scholars* 12,2 (1980): 25-38).

Baity, Philip C. (1975) *Religion in a Chinese Town. Asian Folklore and Social Life Monograph* 64. Based on 1968 fieldwork in Tanshui and Peit'ou (within Daiba Guan) and rejecting the "great" (orthodox, textual) traditions in favor of trying to analyzing how Taiwanese villagers understand the domain of religion, B argues that for Taiwanese villagers Buddhism, Confucianism and Taoism are functionally interdependent, not three distinct competing systems. No one offers a full range of the rites felt to be necessary. Moreover one kind of priest often participates in rites of the others. Even though the introduction by the Japanese overlords of "orthodox Buddhism" led to great changes in the kinds of temples which prospered in the first half of the twentieth century, accommodations to and by the other traditions were made, and distinct niches were negotiated.

Barclay, George W. (1954) *Colonial Development and Population in Taiwan* (Washington, NY: Kennikat) notes considerably higher fertility in southern Taiwan than in northern Taiwan, which he found surprising: "One would not expect to find 'regional' differences, which would most likely stem from long tradition and established usage," not someplace "small in size and new in its settlement" (p. 355). Wolf (1981:356) attributes the difference to marked differences in the rates of *simbua* marriage, although this merely moves the question of why there are differences from fertility to marriage patterns.

Barrett, Richard E. (1980) "Short-term trends in bastardy in Taiwan," *Journal of Family History* 5:293-312, reviews data relating increased illegitimacy during Japanese colonial control of Taiwan (an increase from 2.3% of recorded births in 1906 to 4.0% in 1940, with births to concubines increasing from .9% to 1.7%). B claims that "rise in illegitimacy during the colonial period does not appear to have been directly associated with any 'modernization' of social conditions" (p. 310), although his data show illegitimacy rates in cities twice as high as rates in the countryside. B attributes post-World War II declines (to around 1.5%) to increased availability of contraception and abortion, and to later marriage age.

Barrett, Richard E. (1988) "Autonomy and diversity in the American state on Taiwan," pp. 121-137 in E. Winckler & S. Greenhalg, *Contending Approaches to the Political Economy of Taiwan*. (Armonk, NY: M. E. Sharpe) reviews the history of liberal US officials (in the Joint Commission on Rural Reconstruction, in particular) pressing reforms on a dependent KMT during the decade and a half after the end of the Second World War. Lack of U.S. military bases on Taiwan, lack of interest by U.S. companies in Taiwan as either a market or a source of cheap labor, a bureaucratic New Deal ethos, and Japanese colonial records combined to provide relative autonomy to US officials seeking to build a bulwark against communism, and also provided unusual accountability for foreign aid funds.

Barrett, Richard E. (1990) "Seasonality in vital processes in a traditional Chinese population: Births, deaths and marriages in colonial Taiwan, 1906-1942," *Modern China* 16:190-225 attributes "the similarity between colonial Japanese and Taiwanese seasonality in birth" to climate (p. 219), seasonal differences in marriage to (Chinese) culture. B attributes seasonal differences in death to nature.

Barrett, Richard E., and Martin K. Whyte (1982) "Dependency theory and Taiwan: a deviant case analysis," *American Journal of Sociology* 87:1064-1089, use economic development in Taiwan to challenge the predictions of dependency theory "that foreign economic penetration leads to slow economic growth and also to heightened inequality. Since the early 1950s, Taiwan has received massive foreign aid and investment, but it has also had one of the highest sustained rates of growth in the world, while income inequality on the island has decreased substantially.... A variety of factors—including the nature of the Japanese colonial experience, the [initial] emphasis on labor-intensive enterprises, and the absence of an entrenched bourgeoisie—created a situation in which both rapid growth and increasing equality could occur" (p. 1064). They stress the substantial investments in rural infrastructure and increased agricultural production preceded industrial "takeoff," and "question the importance of direct government redistributive policies and trade union pressures in modifying inequality" (p. 1086).

Bauer, Wolfgang (1979) "Chinese glyphomancy (*Ch'a-tzu*) and its uses in present-day Taiwan," pp. 71-96 in S. Allan & A. Cohen, *Legends, Lore and Religion in China* (San Francisco: Chinese Materials Center), outlines analysis of writing without providing any information on how data was collected from whom where.

Bello, Walden, and Stephanie Rosenfeld (1990) *Dragons in Distress: Asia's Miracle Economies in Crisis,* San Francisco: Institute for Food and Development Policy, argue that economic development in S-ingapore, South Korea, and Taiwan are not models for other "developing" countries, because the industrialization in the "little dragons" was only possible in a time when the United States permitted exports to the US from Asian-Pacific allies in the Korean and Vietnamese wars, while permitting barriers to imports, and because of the high costs in pollution and in exploitation of the agricultural sector and short-term women's labor. B&R supplement their own interviews and official data by drawing heavily on unpublished research by others, especially Ph.D. dissertations.

Bennett, Gordon (1970) "Student attitudes in Taiwan," *China Quarterly* 44:353-354, suggests Appleton (1970a,c) transported culturally invalid indicators of "democratic" and "conservative" attitudes, and used his invalid survey results to make invalid inferences about common ancestry ("one China") and of the viability of the KMT.

Bessac, Frank B. (1964) "Some social effects of land reform in a village on the Taichung plain," *Journal of the China Society* 4:15-28, discusses some breakdown of traditional authority in the countryside, and increasing agnosticism. Although joint family arrangements retained prestige, "almost without exception" married brothers did not reside together in the absence of a parent (p. 27). Also see B's "An example of social change in Taiwan related to land reform," *University of Montana Contributions to Anthropology* 1(1967):1-31.

Bessac, Frank B. (1969) "The effect of industrialization upon the allocation of labor in a Taiwanese village," *Journal of the China Society* 6:13-52. After asserting that land reform increased stability and egalitarianism in rural Taiwan, B noted a "generalized disquiet" and concern with over-population. He further noted that rural factories were absorbing underemployed farm labor along major roads. Indeed, he questioned whether the Daidiong village he had studied could still legitimately be described as "rural" (rather than an exurb). B questioned whether Taiwanese women who worked in factories before marriage would be willing to take over working in the fields after marriage, although he was generally optimistic about rural industrialization and the adaptability of joint families as "a help, not a hindrance to capital formation and risk-taking" (p. 34).

Bloom, Alfred H. (1979) "The impact of Chinese linguistic structure on cognitive style," *Current Anthropology* 20:585-586. Based on survey data from Hong Kong and Taiwan B argues that the lack of the syntax of counterfactual assertions makes it difficult for native speakers of Chinese languages to solve certain kinds of abstract problems, especially counterfactuals (i.e., that the language won't let them think "what if x" if x is known to be impossible). B elaborated his thesis in *The Linguistic Shaping of Thought: A Study of the Impact of Language on Thinking in China and the West* (Hillsdale, NJ: Erlbaum, 1981). B's measures and interpretations were challenged decisively by Terry Kit-Fong Au in "Chinese-English counterfactuals: the Sapir-Whorf hypothesis revisited," *Cognition* 15(1983):155-87.

Bosco, Joseph (1992) "Taiwan factions: *guanxi*, patronage and the state in local politics," *Ethnology* 31:157-183, discusses the background to vote-buying in a 1985 Farmers' Association election in Wandan, Bindong. After being expelled from China, "by keeping local political leaders [in each locality] divided into two nonideological camps and maintaining the role of kingmaker in the nomination process, the KMT inserted itself into a social environment in which it not only had no previous support, but after the [suppression of] the rebellion of 1947, was the target of resentment.... Factions gave a democratic appearance without threatening KMT power. Over time, however, the factions have taken on a life of their own. The KMT has lost control over local factions." (p. 178). B sees in factions "a re-emergence of a force nearly wiped out when land reform eliminated local landlords" (p. 178), i.e., rural leaders—who are not necessarily descended from landlord families.

Buxbaum, David C. (1968) "A case study of the dynamics of family law and social change in rural China," pp. 217-260 in D. Buxbaum, *Chinese Family Law and Social Change*. Seattle: University of Washington Press. Although B notes that interview data are not wholly consistent with official household records, he uses the latter to show changes in Ying-Ke. Half the marriages in 1907 were patrilocal, in contrast to 73% in 1966. Adoption of girls (*simbua*) decreased from a high of 47.4% in 1913 to 17.6% in 1966. Most marriages were arranged, although bride and groom usually met and had some semblance of veto power. There was also a slight longitudinal increase of same-surname marriage (to about one percent of marriages). Also see B's (1966) "Chinese family in a common law setting," *Journal of Asian Studies* 25:621-644; and (1972) "From contract to status: trends in Chinese family law from 1868-1968," pp. 203-247 in Buxbaum & F. Mote, *Transition and Permanence: Chinese History and Culture: A Festschrift in Honor of Dr. Hsia Kung-Ch'uan* (Hong Kong: Cathay Press).

Cernada, George P. (1970) *Taiwan Family Planning Reader: How a Program Works* (Daidiong: Chinese Center for International Training in Family Planning), reviews population policy, tactics, administration, and program evaluation, as these topics have been studied by Ronald Freedman and his many University of Michigan students.

Chan, Steve (1988) "Developing strength from weakness: the state in Taiwan," *Journal of Developing Societies* 4:38-53, contends that "one needs to go beyond the mere assertion of state autonomy and strength to examine what the state actually does with its autonomy and strength. Furthermore, one needs to resist the temptation of crediting all observed successes in dependent development to the state" in that Taiwan and Hong Kong had no weaker or autonomous state structures than, say Colombia or Brazil, and possessed fewer natural resources, had a smaller internal market, and are further from the main trading partner, the USA (p. 51).

Chang Kung-Chi (1986) "Discerning the multiple cosmologies and identifying their interrelationship in a *tang-ki*'s divinatory process," *Bulletin of the Institute of Ethnology, Academia Sinica* 61:81-103 (in Chinese), interprets four cosmologies, "three of which are full-blown with quite a number of cognitive items" in 91 cases recorded from a *dang-gi*'s altar in Chu-bei, a small town in northern Taiwan. "While attributing certain categories of problems to the functioning of a particular cosmology, both the *tang-ki* and his clients have expressed their own 'patterns of attribution' by differing degrees" (p. 103) in a compartmentalized, unintegrated set of cosmologies.

Chang Ly-Yun (1989) "Life stress research in Taiwan" *Bulletin of the Institute of Ethnology, Academia Sinica* 68:189-226 (in Chinese), dismisses research on social stress that has been done on Taiwan because of the inappropriateness of using life stress scales developed in the West to "Chinese society" without first assessing "what the Chinese care about, what are considered as stressful in what way stress is expressed, and how it can be efficiently detected" (p. 226).

Chang Ming-Cheng (1987) "Changing family network and social welfare in Taiwan," *Conference on Economic Development and Social Welfare in Taiwan* (Daiba: Academia Sinica Institute of Economics) 2:459-482. In 1986, more than a tenth of widows aged 75 or more lived alone. The percentage of husbands' parents who lived alone increased from 20% in 1980 to 27% in 1986.

Chang Peng-Yuan (1983) "Sino-American scholarly relations as seen from Taiwan, 1949-1979," *American Asian Review* 1:46-86, documents the influence of American government and foundation money in nourishing social science in universities on Taiwan. 22.5% of students from the Republic of China studying abroad in 1969-72 were engaged in social science. Half the sociology faculty had studied abroad (78% of these in the US), and nearly two-thirds of the citations in sociology articles written in 1981 in Taiwan were to English-language works. (Also see Lung 1968, Maykovich 1987.)

Chang Shiao-Chun (1974) "A study of urban housewife's role in modern society," *Bulletin of the Institute of Ethnology, Academia Sinica* 37:39-85 (in Chinese), reports the results of a survey of 300 urban housewives from the Yenpin and Ta-an districts of Daiba. Nearly two-thirds of respondents rejected traditional roles of silent support for husband's decisions.

Chang Shun (1983) "Medical behavior and medical system of Taiwanese peasants." *Bulletin of the Institute of Ethnology, Academia Sinica* 56:29-58 (in Chinese). Based on fieldwork in Yang-Chi, Daiba, C discusses the reasons for shifting among sacred, secular, and western medical systems. C finds that a functional specialization has emerged. Most informants considered that each kind of medicine was more efficacious for some medical problems (or phases of medical problems) than the others, reducing the direct competition among the different medical systems.

Chang Ying-Chang (1973) "Temples, ancestral halls and patterns of settlement in Chushan," *Bulletin of the Institute of Ethnology, Academia Sinica* 36:113-40. Village temples appeared before the development of ancestor halls, so social organization based on locality preceded organization based on kinship in the Choshui valley. Ancestor halls appeared only in the late Qing and Japanese periods. C notes that it took a long time for settlers to create families that could develop patrilineages, given the atomistic migration to Taiwan (in contrast to the "frontiers" of southeastern China in Freedman's schema). Common trust land is the second prerequisite C sees, and he asserted that "the annual rites of ancestor worship and communal feast are now tending to disintegrate with the loss of trust land" (p. 140). Neither temples nor lineage halls developed in nearby areas without irrigation and intensive agriculture.

Chao Yu-Mei (1985) "Changes in the family system in Taiwan," *American Asian Review* 3:85-105, discusses with official statistics the effects of education, family planning, land reform, equal inheritance legislation, divorce law, and the growth of housing projects. Why the article is subtitled "some personal experiences" is a puzzle, since no personal experiences are related within the article.

Chen Chao-Chen (1961) *Land Reform in Taiwan* (Daiba: China Publishing), estimates that land reform affected 43% of 660,000 farm families and 75% of 410,000 part-tenant/part-owners and that land prices were about 20% of the pre-reform valuation. C reported a savings rate by new farmers in the 1952-62 period of 49% in "Land reform and agricultural development in Taiwan," 126-153 in [the proceedings of a] *Conference on Economic Development of Taiwan* (Daiba: China Council, 1967).

Chen Cheng-Hsiang (1960) *Place Names of Taiwan (Daiba*: Fu-Min Geographical Institute of Economic Development) (in Chinese), discusses strata of imposition by rulers of "meaningful" names for meaningless (to them, but not earlier strata of population) names of places. Holo migrants translated or transcribed many aboriginal names along with recycling many placenames from Fujien. Qing, Japanese, and mainlander overlords did the same thing to some Holo names which didn't make sense to them. There were only a dozen names of Chinese settlements in the oldest geography text (1603). C attested 7700 different names used for 17,800 places. The most complete account is contained in Lin (1937).

Chen Chi-Lu (1970) "The Taiwanese family," *Journal of the China Society* 7:64-79, reviews historical data on household size, concluding the average rural household contained seven persons, the average urban household five. Using Beijinghua descriptive labels, C discussed the "exotica" of Taiwanese household composition, i.e., concubines, posthumously adopted sons, uxorilocally-resident sons-in-law, and adopted daughters-in-law, and concluded with a discussion of inheritance norms and meal rotation (which he considered a venerable Chinese institution, rather than a post-industrial innovation).

Chen Chi-Nan (1980) "The structural transformation of Chinese society in Taiwan during the Qing period," *Bulletin of the Institute of Ethnology, Academia Sinica* 49:115-147 (in Chinese), provides an ethnohistorical account of what C considers indigenization of Chinese Taiwan during the post-colonial period between the Dutch and Japanese. During the 19th century strife between Hakka and Hokkien groups, and between different places of origin (or descent) in China declined. (Some incidents of conflict between those with differing territorial affiliations on Taiwan occurred.) Popular temples became a basis for inter-village cooperation. New lineages organizations were "planted" with no necessary basis in common descent. C concludes that there is no one simple basis of Taiwanese social structure, with the importance of lineage, village, ethnolinguistic group, et al. varying within Taiwan.

Chen Chi-Yen (1950) "The family system of Ta-Ts'un village," *Quarterly Review of Taiwan Culture* 6:55-67, reports that the average household size in this Daidiong village in 1950 was 6.2 persons, in contrast to 7.2 in 1936. 39% of 2969 households were members of one clan (Lai) with 15% belonging to the next most numerous clan (Huang).

Chen Chung-Min (1967) "Ancestor worship and clan organization in a rural village of Taiwan," *Bulletin of the Institute of Ethnology, Academia Sinica* 23:192-224, describes clan and household ritual performance in a one-surname-dominant Hokkien village in Jianghua Guan. In this community the male adults are gradually giving up the obligations and privileges of the ancestral rites. The duties are being taken over by female adults.

Chen Chung-Min (1977) *Upper Camp: A Study of a Chinese Mixed Cropping Village in Taiwan. Academia Sinica Monograph 7*, compares a sugar-producing village on the southern Jianan plain (Dailam Guan) in which he did fieldwork in 1969-71 with two other villages in the area which are not involved in sugar production. C describes how the state (first the Japanese, then the Chinese) dictated sugar-cane production (mandatory three year crop rotation) by withholding irrigation water, so that rice could not be grown. C shows that national sugar company representatives (*g(/h)uan-liao-wi-g(/h)uan*—commissioner in charge of raw materials), who organize and supervise harvest teams and controls loans, become leaders in local politics. All three villages have diversified economies, and do not differ in family and kin organization—with nuclear families and arranged marriages predominating and lineage organizations declining. The local Chia-Fu temple was increasingly prosperous and an important source of loans to farmers.

Chen Chung-Min (1981) "Government enterprise and village politics," pp. 38-49 in E. Ahern and H. Gates, *The Anthropology of Taiwanese Society* (Stanford University Press), describes the political prominence—as protector and mediator—of the Taiwan Sugar Company representative in the Dailam village described in Chen (1977). "Because the commissioner occupies such a strategic position between the sugarcane farmers and the TSC, it is he, not the lineage elders or the village mayor, who functions as the real leader in Upper Camp. All his counterparts in the seven villages surrounding Upper Camp are power figures in their respective villages as well.... Unlike other political leaders such as the village mayor, the commissioner knows very well that he is not in a position to 'rule' his village... that he has to earn his villagers' respect and support in order to carry out effectively [his] job" (pp. 47, 49).

Chen Chung-Min (1985) "Dowry and inheritance," pp. 117-127 in J. Hsieh & Y. Chuang, *The Chinese Family and Its Ritual Behavior* (Nankang:Academia Sinica), criticizes other work on Taiwan/China for largely ignoring dowries while focusing on brideprice. [This should be seen in the contest of British social anthropologists having proclaimed that dowry and brideprice are mutually exclusive social arrangements.] C observed substantial dowries in Jianghua and Dailam in 1969-71, and contends that the dowry is a (complete) prepayment of the woman's inheritance (brideprice is a partial prepayment of the son's inheritance). C concludes, "We cannot fail to notice that a daughter's obligations toward her natal family and parents are largely terminated when her bridal sedan departs from the home, whereas a son's responsibilities toward his parents are just beginning when he receives his share of the inheritance. Put in another way, one can say that a daughter's share (in the form of her dowry) is smaller than her brother's because they have different obligations toward their natal family and not simply because the one is female and the other male" (p. 127).

Chen, Edward I-Te (1972) "Formosan political movements under Japanese rule, 1914-1937," *Journal of Asian Studies* 31:477-497, relates the organizational efforts to preserve Taiwanese cultural identity and to achieve self-rule during the period of Japanese civilian rule. The leaders were educated in Japanese universities and influenced by Japanese liberalism. Given the tightness of Japanese colonial rule, they disavowed violence and sought change through legal means, yet "behind the facade of lawfulness one could easily detect a strong current of national consciousness among their followers intensified by their resentment of alien domination" (p. 495). As circumscribed as the organization had to be, "they preserved the cultural identity of Formosans in the face of all-out Japanese efforts for assimilation, and they helped Formosans to learn about the many hitherto totally alien concepts of democracy, such as home rule, popular election, and universal suffrage. Formosan desire for self-determination today has its deep roots in the days of Japanese rule" (p. 496).

Chen Hsi-Huang (1975) "Economic analysis of small farms," pp. 378-389 in T. Yu & Y. Yu, *Essays on Taiwan's Agricultural Development* (Daiba: Lien Ching), challenges the contention (by Yang 1970, et al.) that small farms are less efficient by showing that the value of output per hectare of farms of less than half a hectare was NT$40,900 in contrast to NT$26,700 for larger farms. However, the output per man was NT$20,000 in contrast to NT$25,000 for larger farms.

Chen Hsiang-Shui (1977) "Land reform in Green-Tree Village," *Bulletin of the Institute of Ethnology, Academia Sinica* 43:65-84 (in Chinese), argues that there is only an indirect relationship between land reform and increased productivity, that trends in the latter preceded land reform, and that they depended on the acceptance of technological changes such as hybrid seeds, fertilizers, and insecticides. However, the delegitimation of landlords had important effects. After land reform, the tenants in the village studied united themselves as one group to resist the landlords in religious and political activities, expressing long-rooted discontents. They asked landlords to carry the deities' sedan-chairs in processions; they forced landlords to join in working on the temples, voted against the landlords in local elections, and elected a village head who was not a landlord.

Chen Hsiang-Shui (1984) "The social organization and adaptation of new Chinese immigrants in New York City," *Bulletin of the Institute of Ethnology, Academia Sinica* 57:31-55, contrasts the family-based organization of recent emigrants from Taiwan with the traditional North American Chinatowns. The greater education, more balanced sex ratio, family orientation, and more common technical/professional skills of recent immigrants (in Queens) differ markedly from the mostly male, uneducated, single (or separated from wives left in China) laborers concentrated in traditional Chinatowns. The newer immigrants' adaptations to different problems and opportunities differ from the coping and entrepreneurial strategies of urban ghetto life. The argument is elaborated in

C's (1992) *Chinatown No More: Taiwan Immigrants in Contemporary New York*, (Ithaca, NY: Cornell University Press, 1992), a description of 18 months of fieldwork between 1984 and 1987 with a snowball sample of a hundred households in the Flushing amd Elmhurst sections of the borough of Queens. It appears that the snowball was primarily of those who had been sojourners on Taiwan (mainlanders) rather than Taiwanese. C found *hui* rotating-credit associations of practically no importance in capitzliation of businesses owned by emigrants from Taiwan.

Chen Shao-Hsing (1966a) "Taiwan as a laboratory for the study of Chinese society and culture," *Bulletin of the Institute of Ethnology, Academia Sinica* 22:1-47 (in Chinese), contends that "the remarkable social change that took place in Taiwan during the Japanese rule is not Japanization, but is a modernization of a Chinese society.... The new cultural traits adopted by the Taiwanese were not Japanese cultural traits, but were western, modernized cultural traits, which the Japanese themselves had adopted only shortly before. The Taiwanese adopted them voluntarily and selectively" (p. 3). Despite its "mean and simple" culture, Chinese society can be studied on this "tiny and insignificant island" (p. 4). The case of Taiwan shows that Confucianism does not necessarily prevent modernization of Chinese society. C claims that unbalanced development forced from above was succeeded by balanced development from below as "the principles of government of the people, for the people, and by the people are being promoted" (p. 8).

Chen Shao-Hsing and Morton H. Fried (1968-70) *The Distribution of Family Names in Taiwan* (Daiba: Chinese Materials and Research Aid Service Center), detail the frequency of surnames in Taiwan based on 1956 census data. Data are presented in the first volume, mapped in he second, and discussed in the third,

Chen Wen-Yen (1989 "1988 Taiwanese-American Summer Conference survey report," *North American Taiwanese Professors' Association Bulletin* 8:30-36, report results of a survey of 628 Taiwanese-Americans attending four regional Taiwanese summer camps, find g them to be highly educated, affluent. married, with two children, little involved in local community activities other than Taiwanese organizations, dissatisfied with reforms in Taiwan, and supporting independence for Taiwan. 53% of the sample reported being satisfied or very satisfied with their adjustment to American life in contrast to 2% who reported themselves dissatisfied (the remainder characterized their adjustment as acceptable). Language was regarded as the major difficulty encountered in living in the USA.

Cheng Li and Lynn White (1990) "Elite transformation and modern change in Mainland China and Taiwan: empirical data and the theory of technocracy," *China Quarterly* 121:135, compare the increasing technocratic dominance of PRC and ROC governments. For Taiwan, L&W stress the importance of the group involved in the periodical *Dai-Ha Tza-Ji (Intellectuals)* during the late 1960s and early 70s, and cooptation by Chiang Ching-Kuo. "A dramatic decrease in average age, an increase in educational level and a rise in the percentage of native Taiwanese are the major trends of elite transformation in Taiwan" (p. 9) T&W argue that the ideology of technical expertise is replacing Maoism and KMT "nationalism" on the two sides of the Taiwan straits, despite the continued lip service to the old ideologies.

Cheng Mei-Neng (1974) "Agricultural policies and socio-economic change of rural society in Taiwan," *Bulletin of the Institute of Ethnology, Academia Sinica* 37:113-143 (in Chinese), shows the relationship between government regulation of agricultural production (and landholding) and the redistribution of wealth from the agricultural sector.

Cheng, Robert L. (1979) "Language unification in Taiwan," pp. 541-78 in W. McCormack & S. Wurm, *Language and Society* (The Hague: Mouton), describes KMT language policy and the attempt to extirpate languages other than Beijinghua. C advocates recognizing and maintaining bilingualism instead.

Cheng, Robert L. (1985a) "A comparison of Taiwanese, Taiwan Mandarin, and Peking Mandarin," *Language* 61:352-377, outlines the language distribution on Taiwan and the differing features of Beijing Beijinghua, Daiba Beijinghua, and Daiba Holo. (Also see Kubler 1979, 1985; Tse 1986.)

Cheng, Robert L. (1985b) "Group interests in treating words borrowed into Mandarin and Taiwanese," *Anthropological Linguistics* 27:177-189, examines the borrowing of English words into Beijinghua and the borrowing of English and Japanese words into Holo, offering linguistic structural explanation of the relative resistance to borrowings from English.

Cheng, Robert L. (1987) "Borrowing and internal development in lexical change: a comparison of Taiwanese words and their Mandarin equivalents," *Journal of Chinese Linguistics* 15:105-131, discusses Beijinghua "equivalents" of words found in Holo texts and argues that content words in the two languages are more likely than function words to share common ancestry.

Cheng Tun-Jen (1989) "Democratizing the quasi-Leninist regime in Taiwan," *World Politics* 41:471-499, questions the inevitability of democracy stemming from economic development, outlining ways in which opposition parties have been limited as the KMT has indigenized, while retaining the "Republic of China representatives" as an overwhelming majority in legislatures and preventing labor union-organization.

Chiang Tao-Chang (1980) "Walled cities and towns in Taiwan," pp. 117-141 in R. Knapp, *China's Island Frontier: Studies in the Historical Geography of Taiwan* (Honolulu: University of Hawaii Press), discusses the building of walls around cities in the 18th century. "If a place had a wall, it would grow faster than neighboring settlements which had no protection" (p. 140). Many were torn down during the Japanese era, and "the former sites of these walls in Gilan and Daiba provide broad encircling boulevards quite unlike the maze of internal streets" (p. 141). Cf. Lamley (1977). On the lateness (post-Ming dynasty) of walled cities in contrast to China, including Hainan, see Chang Sen-Dou (1963) "Historical trends of Chinese urbanization," *Annals of American Geographers* 53:109-43, especially figures 22 and 23.

Chin, Ai-Li S. (1966) *Modern Chinese Fiction and Family Relations* (Cambridge, MA: Center for International Studies), provides a brief discussion of family relations and structures in fiction from Taiwan and from China.

Chinn, Dennis L. (1979) "Rural poverty and the structure of farm household income in developing countries: evidence from Taiwan," *Economic Development and Cultural Change* 27:283-301, reports that the proportion of household income for females living on farms derived from nonfarm work increased from 11% in 1960-2 to 31% in 1970-2 (as the number of off-farm workers increased by about 50%).

Chiu Hai-Yuan (1976) "Social attitude in Yen Village," *Bulletin of the Institute of Ethnology, Academia Sinica* 42:97-117 (in Chinese), reports that "the average educational level of family members, cognitive span, exposure to mass media, and religious affiliation have important effects on individual modernity. Expected number of children and aspiration about educational level of one's children are also significantly related to one's individual modernity. In addition, more perceived alienation is found among the people with higher modernity. Effects of different mass media and of subcategories of folk religion on individual modernity are also detailed" (p. 117).

Chiu Hai-Yuan and Shu-Ling Tsai (1988) "Taiwanese college students' attitudes toward social equality," *Bulletin of the Institute of Ethnology, Academia Sinica* 66:105-131 (in Chinese), reports a survey of 1618 freshmen and seniors. Seventy percent regarded the ROC political institutions as unfair; 60% regarded the economy as unfair; 75% recognized political, economic, and ideological conflict. Background variables explained little variance in perceptions of unfairness or in the attribution of poverty to bad luck and personal shortcomings.

Chou Nih-Er, Cal Clark, and Janet Clark (1990) *Women in Taiwan Politics* (London: Lynne Rienner). Based on interviews with all the women serving in the principal assemblies in Taiwan in 1985, a random matched sample of male legislators, and two smaller samples of women candidates who lost elections and women members of the 1970 assemblies, CCC find that although "modernization" had broken down some obstacles of traditional gender patterns, most women had been able to become active in politics only with special circumstances, and faced continued discrimination as women.

Chow, L. P. (1970) "Abortion in Taiwan," pp. 251-259 in R. Hall, *Abortion in a Changing World* (New York: Columbia University Press), reports on 1965 and 1967 island-wide surveys of women, finding a ratio of 12.9 abortions per one hundred live births. Twenty percent of abortions were performed by midwives.

Chu, Godwin C. (1968) "Impact of mass media on a gemeinschaft-like social structure," *Rural Sociology* 33:189-199, reports (in Parsonian jargon) modest correlations (C between .11 and .27) of rank in the economic hierarchy, an affiliative hierarchy (indicated by invitations to festivals), and an instrumental hierarchy (indicated by being asked for advice) in four villages near Sheng Keng. He concludes that persons with information from mass media will not be asked for advice if their economic or family status isn't also relatively high.

Chu Hai-Yuan (1985) "The impact of different religions on the Chinese family in Taiwan," pp. 221-231 in J. Hsieh & Y. Chuang, *The Chinese Family and Its Ritual Behavior* (Nankang:Academia Sinica), reports that despite holding different views on some aspects of family life, Christians and adherents of Taiwanese folk religion both consider

Chinese family the system superior to what they view as the Western system in a 1971 survey. Few differences on sexual attitudes and behavior were discernable. "Animists" value education more than do Christian Hokkien-speaking Taiwanese, and more strongly   preferr sons (necessary for future ancestor worship).

Chu Pao-Tung (1969) "Buddhist organization in Taiwan," *Chinese Culture* 10:98-132, surveys temples on Taiwan and contrasts Japanese with Chinese Buddhisms.

Chu, Solomon (1974) "Some aspects of extended kinship in a Chinese community," *Journal of Marriage and the Family* 36:628-33, reports findings from the University of Michigan study of family planning initiatives in Daidiong in 1962-3 which indicate persistence of a stem-nuclear-stem cycle of family structure. Chu stresses that because the formation of extended families is a process, cross-sectional data underestimates the prevalence of extended families, e.g. 35% of currently nuclear family households earlier lived with husband's relatives.

Chuang Ying-Chang (1972) "The adaptation of the family to modernization in rural Taiwan" *Bulletin of the Institute of Ethnology, Academia Sinica* 34:85-98 (in Chinese), discusses the increase in complex family forms, including "family federation," which aid entrepreneurial endeavors. Fission into atomistic nuclear families has not been a part of industrialization in Taiwan. Marriages for two-thirds of the women and 55% of the men in the Lamdao Guan village of She-Liou were arranged. 24% of the men and 18% of the women married a partner within the same village. Exogamy beyond the *guan* involved 25% of the husbands and 36% of the wives.

Chuang Ying-Chang (1973) "Temples, ancestral halls, and patterns of settlement in Chu-Shan," *Bulletin of the Institute of Ethnology, Academia Sinica* 36:113-140 (in Chinese), reviews historical records on temples and ancestral halls in the Chingshui valley in Lamdao Guan village in relation to changing primary products, arguing that rural cohesion in Taiwan is territorially-based rather than kinship/lineage-based. "Village temples appeared in the early stages, before the development of ancestor halls, which shows that social organization based on locality came before that based on kinship" (p. 139). Moreover, "temples as well as ancestor halls failed to develop in communities without irrigation and intensive agriculture" (p. 139), both of which required extensive local cooperation. "Ancestor halls appeared only in the later stages during the Late-Ching [Qing] and Japanese Occupation Period. Lineage began to develop, based either on common surname or origin or descent group propagated by one founding father who migrated to the area in early days" (p. 340).

Chuang Ying-Chang (1976) "Economic development and the change of family structure in rural Taiwan: A case from Shei-Liau, Nan-T'ou Hsien [Lamdao Guan]," *Bulletin of the Institute of Ethnology, Academia Sinica* 41:61-77 (in Chinese), shows that price control along with land taxes made agriculture a poor investment in Shei-Liau. Coupled with regularly decreasing average size of household farm land, these factors encouraged workers to migrate to cities during the 1960s. Migration led to a diversification of family types, in particular to more federal-type families (i.e., a residentially-dispersed family which continues to hold common property). Rotating support for elderly parents all but disappeared: "Due to industrialization of agriculture and the advent of professional cultivation teams, old parents can still manage the farmland even after the division of the family and the departure of sons. There is therefore no need to depend on sons by the rotating system to keep the farms going. They can live by themselves or live together with one of their sons. Consequently, this has resulted in the conversion of the conditional stem family into nuclear or standardized families" (p. 77).

Chuang Ying-Chang (1977) *Lin I-P'u: The Socioeconomic History of a Taiwan Township.*(Nankang: Academia Sinica) (in Chinese), reviews historical data (in particular a 1937 Japanese investigation) on the late-19th century development of lineage organization by Hokkien-speakers on Taiwan, and their subsequent weakening by Japanese and KMT policies. Also see C's "The formation of lineage organization on Taiwan and their special characteristics," pp. 93-124 in Li Yih-Yuan et al, *Hsien-tai-hua yu Chung-kuo Wen-hua* (Daiba: Kueir-Kuan, 1985).

Chuang Ying-Chang (1985) "Family structure and reproductive patterns in a Taiwanese fishing village," pp. 158-161 in J. Hsieh & Y. Chuang, *The Chinese Family and Its Ritual Behavior* (Nankang: Academia Sinica), reports universal acceptance of birth control methods, lowering of the ideal number of children and weakening of son preference among 90 women in the fishing village of Nan-T'sun. Although behavior (use of birth control) is changing faster than values (family size and son preference, especially by women), C could find no relationship between reported values and birth control behavior. Women's participation in outside activity is correlated with less concern to have sons.

Chuang Ying-Chang (1987) "Ching dynasty Chinese immigration to

Taiwan," *Bulletin of the Institute of Ethnology, Academia Sinica* 64:179-203, deals primarily with court policy toward Taiwan, which was "to guard it and seal it off; the court did not mean to encourage people to develop Taiwan" (p. 185). Villages had to protect and police themselves. Thus, "residents clearly did not take mainland ancestral homes or the worship of gods from ancestral areas as the focus of group cohesion. Instead, they gradually adopted the villages in which they resided, or some other geographic administrative unit, as their acknow-ledged point of orientation" as Taiwan changed from "an immigrant society to a residentially stable, nativized society" (p. 195). At the time of the 1874 Japanese invasion, "official rule extended over only one-third of the island" and only in the final two decades of Qing claimed jurisdiction, did production of tea, sugar, and camphor involve offi-cially-sanctioned pacification/sinification of the aboriginal population.

Chuang Ying-Chang (1988) "Settlement patterns of the Hakka migra-tion to Taiwan" *Bulletin of the Institute of Ethnology, Academia Sinica* 34:85-98, presents a case study of the T'ou-Fen Ch'en Family. Early immigrants were not part of major land-opening households. The used common surnames to organize contract lineages that were ostensibly for the purpose of ancestor worship, but which were more like a land in-vestment team, concentrating capital, buying and cultivating land, and distributing the surplus rent by lots to members of the lineage organiza-tion. By the third generation, in the mid-19th-century, "Han Chinese society on Taiwan had already embarked on a path of development in-dependent of that of mainland China" (p. 197).

Chun, Allen J. (1990) "Being and nothingness in Chinese kinship," *Reviews in Anthropology* 15:69-80, criticizes the Freedman tradition in a survey review of three books, including Wolf and Huang (1980). They showed that *simbua* marriage result in lower rates of fertility and greater sexual incompatibility without explaining why *simbua* "as a social institution or customary practice has existed, why it exists among certain Chinese ethnic groups and not others [viz., Hakka on Taiwan], why it has continued to exist in spite of the obvious sexual dissatisfaction, or why it has so completely disappeared during the 'modern' era of free association (non-parentally-arranged) marriages" (p. 75).

Clark, Cal (1989) *Taiwan's Development: Implications for Contending Political Economy Paradigms* (New York: Greenwood), uses data from Taiwan as a critical case study to criticize and synthesize developmen-talist, dependista, and statist explanations of economic development and the possibilities of overcoming obstacles to it. For C, "the keystone of

Taiwan's success story appears to be the flexibility and continuing restructuring that occurred in both the economy and the polity" (p. 220), enabling rapid production adjustment to changes in world market conditions. While nominally recognizing "the entrepreneurial efforts of business men and the hard work and skills of workers and farmers" (p. 221), C focuses on the state (returning "the political" to "political economy," he boasts) and attributes wisdom to a democratizing KMT state (which he characterizes as including "periodic regime change" on p. xv). Parts of the book were published as "Economic development in Taiwan," *Journal of Asian and African Studies* 12 (1987):1-16, and "The Taiwan exception: implications for contending political paradigms," *International Studies Quarterly* 31 (1987):327-356.

Cohen, Marc J. (1988) *Taiwan at the Crossroads: Human Rights, Political Development and Social Change on the Beautiful Island* (Washington, D.C.: Asia Resource Center) provides a comprehensive overview of the first four KMT decades of economic and political development and of the ROC's international relations and status. Various forms of censorship, surveillance, and punishment of what the KMT brands "thought pollution" are examined in detail. There are also chapters on the degradation of the physical environment, on women's role as a labor reserve, on the plight of the "original people" (i.e., Polynesians), and on organizations in the overseas diaspora of Taiwanese. With Emma Teng, C edited a collection of Chinese, Taiwanese, and Western diplomatic documents on Taiwan sovereignty, *Let Taiwan Be Taiwan* (Washington, D.C.: Center for Taiwan International Relations, 1990). He also prepared a hundre-page popularization of Taiwan at the Crossroads, *The Unknown Taiwan* (Daiba: Coalition for Democracy, 1992).

Cohen, Myron L. (1968a) "Family partition as contractual procedure in Taiwan," pp. 176-204 in D. Buxbaum, *Chinese Family Law and Social Change* (Seattle: University of Washington Press). In the Hakka-speaking Go'hiong village C studied, in the mid-1960s most persons were members of joint families. "Improved methods of communication have widened the range of kinsmen with whom significant interaction is possible," (p. 196), reducing the importance of co-residence for various forms of co-operation. C shows the influence of customary patterns on contracts, and includes six abridged family division documents. In particular, although the lineage could not longer be endowed with land after the Land Reform acts, when families divided land could be held in trust.

Cohen, Myron L. (1968b) "A case study of Chinese family economy and development," *Journal of Asian and African Studies* 3: 161-180, argues that "given the proper economic circumstances, non-elite groups may also develop complex family organization." In Yen Liao, "multi-enterprise families played a key role in diversifying the economy. In an environment where credit was weak, the flow of productive resources within joint families formed one of the most dependable lines of capital transmission. In the contest of the joint family, agricultural and non-agricultural enterprises mutually supported each other" (p. 179).

Cohen, Myron L. (1969) "Agnatic kinship in South Taiwan," *Ethnology* 8:-167-182, describes kinship organizations (with corporate holdings and ancestor worship) which are not necessarily based on demonstrable common descent or on propinquity within the same locale. Fusion into lineages rather than fission of large and venerable ones differentiates Taiwan from the mainland (pre-Mao) norm. Despite the distribution of corporately-held land, the most important economic function of lineage organizations, four of five in the Hakka village which C studied (1964-7) continued to function, holding periodic ancestral rites.

Cohen, Myron L. (1970) "Developmental patterns in the Chinese domestic group," pp. 21-36 in M. Freedman, *Family and Kinship in Chinese Society* (Stanford University Press) and pp. 183-198 in A. Wolf, *Studies in Chinese Society* (Stanford University Press), distinguishes domestic units (*bang* [*fang*]) from the family (*ge* [*chia*]). C argues that the relationship between *ge* members was quite flexible (without systematic examination of any data, although the interpretations bear some relationship to 1964-5 fieldwork in the Go'hiong village he calls Yen-Liao). The distinction is not precisely based on co-residence, especially anywhere from which young men go out as unmarried workers and remit some of their income. "Most men seeking employment and opportunities away from their birthplace remained members of their original chia group" (1978:197). Indeed, C suggests that co-residence had a centripetal force that migration to take advantage of economic opportunities did not: "Factors leading to early *fen-chia* [*huen ge hue*] were associated mainly with membership in a common household. It was under one roof that conflicts of interest were likely to emerge quickly; when members of a chia group lived together, dissatisfaction over distribution of chia resources or other situations increased tensions between the fang could appear more rapidly and with greater force" (p. 198). An earlier version was contained in C's (1967) "Variations in complexity among Chinese family groups: the impact of modernization," *Transactions of the New York Academy of Sciences, Series 11*, 29:638-644.

Cohen, Myron L. (1976a) *House United, House Divided: The Chinese Family in Taiwan* (New York: Columbia University Press). This study of 27 families in Yen-Liao, an inland Hakka-speaking Go'hiong village in which half the families have permits from the Taiwan Tobacco and Wine Monopoly to grow and process tobacco, elaborates the fission-fusion process described in Cohen (1969). Such family enterprises conduce to maintaining large joint families more than does rice-growing (for neighboring Hakka and Hokkien communities). C argues that co-residence is too restrictive a criterion for family (*ge* [*chia*]). Component nuclear households (*bang*) of those involved in tobacco (which is both capital- and labor-intensive) remain linked by shares in common property and identify with a *ge* which is central for weddings, funerals, and New Year celebrations. C details the economic assets brides bring with them, and shows that wealth transmitted during the engagement and wedding becomes her private property (*pin-gum*), controlled by her until such time as the *ge* divides (at which point the husband and wife have joint control of it). Control of such wealth enhances the status of Hakka women (especially in contrast to the *simbua* arrangements of women from some landless Hokkien families in northern Taiwan) and gives women a vested interest in maintaining the joint family (and, thereby, continued exclusive control of her *pin-gum*). Also see C's (1976b) "Mei-Nung: state and community in rural Taiwan,"*Third World Review* 2,1:1-22 and Diamond (1977).

Cole, Allan B. (1967) "The political roles of Taiwanese enterprisers," *Asian Survey* 7:645-654, describes the "web of connections in official circles" of mainlander and Taiwanese businessmen. "The two most common processes where special persuasion may be used are tax assessment and the securing of licenses and permits. At any administrative level bribery may be employed to speed up bureaucratic procedures, which can be agonizingly slow or at times amazingly expedited. The main alternative, other than accepting delay, is to work through old friends, or at least through persons who are obligated" (p. 652).

Coombs, Lolagene C., and Ronald Freedman (1979) "Some roots of preference: roles, activities and familial values," *Demography* 16:359-374. By 1976, contraception was used by most people in all social strata in Taiwan, but to attain differing preferences in number of children. Variance in views of ideal family size depended on the extent of the wife's activities outside the family (mass media exposure as well as working outside the home), experience in nuclear rather than extended families, active participation in choice of a husband, less involvement in religious observances and beliefs of a familial character, and less perceived importance of a male heir. These predictors (which are more highly correlated to husbands' than to wives' education) suggest to C&F that "it is changes in relations to the outside modernizing world rather than in internal familial role relationships which are important for preferences" (p. 372).

Coombs, Lolagene C., and Te-Hsiung Sun (1981) "Familial values in a developing society: a decade of change in Taiwan," *Social Forces* 59:1229-1255. Based on four island-wide surveys conducted between 1965 and 1976 C&S show that "attitudes toward personal control of the childbearing process were among the first to change.... Individual reproductive goals, however, lagged behind those perceived as in the best interest of the general population.... [Nonetheless,] increased used of contraception and considerable reduction in the birth rate have occurred even though many familial values have not undergone great change. Although they lag behind other changes, attitudes, values, and norms do change gradually as economic development occurs and family needs become different" (p. 1252). Significant fertility decline occurred without changes in family patterns and organization (in particular filial piety/obligation) which demographers expect to precede demographic transition in developing societies. Other reports of this research include Coombs and Sun ,"Family composition preferences in a developing culture: The case of Taiwan, 1973," *Population Studies* 32 (1978):43-64; Sun, H-S Lin & R. Freedman, "Trends in fertility, family size preferences and family planning practices in Taiwan 1961-76," *Studies in Family Planning* 9 (1978):54-70; Coombs, "Prospective fertility and underlying preferences: A longitudinal study of Taiwan," *Population Studies* 33(1979):447-455; and Ronald Freedman, L. Coombs, M. C. Chang and T-H Sun, "Trends in fertility, family size preferences, and practices of family planning: Taiwan 1965-1973," *Studies in Family Planning* 5(1974):270-288.

Crane, George T. (1982) "The Taiwanese ascent: system, state, and movement in the world economy," pp. 93-113 in Edward Friedman, *Ascent and Decline in the World System (=Political Economy of the World-System Annual* 5 [Beverly Hills: Sage]), attributes the advancement from the periphery to semi-periphery of "the world system" to (first) Japanese imperial policy and later KMT state capitalism with fortuitous timing for entering international competition and the support of massive US aid. C contrasts Taiwan's high economic status with the low political status of the Republic of China, noting that the latter is underemphasized in the model of a "world system" by Wallerstein et al.

Crissman, Lawrence R. (1972) "Marketing on the Changhua Plain, Taiwan," pp. 215-260 in W. Willmot, *Economic Organization in Chinese Society* (Stanford University Press) finds the size of standard marketing areas in Jianghua to differ from those derived by Skinner, and tries to explain the distribution of market towns on the basis of optimal transportation networks between towns (Christaller's "traffic principle") with many historical "exceptions." Further data is analyzed in "Specific central-place models for an evolving system of market towns on the Changhua Plain, Taiwan," *Regional Analysis* 1:183-218, and (1976b) "Spatial aspects of marriage patterns as influence by marketing behavior in West Central Taiwan," *Regional Analysis* 2:123-148.

Crissman, Lawrence R. (1981) "The structure of local and regional systems," pp. 89-124 in E. Ahern and H. Gates, *The Anthropology of Taiwanese Society* (Stanford University Press), outlines the kinds of social relations in Taiwan, emphasizing that "much of Taiwanese local and regional organization [including villages and factions] is in fact noncorporate—i.e., it is not formally organized at all, and to the extent that it is structures in any definable sense, it is governed by normative relations that do not involve legal obligations or formal sanctions" (p. 90). In the Jianghua plain, C found that "brides are usually acquired within regions roughly the size of—though rarely corresponding to—intermediate marketing areas" (p. 120). He asserts that Christaller's "marketing principle" of a hierarchical distribution of market centers with optimal convenience of access for a dispersed rural population fits the distribution of road systems and optimally-centered markets on the Jianghua plain, but cautions against over-emphasizing the spatial aspects of social and administrative units.

Crittenden, Kathleen S. (1987) "The social impact of attribution of good and bad events: another look at the Chinese case," *Journal of Sociology* 23:107-125. On the basis of a survey of 389 students, C reports that "a self-effacing attributional pattern implies less productivity but greater social responsibility than a self-enhancing pattern" of presentation (p. 115). Although there is situational variability in whether harmony or productivity is the highest value, in general judgements of likability and competence are inversely related.

DeGlopper, Donald R. (1972) "Doing business in Lukang," pp. 297-326 in W. Willmot, *Economic Organization in Chinese Society* (Stanford University Press) also pp. 291-320 in A. Wolf, *Studies in Chinese Society* (Stanford University Press, 1978), reports 1967-8 fieldwork among businessmen in what had been the second largest city in Taiwan before the redirection of trade to the north (Japan)." Businessmen were unanimous in asserting that such categories as surname [, sworn brotherhoods,] or neighborhood, in and of themselves, were of no importance in doing business"(1978:296). What was viewed as vital was *hsin-yiong*—a reputation for reliability and creditworthiness, although informal relationships are essential to credit and mutual assistance. In the businessmen's view "it is better to have limited relations with a lot of people than very close ties with only a few" (1978:317). Industriousness and frugality, in their view, are not sufficient for success in business (since these qualities are so common as to be taken for granted). Cleverness and maintaining one's autonomy to see and seize opportunities are the key to success.

DeGlopper, Donald R. (1974) "Religion and ritual in Lukang," pp. 43-69 in A. Wolf, *Religion and Ritual in Chinese Society* (Stanford University Press), contends that not only is there great individual and communal variation in religious beliefs and practices on Taiwan, but that the variation is not systematic or explainable. Lugang, a city in Jianghua Guan, supports 39 neighborhood-based temples as part of a cult of its past glory.

DeGlopper, Donald R. (1977) "Social structure in a 19th century Taiwanese port city," pp. 633-650 in W. Skinner, *The City in Late Imperial China* (Stanford University Press). Using a Simmelian social algebra D concludes, "the social structure of Lukang [c. 1890] consisted of overlapping groups, each recruited on different principles and each acting in a different sphere. On different occasions people defined themselves as members of different groups and within each sphere the groups were opposed to each other. Within the city, groups cut across each other, and both the limited opposition of the groups and the ultimate solidarity of the city were expressed in periodic public rituals. Relations with groups outside the city were restricted to economic exchange, political negotiation, or to open and unrestrained conflict" (p. 650). Also see his "Lu-kang: a city and its trading system," pp. 143-65 in R. Knapp, *China's Island Frontier: Studies in the Historical Geography of Taiwan* (Honolulu: University of Hawaii Press, 1980).

DeGlopper, Donald R. (1977) "Old medicine in a new bottle," *Reviews in Anthropology* 4:349-359, follows Gallin (1975) in stressing that using a medical practitioner does not imply any salient belief in the efficacy of the kind of medicine practiced. Just as DeGlopper (1974) contended that there is not a single "Chinese religion," he here concludes that there is "no single, pristine Great Tradition of Chinese medicine. There are several distinct schools, and when you look at what actual practitioners are doing, the variety is even greater" (p. 356). Moreover, "a tendency to try to keep one's options open and to prefer multi-causal explanations is common among ordinary people" on Taiwan (p. 357).

DeGlopper, Donald R. (1979) "Artisan work and life in Taiwan," *Modern China* 5:283-315, reports on a study of eighteen furniture firms in Lugang, c. 1968, arguing that craftsmanship is not archaic or backwards, and that small firms are very common in Taiwan. D argues that cabinetmaking represents "more of a job than a vocation" (p. 313), yet that "the cabinetmakers of Lugang do share a clear sense of themselves as a distinct group with its own values and ideal personality" (p. 310).

Devoe, Pamela A. (1981) "The effect of technoeconomic change on Taiwanese women and their role in society," *Asian Thought & Society* 6:148-155, outlines effects of compulsory education, increased participation in a money economy, mass media, and labor-saving devices on women in a Hualien village, c. 1977-78. Data derive from a survey of 661 junior high school students. Females reported a greater interest in and expectation of higher education than males. As D notes, many female students had been selected out of education and weren't in school to be sampled. D discusses the reduction of adult female sociation deriving from increased availability of "home conveniences" such as running water and washing machines.

Devoe, Pamela A. (1987) "Structural considerations in the contemporary farm family: survival of the large family ideal," *International Journal of the Sociology of the Family* 17:57-65. Based on interviews with members of 96 farm families in Jianghua guan, D finds a persistence in positive valuation of the extended families.

Diamond, Norma (1969) *K'un Shen, A Taiwan Village* (New York: Holt, Rinehart & Winston), provides a brief ethnography of a fishing village in Dailam that was minimally impacted by the KMT retreat to and domination of Taiwan. D gives special attention to the local Lung-Shan temple and the pantheon of locally-recognized deities. K'un Shen is characterized by weak agnatic groupings and a lack of corporate ownership of the means of production (fishing ponds, boats and equipment rather than land in this case). A very concise account of the typical life cycle is followed by an incisive discussion of Japanese influence on matchmaking practices. D also shows the fusion of lineages in worship and a general reliance on non-kin exceptional markedly contrasts with "traditional [Confucian] China," even though K'un Shen in the mid-1960s was not involved in the industrialization that affected many parts of the country: it was a traditional Taiwanese fishing village.

Diamond, Norma (1970) "Fieldwork in a complex society," pp. 113-141 in G. Spindler, *Being an Anthropologist* (New York: Holt), discusses fieldwork in a patriarchal society with written records by a young, female anthropologist, struggling to gain fluency in Hokkien and in "the national language," and confronted by "many who find it difficult to understand why, with our power and influence, we do not exert some kind of pressure to make Taiwan conform more to the democratic model, more like the ideal American that they believe exists" (p. 132). She noted that "not till the end of my fieldwork did I become aware of the fact that there was a sizable group of former villagers living in Tainan and elsewhere who still maintained significant ties to the village, and who were considered to be under obligation to contrbute to the temple, as if they were still residents in K'un Shen" (p. 141).

Diamond, Norma (1973) "The middle class family model in Taiwan: woman's place is in the home," *Asian Survey* 13:853-872, reports a survey of 112 full-time working wives, 20 part-time, and 108 housewives. Working wives were twice as likely as housewives to receive household assistance from their mother-in-law, and twice as likely to have husbands doing some cooking and housecleaning, but less help with childcare. 72% of the households with working wives were nuclear, in contrast to 65% of those with housewives. D concludes that middle-class women in Taiwan are "permitted low paid and rather uninteresting jobs before marriage and defined as a source of domestic labor after, regardless of training, talents or social class. Many in the urban situation are cut off from social participation of any sort and forced into an isolation [alone at home] which has few if any precedents in the traditional society" (p. 872) of fairly intensive village interaction and larger households.

Diamond, Norma (1975a) "Women under Kuomintang rule: variations on the feminine mystique," *Modern China* 1:3-45, discusses the continued oppression of women as women across class lines in the militaristic and repressive rule of the KMT on Taiwan. The exclusion of women from upper level positions, the firing of women when they marry, the occupational segregation into "pink collar" positions, lack of day-care service, along with cultural and social pressure to focus on child-rearing combine to make it difficult for women to have rewarding careers. "Suitable outside employment is less available for middle-class women. The occupations still open to women conflict with middle-class status" (p. 41). New urban, middle-class housewives, especially among immigrants to Daiba, are physically and socially isolated from contact with anyone except their own young children. "It is only very recently that women in Taiwan society have borne so much of the responsibility alone for child care and domestic tasks" (p. 40).

Diamond, Norman (1975b) "China's cities," *Reviews in Anthropology* 2:539-544, criticizes Feuchtwang (1974) for ignoring the function of temples in reaffirming Taiwanese ethnicity and fostering native Taiwanese leadership and Speare (1974) for misestimating the status (educational and other) and "modernity" of attitudes of rural-urban migrants in Taiwan. D deplores a general confusion of "development" with westernization in the literature on Taiwan and China, and the failure to see that the revolution in China was not urban-based.

Diamond, Norma (1977) "Prosperity on Tobacco Road," *Reviews in Anthropology* 4:9-16, argues that the tobacco-growers of Yen-Liao (studied by Myron Cohen) living in complex households are petty capitalists rather than peasants. D suggests "agro-business families" for people who are neither gentry nor traditional (rice-growing) peasants. "In the more complex households there is sufficient woman-power to free some of the women for work other than domestic chores" (p. 10). D also discusses women's economic assets as an explanation for their higher status in Hakka communities.

Diamond, Norma (1979) "Women in industry in Taiwan," *Modern China* 5:317-340, reports on the status of 134 young, unmarried women working in a Dailam factory in 1970 and aspiring to middle class marriage after some years of labor to repay parents for the cost of raising them. Those living in factory dormitories remitted 46% of their gross earnings, those living at home 70-80%. Only 23% of the money was put aside for future dowries. The bulk financed the education or establishment of the workers' brothers. For the most part, the young women maintained traditional views about the appropriateness of female subordination.

Eberhard, Wolfram (1962a) "Social mobility among businessmen in a Taiwanese town," *Journal of Asian Studies* 21:327-339; reprinted pp. 178-193 in E's *Settlement and Social Change in Asia* (Hong Kong University, 1967), reports a survey by Ch'en Shou of 157 merchants in Chingmei in Daiba Guan. Half were sons of businessman. Of those who started businesses (often quite small shops), less than 10% received loans. More than two-thirds of those starting business used their own savings and their father's savings. New businesses were no more likely than old ones to seek objects of modern technology and industry. E concluded, "Small towns have no real patriciate, only a small sector of businessmen with a family tradition in business," and that many of those starting businesses are farmer's sons (p. 192).

Eberhard, Wolfram (1962b) "Labour mobility in Taiwan," *Asian Studies* 2: 38-56; reprinted pp. 150-177 in E's *Settlement and Social Change in Asia* (Hong Kong University, 1967), reports on a sample of 2,000 applications at a government Employment Office. E presents descriptive statistics about this very biased sample. He was surprised that educated Taiwanese had been in and/or sought sales or higher blue-collar positions, speculating that "the development of the labour market has lagged behind the spread of higher education" (p. 153). E mentions but does not cross-tabulate thnic disparities. Explanations for leaving previous jobs suggest that education and illness are socially accepted reasons.

Eberhard, Wolfram (1963) "Auspicious marriages: a statistical study of a Chinese custom," *Sociologus* 13:49-53; reprinted pp. 201-207 in E's *Studies in Chinese Folklore and Related Essays, Indiana University Folklore Institute Monograph* 23 (1970), examines astrological signs of 2329 couples in Dailam in which the woman was born after 1911 and data on 634 Jungs in Kwantung between 1600 and 1899 to show that despite the widespread interest and expressed belief that some combinations are auspicious and others are not, the marriages contracted are randomly distributed (one of twelve inauspicious combinations occurred less than would be expected by chance, and one of twenty of these single tests would be expected to appear "statistically significant" by chance). Also see E's (1971) "Aspirations concerning marriage and married life among contemporary Taiwanese," pp. 325-369 in E's *Moral and Social Values of the Chinese* (Daiba: Chinese Materials and Research Aids Service Center).

Eberhard, Wolfram (1964) "Business activities of a small Chinese merchant," *Monumenta Serica* 21: 345-65; reprinted pp. 194-203 in E's *Settlement and Social Change in Asia (*Hong Kong University, 1967), analyzes the account book of one Daiba small merchant for a six-month period in 1911-12. "Such a store tended to serve 65 to 75 persons (families?) to such a degree that the store regarded them as customers.... The customers seemed to belong mainly to the lower classes of the local population," and "The store tended to buy its supplies from small suppliers, in small amounts" (pp. 202-3).

Eberhard, Wolfram (1965a) "Oracle and theater in China," *Asiastische*

Studien 18/19:11-18; reprinted pp. 191-199 in E's *Studies in Chinese Folklore and Related Essays, Indiana University Folklore Institute Monograph* 23 (1970), quotes eleven unfavorable sayings from the oracular texts of a Daiba Guan-Ti temple and discusses the references in oracles to well-known plays.

Eberhard, Wolfram (1965b) "Chinese regional stereotypes," *Asian Survey* 5:596-608, reports a survey of 97 college students in Taiwan in 1964 and 13 in the San Francisco Bay Area in 1953. The one-fifth of the respondents whose "regional origin" was coded as "Taiwan," knew fewer of the "well-known and clearly established stereotypes" of regions of China than those from other regions. "The most complete answers were given by Southern Chinese, the least complete by Taiwanese" (p. 596). Taiwan itself was not considered a region of China, and stereotypes of it were not included.

Eberhard, Wolfram (1966) "Fatalism in the life of the common man in non-Communist China," *Anthropological Quarterly* 39:148-160; reprinted pp. 177-189 in E's *Moral and Social Values of the Chinese* (Daiba: Chinese Materials and Research Aids Service Center, 1971), makes some general comments on various forms of divination, and then suggests behavior was not bound by such consultations, using his findings of "no statistically significant of marriages which according to the calendar would be inauspicious and no preference for auspicious marriages" (p. 186), based on records of more than 10,000 marriages— which is 7,000 more than claimed in the more systematic presentation in Eberhard (1963).

Eberhard, Wolfram (1967a) "Family planning in a Taiwan town," pp. 204-254 in *Settlement and Social Change in Asia* (Hong Kong University), reports a comparison of population register data on women living in Do-Hn born between 1911 and 1946 with Family Planning Association records. Differences in class, ethnicity, and the highly inter-correlated variable of mainlander/Taiwanese ethnicity differentiated acceptors from rejectors of family planning. "In contrast to other countries, the more highly educated group of the urban population seemed - typically to have more children than the less educated urban people" (p. 219). E suggests that a decrease in the interval between bearing children "might mean that traditional restrictions on intercourse were observed less frequently in those more modernized groups.... Relatively quick succession of births occurred with particular frequency among civil servants" (p. 216). 9% of married women had given away one or more child in adoption—for economic reasons. 1% of boys had been given away to another member of the same family, including even some first sons.

Eberhard, Wolfram (1967b) "Topics and moral values in Chinese temple decorations," *Journal of the American Oriental Society* 87:22-32; reprinted in E's *Moral and Social Values of the Chinese* (Daiba: Chinese Materials and Research Aids Service Center, 1971), discusses the relationship of Daiba temple paintings to literature (including opera) rather than to the resident divinities of a temple.

Eberhard, Wolfram (1970a) *Studies in Taiwanese Folktales . Asian Folklore & Social Life Monographs* 1. 394 native speakers of Hokkien in Daiba were asked to tell one of four widely-known stories which they liked best: Grandaunt Tiger (pan-Asian), Treasure Bowl (pan-Chinese), Peach Boy (Japanese), and Duck King (Taiwanese). E analyzes choices of tale and variants in telling with socio-demographic characteristics.

Eberhard, Wolfram (1970b) *Studies in Hakka Folktales; Asian Folklore & Social Life Monographs* 61 (Daiba: Chinese Association for Folklore). 534 native Hakka speakers in Daiba, Gu-D'ing, Miaoli(n), Dao-Yüan which stories they knew, which they liked, and why. E found few distinctively Hakka tales (some about the origins of the Hakka and Hak-ka heroes), few about deities (none about Buddhist deities), demons, or ghosts, many about animals. There was some sex-specificity, and rural informants had a richer repertoire than urban ones. Tales tended to be very moralistic, extolling harmony and filial piety. Also see E's (1972) *Taiwanese Ballads, Asian Folklore & Social Life Monographs* 22.

Eberhard, Wolfram (1971) "A comparison of dreams of San Francisco Chinese-Americans with dreams of Taiwanese," pp. 13-59 in E's *Moral and Social Values of the Chinese* (Daiba: Chinese Materials and Research Aids Service Center), contrasts surveys in the two places. Also see "Chinesiche Traume ais soziologischges Wuellen-material," pp. 97-134 in the same volume (including an English synopsis).

Eberhard, Wolfram (1972a) *The Chinese Silver Screen: Hong Kong and Taiwanese Motion Pictures in the 1960's, Asian Folklore & Social Life Monographs* 23, contains plot summaries of 329 films shown in Daiba between 1960 and 1971, and summarizes the portrayal of family and social life in the 181 which he saw. E found films made in Hong Kong to be more permissive in sexual matters than those made in Taiwan.

Eberhard, Wolfram (1972b) *Predigten an die Taiwanesen. Asian Folklore & Social Life Monographs* 33, contains translations into German of Buddhist sermons from Taiwan.

Eberhard, Wolfram, and Frank Huang (1968) "On some Chinese terms of abuse," *Asian Folklore Studies* 27:25-40, reprinted pp. 319-34 in Eberhard, *Moral and Social Values of the Chinese* (Daiba: Chinese Materials and Research Aids Service Center, 1971), analyze 325 insults H collected in conversations among Taiwanese students at Berkeley. The modal theme was stupidity (15%, followed by dishonesty/unreliability (12%) and improper behavior (10%). Domesticated animals recurred in the imagery of the insults. Instead of the more - typical practice of generalizing from Taiwan to all of China, E generalizes from Taiwanese in Berkeley to all of China.

Farris, Catherine S. (1989) "The social discourse on women's roles in Taiwan," *Journal of Oriental Studies* 27:76-92 and *Michigan Discussions in Anthropology* 9(1990):89-105, discusses official governmental representations of the status of women in Taiwan, mass magazine representations, and something of the history of feminist movements in Taiwan. F calls attention to the lack of discussion of Japanese influences (such as forbidding footbinding and establishing compulsory education for women) in all three discourses. Contrasting to the continuing low divorce rate in Taiwan, she finds a lot about "internal" or "Chinese-style" divorce in the popular women's magazines. Insofar as the phrases are all Beijinghua (not including Holo parallels like *buo dong bang*), one might wonder about the elite/popular origins (and resonances) of the discussions.

Farris, Catherine S. (1988) "Gender and grammar in Chinese with implications for language universals," *Modern China* 14:277-308. On the basis of undescribed research on an unspecified sample of Beijinghua-speakers in Daiba, F analyzes the sexual (more properly, marital) status of women embedded in life cycle words, forms of address and reference (which are not distinguished from each other), pejoratives, occupational terms, and covert gender-marking of identities.

Farris, Catherine S. (1991) "The gender of child discourse: same-sex peer socialization through language use in a Taiwanese preschool," *Journal of Linguistic Anthropology* 1:198-224, contrasts videotapes of (older) girls and boys in a Baeijinghua-speaking Daiba preschool with the familiar contrast of male direct, female indirect styles of speech that were a cliche of Western feminist sociolinguistics prior to Deborah

Tannen's recognition that boys and girls are direct about different things (in *You Just Don't Understand*, New York: Morrow, 1990).

Fei, John C. H., Gustav Ranis, and Shirley W. Y. Kuo (1979) *Growth with Equity: The Taiwan Case* (Washington, D.C.: World Bank), mark 1968 as a watershed between agricultural and industrial development, as labor scarcity succeeded years of labor surplus. Family income in rural households rose steadily until 1968, and then remained virtually constant. Until 1968 urban family income had been virtually constant, but had "significant improvement thereafter" (p. 312), as a gap between urban and rural family income widened. In the countryside, "because nonagricultural income was more equally distributed than agricultural income, the growth of rural industries and services made a substantial contribution to FID [family income distribution equity].... The steady increase of opportunities in rural by-employment available to members of rural families, especially the poorer ones, greatly contributed to the complementarity of growth and FID" (p. 315).

Feuchtwang, Stephan (1974a) *An Anthropological Analysis of Chinese Geomancy* (Vientiane, Laos: Vithagna), lays out in great detail an indigenous model of geomancy (hong sui). The extent to which it is based on fieldwork in Taiwan and the New Territories of Hong Kong and/or is derived from archival materials is not clear. There is no statement of method and is a singular lack of documentation for a dissertation (it was an M.A. thesis, supervised by Maurice Freedman).

Feuchtwang, Stephan (1974b) "Domestic and communal worship in Taiwan," pp. 105-130 in A. Wolf, *Religion and Ritual in Chinese Society* (Stanford University Press), describes calendric rites and funerals in Daiba as reflections of imperial Chinese in the hierarchy of supernatural beings. Why an organization with so little demonstrated salience on Taiwan even a century ago as the Qing bureaucracy should be the basic reality symbolized in a vibrant and revitalizing religion in another state a century later is a question F does not ask. The style of argumentation is exemplified in this summary: "The rhythm of the ritual calendar and of every religious ceremony is a movement between the interiorizing of a central authority and the externalizing of a mass of subjects,"

Feuchtwang, Stephan (1974c) "City temples in Taipei under three regimes," pp. 263-301 in M. Elvin and G. W. Skinner, *The Chinese City Between Two Worlds* (Stanford University Press), describes the changing fortunes of Daiba temples with the varying attempts at restriction by Qing, Japanese, and KMT regimes, and an increasingly successful development by mainlanders of a KMT state cult. Local temples in poorer and older parts of the city have declined as the rapid growth of Daiba and increased availability of cheap transportation dissolve local communities. "The gods of the new temples have no local significance, nor are they branches of older cults. They stand for power on a national scale. The morality preached in their name, and the stress of their religious style, is on the individual as a universal atom, receptacle of and responsible for 'society' and 'Chinese culture,' and duty-bound to perform good works" (p. 301),

Feuchtwang, Stephan (1977) "School-Temple and City God," pp. 581-608 in W. Skinner, *The City in Late Imperial China* (Stanford University Press); also pp. 103-130 in A. Wolf, *Studies in Chinese Society* (Stanford University Press, 1978), contrasts Qing historical data from Ning-Bo and from Taiwan (rain ceremonies —1978: 124-5), arguing that the ostensibly "Confucian" state cult included popular, Buddhist and Taoist components. "The managers of society necessarily looked to religious arenas outside the strict confines of official religion" (p. 103). "*Shen* and *kuei* can become gods and demons... and can be brought under control through the officials of a supernatural bureaucracy. Taoist priests perform rites in the names of these gods and demons, officials do not" (p. 127). Just what derives from 1966-8 fieldwork on Taiwan is not clearly demarcated.

Feuchtwang, Stephan, and Wang Ming-Ming (1991) "The politics of culture or a contest of histories: representations of Chinese popular religion," *Dialectical Anthropology* 16:251-272. W discusses shifting PRC regime repression and permission to consider folk/peasant traditions useful in positing a Chinese essence and deriding individualistic "counter-revolutionary superstitions" (especially divination). F discusses American representations of "Chinese" religion, based on fieldwork on Taiwan rather than in the PRC (specifically, Wang Shih-Ching 1974, Ahern 1981, Weller 1987, Sangren 1987, Jordan and Overmyer 1986) without any consideration of the parallel essentializing of "Chinese" unit and attempt to suppress local "superstition" by the KMT. A summation of F's two decades of essentializing of "Chinese" religion from mostly Taiwanese materials is contained in his book, *The Imperial Metaphor: Popular Religion in China* (New York: Routledge, 1992).

Freedman, Deborah S. (1975) "Consumption of modern goods and services and its relation to fertility: a study from Taiwan," *Journal of Development Studies* 12:95-117, shows from islandwide survey data "that couples whose consumption patterns emphasize modern goods and services also exhibit modern fertility behaviour, i.e., they cite a somewhat lower ideal family size and are considerably more likely to be using contraception," suggesting to her that "economic development, by fostering new wants, may encourage couples to limit family size" rather than expenditures for additional children (p. 95).

Freedman, Maurice (1968) Foreword to *The House of Lim* by Margery Wolf (London: Prentice-Hall), goes beyond Wolf in claiming Taiwanese data for the study of China, dismissing the prevalence of *simbua* marriage as a difference of quantity not of quality of social structure. F questions Wolf's analysis of the division of families (*huen ge hue*) as a product of women's inability to get along with each other. Quarrels between women may provide the occasion, but "while the quarrels precipitated by women are often seen as the major causes of the disruption of Chinese families, it is to the brittle relationship between brothers that we must look for an understanding of why, in spite of the great pride taken in large families, they are nonetheless very rare" (p. xi). F suggests the cultural contradiction between requirements that the older yield to the whims of younger brothers as children and that the younger brother defer to elder brothers when all are adults is the psychodynamic background for later conflicts which are blamed on wives. Wolf (1970) appears to have accepted this view)

Freedman, Ronald, John Y. Takeshita, and T. H. Sun (1964) "Fertility and family planning in Taiwan: a case study of the demographic transition," *American Journal of Sociology* 70:16-27. Based on probability samples of 2432 married women aged between 20 and 39 in 1962-3, FTS report positive correlations between "modernization" indices and use of family planning. "Favorable attitudes to family limitations and attempts to practice it develop in the latter half of the child-bearing period when low mortality permits the survival of the moderate number of children and sons formerly requiring a larger number of births. We do not know whether this represents a change in the desired number of children or simply a different way of reaching the same values" (p. 27).

Freedman, Ronald (1969) *Family Planning in Taiwan: An Experience in Social Change* (Princeton University Press) and a series of articles such as R. Freedman, L. Coombs, M. C. Chang and T-H Sun (1974) "Trends in fertility, family size preferences, and practices of family planning: Taiwan 1965-1973," *Studies in Family Planning* 5:270-288 and T-H Sun, H-S Lin & R. Freedman (1978) "Trends in fertility, family size preferences and family planning practices in Taiwan 1961-76, *Studies in Family Planning* 9:54-70; Coombs (1979) "Prospective fertility and underlying preferences: A longitudinal study of Taiwan," *Population Studies* 33:447-455 report island-wide surveys (1965-1976) Daidiong surveys (1961-1976) of acquiescence in principle to family planning as good for society, followed by increasing personal application. Family size preferences decreased, but not the perceived necessity of producing male heirs for support in old age. With economic development, the expected demographic transition occurred, although contraception was widely accepted prior to the changes in family functions and organization which are supposed (in demographic transition theory) to lead to limiting family size.

Fried, Martha Nemes, and Morton H. Fried (1980) *Transitions: Four Rituals in Eight Cultures* (New York: Norton) contrast rituals connected with birth, puberty, marriage and death in China, Taiwan, the USSR, Cuba, Hausa, !Kung, Tikopia, and Tlingit cultures. Although Taiwan is one of the eight cultures, and China another, Taiwanese materials are often, but not invariably, identified as "Chinese."

Fried, Morton H. (1966) "Some political aspects of clanship in a modern Chinese city," pp. 285-300 in M. Swartz, V. Turner, & A. Tuden, *Political Anthropology* (University of Chicago Press) discusses the continued salience of clan organizations (tight *zho(k)-dong* registered as non-profit corporations and looser *zong-ch'in hue*) in Daiba. F noted that KMT symbols had been co-opted in temple rites, making it difficult for the invited officials to criticize holding them. "Mainlanders show little inclination to seek membership in existing Taiwanese clans," (p. 297) although F claimed they were forming their own. Clans provide semiformal forums for communication between government and the masses, and some limited mediation, but only moderate social control. Leading Daiba politicians, including the then-mayor, were active in their own clan associations, and presumably mobilized that particular base, although F provides no data on political expenditure or clan involvement in campaigns.

Gale, James L. (1975) "Patient and practitioner attitudes toward traditional and western medicine in a contemporary Chinese setting," pp. 195-208 in A. Kleinman et al., *Medicine in Chinese Cultures.* (Washington: U. S. Government Printing Office), reports interviews with 33 Western and traditional Chinese doctors and 55 patients in Daiba in 1972. Practitioners of traditional Chinese medicine were mostly over 50 years old and 11 of 15 were mainlanders. The Western-style doctors were younger, and 14 of 18 were born on Taiwan. Both kinds of doctors reported treating mostly acute illnesses. Direct observation of the Chinese-style doctors and interviews with their patients revealed that they mostly dealt with chronic illnesses associated with pain in the joints or vascular problems. "Although expressing about equal preference for traditional Chinese and Western practitioners... almost all had initially sought care from Western physicians for their present illnesses, which were mainly chronic" (p. 206).

Gallin, Bernard (1960a) "Matrilateral and affinal relationships of a Taiwanese village," *American Anthropologist* 62:632-642, describes economic, social, religious and political aspects of *ch'in-ja* relations, which are, perhaps, especially prominent where there are small clan groupings. In Xin Xing, a village in Jianghua Guan, there were twelve different names among 115 families, and land was not held by *zho*.

Gallin, Bernard (1960b) "A case for intervention in the field," *Human Organization* 18:140-144, relates G's experience being pressed into service to act as a village leader in mediating reparations for the beating of two village residents by men from a neighboring village in a dispute over water rights, discussing how this enabled him to be a participant observer of attempted mediation, and how his intervention in the legal system led to obtaining better and more copious data from villagers.

Gallin, Bernard (1963a) "Cousin marriage in China," *Ethnology* 2:104-108. Based on data from Xin Xing, G argues that cross-cousin marriage is rarely if ever symmetrical. Mother's brother's daughter is favored over father's sister's daughter as a source of brides. The latter choice is disapproved by villagers.

Gallin, Bernard (1963b) "Land reform in Taiwan: its effect on rural social organization and leadership," *Human Organization* 22:109-122, discusses changes in attitudes toward authority/leadership as landlords. Traditionally village leaders and mediators to outside governments, land–lords were expropriated and left. Xin Xing villagers distrust those putting themselves forward for political positions, and those elected lack the legitimacy to resolve intra- or inter-village conflicts.

Gallin, Bernard (1963c) "Chinese peasant attitudes towards the land," *Proceedings of the American Ethnological Society*, pp. 64-71, and pp. 367-375 in J. Potter, M. Diaz & G. Foster, *Peasant Society* (Boston: Little Brown, 1967), interprets the willingness of Jianghua Guan peasants (as well as expropriated landlords) to sell their land and move to opportunities in Daiba as contradicting Redfield's (1956:112, 140) contention that peasants have "an intimate and reverent attitude toward the land; that agricultural work is good and commerce not so good" and "a reverent disposition toward habitat and ancestral ways." G contends that the connection to the land is based on concern for family security without spiritual or emotional attachment. Landholdings are not quickly abandoned as family members begin to work in Daiba, but are relinquished without regret by those well enough established in urban enterprises to move their family to the city. In contrast to reports of Chinese peasants from the mainland, the peasants observed by G gave little consideration seeking to find relatives to buy land at the time they felt secure enough to sell it. As a place "where the lineage is weak, there is virtually unobstructed sale of land to outsiders" (1967:374) in Xin Xing.

Gallin, Bernard (1964) "Rural development in Taiwan: the role of the government," *Rural Sociology* 29:313-323. The departure of landlords who sold out what land was left to them after land reform, and "the reduced prestige of the ones who remain have begun to affect leadership in rural areas, traditionally a function of the landlord class" (p. 323). G argues that increased mandatory education was so remote from rural needs that the increase little affected Xin Xing.

Gallin, Bernard (1966a) *Hsin Hsing, Taiwan* (Berkeley: University of California Press), analyzes changes, in particular erosion of lineage organization's power, brought about by the mainlander government, in a Jianghua village. G describes former landlords withdrawing from local interests as they were forced to take stock in government industrial enterprises for the land they had previously rented and former tenants pressed into migrating to cities to become industrial laborers. The account of religion is superficial functionalism, concerned with "anxiety reduction." G notes that "while the traditional significance attached to some rituals has lessened, that of others has remained the same, and some have even, perhaps, increased in popularity," as emigrants to cities return for the village god's birthday "pai-pai" (p. 269). The pluralism of trying remedies from diverse medical systems described in Daiba occurred in the countryside as early as G's fieldwork.

Gallin, Bernard (1966b) "Conflict resolution in changing Chinese society: a Taiwanese study," pp. 265-74 in M. Swartz, V. Turner & A. Tuden, *Political Anthropology* (Chicago: Aldine), discusses the breakdown in mediation, "the traditional Chinese method for settling local disputes" in Xin Xing during the 1950s and early 60s. G saw a growing individualism with a refusal to submit to mediation or to be bound by the results. Even the underlying principle—"that the goal of the resolution is to enable to persons in conflict to live harmoniously together"

(p. 272)—was losing its taken-for-granted legitimacy in a more and more contractualist gesselschaft (society). Traditional peasant fear of the authorities gave way to attempts to use police and courts, both of which were reluctant to become involved and both of which tried to reinforce the use of mediators, despite their decline in status. Also see G's (1967) "Mediation in changing Chinese society in rural Taiwan," *Journal of Asian and African Studies* 2:77-90.

Gallin, Bernard (1967) "Emerging individualism in changing rural Taiwan," *Journal of the China Society* 5:3-8. Widening networks—both beyond kin and across greater distances—have weakened village organization and solidarity. Parents have relinquished their monopoly of control over marriage, thus avoiding likely challenge of it. G considers this flexibility analogous to willingness to depart from the ideal of the joint family when brothers insist on family division.

Gallin, Bernard (1968a) "Rural to urban migration in Taiwan: its impact on Chinese family and kinship," pp. 261-282 in D. Buxbaum, *Chinese Family Law and Social Change* (Seattle: University of Washington Press). Only 21.6% of Xin Xing migrants to Daiba were landless. All men moved initially without their wives and families. Most return home to worship ancestors, and, over time, brought wives and families to join them the city. These immigrants enrolled their children in public schools (as they would have back in the village). They used *dang-gis* less often, in part, because they lacked a room for rituals to be performed and because of the necessity of cash payment to an urban *dang-gi*. Mostly, however they "do not and many cannot take advantage of the other services available in the urban center; e. g., they make no use of credit facilities, wide organizational networks, or legal facilities" (p. 282).

Gallin, Bernard (1968b) "Political factionalism and its impact on Chinese village social organization in Taiwan," pp. 377-400 in M. Swartz, *Local-Level Politics* (Chicago: Aldine), describes the local factions in Xin Xing after 1959, when direct election of the village head (*tuaen diu*) began. "The traditional concern for consensus has been weakened radically and, to a great degree, has been rendered impractical by the development and penetration of political factions into the rural area.... An official usually considers his mandate to be from, and his main responsibility to be to, the members of the faction that elected him.... The local leaders, because of this partisanship, thus adulterate their traditional effectiveness as mediators and, as a result, the customary means for resolving local-level conflict are becoming increasingly inadequate and local conflict often goes unresolved" (p. 398).

Gallin, Bernard (1975) "Comments on contemporary sociocultural studies of medicine in Chinese societies," pp. 273-280 in A. Kleinman et al., *Medicine in Chinese Cultures*. (Washington: U. S. Government Printing Office), discusses the continued functioning of *dang-gi*, who reinforce moral (familial) behavior, offer explanations that make sense in native terms, and focus on the patient (and his/her milieu) rather than on the disease. A *dang-gi* involves the whole family, or even the whole community in a cure. G notes that Western observers exhibit a kind of euphoric admiration for sacred medical systems reinforcing the moral order they study. He wonders if this is a "reverse ethnocentrism," celebrating the exotic and underemphasizing more mundane medical activities. Taiwanese social scientists are not merely skeptical of, but oblivious to *dang-gi*, denying their continued role. G concludes by cautioning against attributing the same knowledge, perceptions, and beliefs to all members of Chinese societies, even when they engage in similar behavior. "Utilization of the traditional systems does not necessarily imply belief in these forms of medicine. Many people 'go through the motions'" (p. 277).

Gallin, Bernard (1985) "Development and change in Taiwan and Hong Kong: implications for future relations with the People's Republic of China," pp. 47-65 in J. Williams, *The Future of Hong Kong and Taiwan* (E. Lansing, MI: Asian Studies Center), suggests that although the family remains the basic element of Chinese culture in Hong Kong, PRC, and Taiwan, rapid social change "has altered some cultural traits that characterized the 'Chineseness' of the Chinese people as well as created other variations that differentiate Taiwan and Hong Kong from the PRC. Rural-to-urban migration receives special emphasis, having been almost entirely blocked in the PRC and very important in Taiwan and Hong Kong. G also suggests that "the proliferation of religious activity in Taiwan and increased importance of the supernatural might be viewed as a nativist movement to mark and enhance Taiwanese identity (as opposed to mainlanders)" (p. 55).

Gallin, Bernard, and Rita S. Gallin (1974a) "The rural-to-urban migration of anthropologists in Taiwan," pp. 223-248 in G. Foster & R. Kemper, *Anthropologists in Cities* (Boston: Little Brown), provide a narrative account of studying Xin Xing immigrants in Daiba, first directing a team of Taiwanese assistants in survey research (1965-6), and then the more personal relations of a patron which developed in more participant observation fieldwork in 1969. The Gallins found continued involvement in the religious life (especially annual Mahzo processions) of their home village, and also saw remittance back to the village as important to the increased prosperity of Xin Xing during the 1960s. "Struck by migrants' seeming isolation from each other and by the lack of formal linking bonds" in the first urban fieldwork, they discovered later that "migrants, while not forming a cohesive urban community in the narrow sense of the word, turned out to be bound by more formal and informal ties than we had believed" although "outside of the [produce] market, migrants have failed in attempts to organize into a cohesive mutual aid group" (pp. 223-4, 241-2).

Gallin, Bernard, and Rita S. Gallin (1974b) "The integration of village migrants in Taipei," pp. 331-358 in M. Elvin and G. Skinner, *The Chinese City Between Two Worlds* (Stanford University Press), contrast migration to Daiba and Gohyiong of natives of four Jianghua villages. Nearly twice as many from Xin Xing as from the other villages migrated (39% in contrast to 23%). The heaviest migration was immediately after World War II (1945-50). The majority worked as laborers upon arrival in Daiba. "Most long-distance migrants perceive their move as one of economic necessity, although in a strict sense this was by no means the case" (p. 339). There were pull factors of opportunity from the city as well as push factors of poverty from the countryside. Three-quarters of the migrants to Daiba maintained their hold on their village land (c. 1966). There was chain migration to areas of the city and to work in the central market, and a certain amount of cohesion between laborers and businessmen born in Xin Xing." Although "outside the market, Xin Xing laborers have failed to organize themselves into a cohesive mutual-aid group" (p. 353), most return to Xin Xing for the annual procession of Mazho.

Gallin, Bernard, and Rita S. Gallin (1977) "Sociopolitical power and sworn brother groups in Chinese society: A Taiwanese case," pp. 89-97 in R. Fogelson & R. Adams, *Anthropology of Power* (New York: Academic Press), examine the operation of one form of *guan-he* for mutual support.

Gallin, Bernard, and Rita S. Gallin (1982a) "The Chinese joint family in changing rural Taiwan," pp. 142-158 in S. Greenblatt, R. Wilson & A. Wilson, *Social Interaction in Chinese Society* (New York: Praeger), argue that, following an earlier diminution of the importance of kinship in rural Taiwan, the joint family was being revived in Xin Xing during the 1970s because it facilitates economic diversification. The authors suggest that mothers-in-law providing childcare permit more young women to work (70% of the women under age 40 from joint families worked in contrast to 33% from conjugal households). The joint family also increases the pool of venture capital for family economic enterprises.

Gallin, Bernard, and Rita S. Gallin (1982b) "Socioeconomic life in rural Taiwan: 20 years of development and change," *Modern China* 8:205-246. Land reform and consolidation, along with other governmental intervention in the countryside diminished the significance of kinship (especially large lineage organization) during the 1950s and 60s. With the development of small factories in Xin Xing, urban emigration slowed during the 1970s, and some earlier migrants returned, because "job surety in the city became questionable and employment possibilities in the country demonstrable [and/]or skills learned, contacts established, and capital accumulated in the city became actualizable in the [increasingly industrialized] country" (p. 225). Contrary to "modernization theory," joint families became more common (see their 1982a chapter). Moreover, the increased rural prosperity fueled by remittance from urban emigrants and by local industrialization led to a revitalization of Taiwanese religion with more elaborate rites, temple rebuilding and building, rather than declining religiosity and predicted secularism. G&G suggest that dentification with the locality and as Taiwanese in Taiwanese religion may be a covert nativism and protest against mainlander domination.

Gallin, Bernard, and Rita S. Gallin (1985) "Matrilateral and affinal relationships in changing Chinese society," pp. 101-116 in J. Hsieh & Y. Chuang, *The Chinese Family and Its Ritual Behavior* (Nankang:Academia Sinica), contend that, although agnatic kinship remains the most important relationship within villages, affinal relationships have been underemphasized in accounts of Taiwan. In southern Taiwan (in contrast to Kwangtung) "Villagers are unwilling to jeopardize a potentially meaningful and utilitarian relationship by disappointing their affines' expectations" (p. 116). Arthur Wolf (1985a) suggested that these relationships are more important in Xin Xing than elsewhere, because of the lack of lineage organization there, and also that such relationships are of increasing importance (especially where there are weak or no lineage organization), rather than having been missed by earlier fieldwork elsewhere.

Gallin, Rita S. (1983) "Women at work in Hsin Hsing," *Taiwan Review* (spring) 12-15; (1984a) "Women, family and the political economy of Taiwan," *Journal of Peasant Studies* 12:76-92; (1984b) "The entry of Chinese women into the rural labor force: a case study from Taiwan," *Signs* 9:383-398; and "Mothers-in-law and daughters-in-law: intergenerational relations within the Chinese family in Taiwan," *Journal of Cross-Cultural Gerontology* 1:31-49, reports that twice as many Xin Xing women born after 1939 working outside the home as those who were housewives lived in joint households. The presence of a mother-in-law to do "women's work" in the household underlies the new "women's work" in small factories (also see Diamond 1973). Village women used their dowry as venture capital for the family's economic advancement, not to promote their personal independence. Economic contributions by women failed to increase their autonomy. There were fewer arranged marriages, but "once women became members of a family, their goals were defined for, not by, them" (b:396). The continued low status of women "is not simply a legacy of traditional culture. It derives from a system of patriarchal capitalism that reproduces women's subordination to maintain and justify the employment practices that underpin the political economy. To ensure sustained production at low cost during periods of economic growth and political stability during periods of economic recession, the Taiwanese [sic. Republic of China] government encourages an ideological environment that relegates women to menial labor and household tasks. The marriage of patriarchal ideology and contemporary capitalism allows the family, the nation, and the international market economy to take advantage of women's unpaid domestic and underpaid public labor without altering cultural definitions of male and female roles or transforming the structure of male status and authority within the family" (b:398).

Gallin, Rita S. (1989) "Women and work in rural Taiwan," *Journal of Health and Social Behavior* 30:374-385, repeats 1984 comments about political economy and the labor reserve of rural Taiwanese women, reports twice as many women living in nuclear families in Xin Xing in 1979 not working for remuneration than in her 1984 report, and speculates that an "effect of their tradition-bound socialization is to decrease their awareness and attention regarding symptoms," since "the women of Hsin Hsing showed little of the frustration or resentment purported to increase women's susceptibility to disease" (p. 382).

Gates, Hill (1979) "Dependency and the part-time proletariat in Taiwan," *Modern China* 5:381-407, relates the exploitation of women as a reserve of transient, docile, and cheap labor which can be laidoff during recessions to the traditional subordination of women in Chinese societies. G estimates the proletariat consists of about one-fifth of the population; the petty bourgeoisie nearly a half.

Gates, Hill (1981) "Ethnicity and social class,"pp. 241-281 in E. Ahern and H. Gates, *The Anthropology of Taiwanese Society* (Stanford University Press), analyzes historical and functional causes of ethnic consciousness and Taiwanese/ mainlander conflict in relation to class differences. Reviewing various explanations of ethnic conflict offered by social theorists, G stresses that socioeconomic inequality rather than behavioral differences is the base. On Taiwan, the imposition of the foreign elite's language as "the national language," residential segregation, the monopolization of the technocratic and bureaucratic niches vacated by Japanese, the great preponderance of men among the emigré mainlanders, and the continued garrison mentality of armed forces supported by taxes and other expropriation of Taiwanese all contributed to a resentment that can only be covertly expressed (as in folk festivals). The political uses of ethnicity differ by social class (G posits five) within a framework enforced by mainlander military and police power and educational discrimination.

Gates, Hill (1987) "Money for the Gods," *Modern China* 13:259-277, analyzes the ubiquity of cash transactions, particularly around weddings and funerals. In offerings to ancestors/gods, Taiwanese use paper money, while mainlanders from the north prefer imitation-silver ingots. G is particularly concerned that "women can be bought and sold," although "even a bought person remains a person with some rights and capacities that no nonhuman creature or object has [so that] women are not, and have not been, pure commodities in Chinese society" (p. 266).

Gates, Hill (1988) *Chinese Working Class Lives* (Ithaca, NY: Cornell University Press). Life histories of six Taiwanese and three Mainlanders living in Daiba from non-elite (but working class only in a loose sense, since the women were little involved in industrial labor) show disruptions of many childhood expectations. There is some recognition of Taiwanese ethnicity, despite the author's own allegiance to class analysis as more basic.

Gold, Thomas B. (1986) *State and Society in the Taiwan Miracle* (Armonk, NY: M. E. Sharpe), provides a concise account of economic development in Taiwan, with special emphasis on the 1960s expansion of exports and 1970s flexibility to various external shocks (oil shortage, withdrawal of political recognition of a "Republic of China," and increased protectionism in other countries suffering from stagflation). The considerable reliance on nuclear power is clearly described, as is increasingly open popular discontent from 1977 onward. G's field research provides an account of the economic elite and the relationships of the authoritarian government to old and new capitalists in Taiwan. G calls for a challenge with East Asian materials of the dependency theory largely generalized from Latin American materials.

Gold, Thomas B. (1988a) "Colonial origins of Taiwanese capitalism," pp. 101-117 in E. Winckler & S. Greenhalg, *Contending Approaches to the Political Economy of Taiwan.* (Armonk, NY: M. E. Sharpe), suggests that in addition to developments of infrastucture (including human capital), the legacy of Japanese colonialism important to development included removal of the traditional elite, along with its material base, exemplification of the possibilities of business success despite political repression, exemplification of the possibilities of increasing production with new technology, and "Japan left a structure of pervasive political control and penetration down to the grass roots" (p. 116) inherited by the Chinese police state.

Gold, Thomas B. (1988b) "Entrepreneurs, multinationals, and the state," pp. 175-205 in E. Winckler & S. Greenhalg, *Contending Approaches to the Political Economy of Taiwan.* (Armonk, NY: M. E. Sharpe). Using data on economic development on Taiwan (particularly data on foreign investments), G contends that even Evans' retooled dependency theory overestimates the monolithic power of multinational corporations (MNCs) and underestimates the autonomy of governments from MNCs and indigenous bourgeoisies. G asserts Taiwanese consensus with first Japanese and then KMT overlords without any (even anecdotal) data (pp. 182, 203). His view of a KMT conversion experience should be contrasted with Barrett (p. 135 in the same volume).

Gould-Martin, Katherine (1975) "Medical systems in a Taiwan village: *Ong-Ia-Kong*, The Plague God as modern physician in Taiwan," pp. 115-140 in A. Kleinman et al., *Medicine in Chinese Cultures.* (Washington: U. S. Government Printing Office). *"Ong-ia-kong* handles cases Western medicine cannot, either because they are incurable or because they are not part of the complaints that Western medicine recognizes. *Ong-ia-kong* handles underlying conditions—weakness of health or fate and loss of harmony—that Western medicine does not... [and] provides a theory which the patients understand so that they can participate in their own diagnosis and cure.... In his current practice, he does not interfere with Western medicine, he 'patches' it" (p. 135).

Gould-Martin, Katherine (1978) "Hot, cold, clean, poison, and dirt: Chinese folk medical categories," *Social Science and Medicine* 12B:39-46. Drawing on fieldwork in Daiba guan in less-than-obvious fashion, G-M presents an analysis that she rightly labels "abstruse" on the relations between hot/ cold, wet/dry, clean/dirty, and poison/non-poison, seeing poison as an entity caused by yin-yang collision. G-M notes that "the connections drawn will rarely be uttered by rural informants.... it may be difficult to elicit them and in some cases informants will even deny them" and that others told her that their Taiwanese informants did not use the terms yin and yang (p. 44). She provides no reason for confidence in the validity (reality) or the salience of her analysis.

Gourlay, Walter E. (1985) "Hong Kong and Taiwan: the colonial heritage," pp. 1-32 in J. Williams, *The Future of Hong Kong and Taiwan* (E. Lansing, MI: Asian Studies Center), contrasts the development of Japanese Taiwan and British Hong Kong to communist mainland China.

Greenhalg, Susan (1984) "Networks and their nodes: urban society on Taiwan," *China Quarterly* 99:529-542. Using official statistics and "close study" of 73 families in Daiba, Tansui, and Samgia(p), G shows inequities in education, employment and income between mainlanders and Taiwanese as well as much greater religious involvement of Taiwanese.

Greenhalg, Susan (1985a) "Is inequality demographically induced? The family cycle and the distribution of income in Taiwan," *American Anthropologist* 87:571-594. Based on a sample of 80 native Taiwanese families in Samgia(p), Daiba, Tanshui and Yenping, G concludes that the family cycle is more important than class in determining mobility (supporting Chayanov's hypothesis).

Greenhalg, Susan (1985b) "Sexual stratification: the other side of 'growth with equity' in East Asia," *Population and Development Review* 11:265-314, documents increasing inequality between sons and daughters in education, occupation, income, property, control over (choice of) jobs, residences and expenditures.

Susan Greenhalg (1988) "Families and networks in Taiwan's economic development," pp. 224-245 in E. Winckler & S. Greenhalg, *Contending Approaches to the Political Economy of Taiwan.* (Armonk, NY: M. E. Sharpe), reviews evidence for the preponderance (she estimates 95.4%) and efficiency of family-owned firms. "Not only can it maintain greater secrecy about its operations, but it also enjoys greater continuity over time in management and operations" and, through diversification of family enterprises, "substantial protection against failure" (p. 233). Moreover, "in an environment in which bank loans are very difficult for small firms to obtain, use of social networks ensures access to much more capital than would otherwise be available" (p. 234). However, "because it disperses capital rather than concentrating it, the family firm has relatively few resources to invest in upgrading its technology or in R&D of new technology. Nor can it easily achieve the economies of scale that reduce unit production costs" (p. 236).

Gregor, A. James, and Maria Hsia Chang (1985) "The Taiwan Independent Movement: the failure of political persuasion," *Political Communication and Persuasion* 2:363-390, list acts defined by the ROC government as terrorism. They attribute these to the failure of a Maoist revolution by Taiwanese and the "unmanageable frustration among Taiwan's revolutionaries" (p. 378).

Grichting, Wolfgang L. (1971) "Occupational prestige structure in Taiwan," *Journal of Sociology* 7:67-78, reports findings of a nationwide value survey more fully reported in the 588 page privately-printed *Value System in Taiwan*, 1970.

Hanson, Karen J. (1984) "Prosperity and health," *Taiwan Review* (fall) 19-25, summarizes data from her Ph.D. dissertation on increasing preventive health interventions.

Harrell, C[lyde] Stevan (1974) "When a ghost becomes a god," pp. 193-206 in A. Wolf, *Religion and Ritual in Chinese Society* (Stanford University Press), divides the spirits of the dead into private spirits (ancestors), those from whom assistance is solicited (*sin*), and those whose potential harmfulness is forestalled by bribes (*on bao*). "Some Taiwanese can describe a coherent supernatural social order, roughly corresponding to the real social order on earth. Others are not given to such systematic theology, but... [can] classify supernatural beings in terms of their relationships to those who worship them" (p. 193). H describes differentiation in places, occasions, offerings, and organization of worship for ghosts and gods, and discusses intermediate categories of upwardly mobile spirits and the marginal people most interested in them.

Harrell, C[lyde] Stevan (1976) "The ancestors at home: domestic worship in a land-poor Taiwanese village," pp. 373-386 in W. Newell, *Ancestors* (The Hague: Mouton), follows Maurice Freedman (1958) in distinguishing the unity of the lineage from filial obedience to recently deceased forbearers within "ancestor worship." In a place such as "Ploughshare Village" with a mixture of surnames, without established lineage organization and without inherited land, ancestor rites are reduced to domestic cults with simplified offerings and a reduced number of ancestors being commemorated. H notes that tablets of remote ancestors are burnt or buried when their worship is discontinued.

Harrell, C[lyde] Stevan (1977) "Modes of belief in Chinese folk religion," *Journal for the Scientific Study of Religion* 16:55-65, differentiates "intellectual belief", "true belief", from "practical belief", instead of contrasting believers to non-believers. The typology is based on interviews with 66 residents of "Ploughshare Village."

Harrell, C[lyde] Stevan (1979) "The concept of 'soul' in Chinese folk religion," *Journal of Asian Studies* 38:519-528, explores "soul" (*lienghuen*), arguing that it may be multiple in theory, "Chinese people actually behave as if the 'soul' were a single entity.... Contexts in which it is separated from the body are enumerated. The image that emerges of the 'soul' indicates that the Chinese concept *lieng-huen* has a dual nature that incorporates the cultural aspect of being human and the individual personality" (p. 449).

Harrell, C[lyde] Stevan (1981a) "Normal and deviant drinking in rural Taiwan," pp. 49-59 in A. Kleinman & T-Y Lin, *Normal and Abnormal Behavior in Chinese Culture* (Dordrecht: Reidel), notes that "most Chinese adult males, at least in rural areas of Taiwan, do drink and when they do, they drink until at least tipsy, if not downright drunk. If drinking is not a major social problem, then, the reasons must be sought in the ability of the society to put drinking in its place, to define the social context of alcohol consumption so that it becomes... a social activity" (p. 50) by toasting other persons in the context of eating (banquet or festival). "Outside the accepted social contexts, however, drinking becomes dangerous. People who drink too often are dangerous mainly to themselves.... The most deviant drinkers of all, those who drink alone, are posing a direct social danger, and their behavior is strongly condemned" (p. 57).

Harrell, C[lyde] Stevan (1981b) "Effects of economic change in two Taiwanese villages," *Modern China* 7:31-54, contrasts economic development in two Daiba villages. One "looks like the traditional subsistence periphery," the other participates in decentralized industrial production (p. 51). H credits Japanese development of transport infrastructure and agriculture for providing the base for post-dependent development.

Harrell, C[lyde] Stevan (1981c) "Social organization in Hai-shan," pp. 125-147 in E. Ahern and H. Gates, *The Anthropology of Taiwanese Society* (Stanford University Press), contrasts farming Hokkien-speaking villages in Daiba Guan with "Ploughshare Village," whose residents do not own land and are engaged in wage labor. H attributes the absence of lineage organization to the difficulties involved in collective ownership of property other than land and the ease of migration for those not tied to landholdings. Differences in ancestor worship and religious institutions between villages show that "common principles about gods, ghosts, and ancestors are shaped to suit the forms and needs of particular communities" (p. 146)—presumably in history and particular contexts.

Harrell, C[lyde] Stevan (1982) *Ploughshare Village: Culture and Context in Taiwan.* (Seattle: University of Washington Press). With a foreshortened historical perspective, H describes changing patterns of employment, internal stratification, social grouping, family types, and ancestral cults in a former mining town in Haishan now involved in manufacturing, both in local, small, subcontracting enterprises and as a source of labor for larger enterprises in and around nearby Daiba. H discusses the social and economic co-operation of unrelated persons, the simplification of ancestor worship in a locale without established lineage organizations, and the relatively higher status of women in a place where the household is the predominant unit of social organization. Rates of uxorilocal marriage are higher (15%) and rates of minor marriage are lower (35%) than in peasant villages in which the lineage is the major unit of social organization. H also attributes the relative lack of "dependency" symptoms (stratification and comprador capitalism) to the expansion of the (manufacturing) core to such villages, while avoiding examination of politics, local, national, or international.

Harrell, C[lyde] Stevan (1985) "Why do the Chinese work so hard? Reflections on an entrepreneurial ethic," *Modern China* 11:203-226. Contrasting contemporary Taiwanese and 19th century mainlanders to workers on Maoist collective farms, H show that hard work is not an invariant feature of Chinese societies. It does not occur if there is no perceived chance of raising the economic status of the family (not just the individual and also not an abstract collectivity). Perceived entrepreneurial opportunities which have some chance to provide long-term benefit to the family, not just socialization to a "work ethic" is necessary to account for the considerable effort often expended.

Harrell, C[lyde] Stevan (1987) "The concept of fate in Chinese folk ideology," *Modern China* 13:90-109, endeavors to explain how fatalism can co-exist with an entrepreneurial ethic, using data from accounts of "Ploughshare Village" informants on their encounters with *sun(g)-miya* (fortune tellers) and Chinese historical material. H argues that Chinese do not try to change their fate, but operate within what they perceive to be lifelong fate. He also argues that fate relates more to marriage than to economic prosperity.

Harrell, [Clyde] Stevan (1991) "Pluralism, performance and meaning in Taiwanese healing: a case study," *Culture, Medicine and Psychiatry* 15:45-68, examines a case of presumed psychosis in a 16-year-old Taiwanese girl to show the role of performance in creating meaning in a plural medical system. The case illustrates that there is no necessary correspondence between diagnoses, authorities, and therapies; that consensus, if achieved at all, is tenuous and context-dependent; that meaning is created by performance, rather than the other way around; and that understanding of how therapies work depends on their efficacy.

Hchu Hai-Yuan (1975) "Changing social attitudes in Wanhua," *Bulletin of the Institute of Ethnology, Academia Sinica* 39:57-84 (in Chinese), reports the results of an attitude survey which found cohort differences to match the ethnohistorical analyses of Huang (1975) and Wen (1975) in a study of a Daiba precinct.

Hirasawa, Teito (1976 [1917]) *Taiwanese Folkliterature. Asian Folklore & Social Life Monographs* 78/79, discusses six categories of Chinese novels popular in Japanese Taiwan: (1) romances of ideal upper-class lovers (e.g., "The story of lichee"), (2) biographical histories of kings and generals (mostly from the Warring Kingdoms era), (3) tales of gods and spiritual masters (e.g., the Monkey King), (4) tales of detection and judgement of crimes, (5) stories verging on gossip about common people (with ghost marriage comprising a leitmotif), and (6) cautionary tales of sexual excess and adultery. Only work in the fourth category was set in Taiwan.

Ho, Samuel P. S. (1976) "The rural non-farm sector in Taiwan," *Studies in Employment and Rural Development* 32 (Washington: International Bank for Reconstruction and Development), shows that real income doubled in the countryside between 1952 and 1972 (p. 17), showing that successful industrialization does not have to be urban.

Ho, Samuel P. S. (1978) *The Economic Development of Taiwan, 1860-1970* (New Haven: Yale University Press), documents the increased productivity of Taiwanese during the Japanese colonial era. Ho shows the importance of Japanese investment (of the profits of Taiwanese agricultural production) in education, irrigation, road and railway building, of massive U.S. economic aid, of Taiwanese labor-intensive entrepreneurial enterprises, and of KMT policies fostering production for export in the economic development of Taiwan. H notes the disparity between government-sponsored capital-intensive manufacturing and labor-intensive Taiwanese agriculture and manufacturing. Considerable statistical data are included, notably input-output analysis of agriculture (1910-42 and 1951-70) and manufacturing (1951-70).

Ho, Samuel P. S. (1980) "Decentralized industrialization and rural development: evidence from Taiwan," *Economic Development and Cultural Change* 28:77-96, uses material from Taiwan to show that rapid industrialization may be spatially decentralized. These were facilitated in Taiwan "by the presence of a highly commercialized and productive agricultural sector, the development of a diversified agro-industry, and the early development of infrastructure and human capital in rural areas" (p. 93). Ho interprets declining Gini ratios (a measure of societal inequality) as a result of increased non-agricultural activities in rural areas.

Ho, Samuel P. S. (1987) "Economics, economic bureaucracy, and Taiwan's economic development," *Pacific Affairs* 20:226-247, discusses the role of Chinese-Americans in pressing the KMT to reorient the economy toward exports and private enterprise, c. 1958-1961, when import substitution and state capitalism had saturated the domestic market.

Holbrook, Bruce (1974) "Chinese psycho-social medicine: doctor and dang-gi, an inter-cultural analysis," *Bulletin of the Institute of Ethnology, Academia Sinica* 37:85-112, includes a Western comparison of a licensed classical Chinese doctor (*diong-I*) and *dang-gi*, a Chinese comparison of his own tradition and that of *dang-gi*, and a simultaneous Western and Chinese comparison of the two "to extend controlled intracultural comparison to the culture of the investigator." H's formal semantic analysis was criticized by Kleinman (1975) and fiercely defended in Holbrook (1977).

Holbrook, Bruce (1977) "Ethnoscience and Chinese medicine, genuine and spurious," *Bulletin of the Institute of Ethnology, Academia Sinica* 43:129-80, launches a counter-attack to the criticisms by Kleinman (1975). H maintains that *dang-gi* are not part of the same cognitive domain as real Chinese doctors, bonesetters, or herbalists, and accuses Kleinman of confusing unlicensed Chinese doctors with licensed ones, and thereby failing to appreciate the efficacy of traditional Chinese medicine. H rejects Kleinman's claim that the salient distinction is between a "professional" and a "folk" sector, arguing that this distinction entirely lacks salience in Taiwan, and that "there are no native terms for these mystically cognized categories" (p. 151). The native classification contrasts Chinese doctors (*diong-I*) and Western M.D.s (*se-I*) with those misrepresenting themselves as real Chinese doctors (*jia-e diong-I*, a category in which H includes bonesetters) or as real Western doctors (*jia-e se-I* who have purchased or manufactured ersatz degrees) and *dang-gi* who do not dispense medicine. (H questions glossing *dang-gi* as shamans, since he believes shamans seduce or coerce their gods, whereas *dang-gi* are "acts more like one possessed by a somewhat benevolent spirit" (p. 153))

Hong Keelung, and Stephen O. Murray (1989) "Complicity with domination," *American Anthropologist* 91:1028-1030, responds to an attack by Stevan Harrell on Murray and Hong (1988), extending the critique of using Beijinghua and of conflating Taiwan and China.

Hou Chi-Ming (1978) "Human resources mobilization of a developing society: labor utilization in Taiwan," *Asian Thought and Society* 3:131-134, discusses a slight decrease in male labor force participation and a large increase in female participation, and contends that underemployment has decline continuously since 1965, along with the rate of unemployed workers in family enterprises.

Hsiao Chi-Pei (1961) *The Village Leaving of the Farmers in Suburban Taipei* (Daiba: Fu-Min Geographical Institute of Economic Development). This pamphlet describes the effects of the capital's growth and incipient industrialization in the neighboring countryside.

Hsiao, Hsin-Huang Michael (1981) *Government Agricultural Strategies in Taiwan and South Korea: A Macrosociological Assessment; Institute of Ethnology, Academia Sinica Monograph 9*, contrasts the policies of two regimes promoting industrial production. Having been pushed out of China by a peasant revolution, the KMT sought to break rural power bases in its refuge. Officials lacking ties to local landowners in Taiwan, unlike in Korea, centralized and industrialized the interests of the former landowner. Some peasant tenants became landowners, as agriculture became less important in Taiwan's anti-agricultural, pro-industrial export strategy. H contends that U.S. surplus food further depressed Taiwanese agricultural earnings and dependent, uneven development. Also see H's (1986) "Development strategies and class transformation in Taiwan and South Korea," *Bulletin of the Institute of Ethnology, Academia Sinica* 61:183-217 and Joseph A. Yager, *Transforming agriculture in Taiwan: The Experience of the Joint Commission on Rural Reconstruction* (Ithaca, NY: Cornell University Press, 1988).

Hsiao, Hsin-Huang Michael (1990) "The Farmers' Movement in Taiwan in the 1980s," *Bulletin of the Institute of Ethnology, Academia*

Sinica 70:67-94), reviews structural impediments to farmers organizing for collective action, and chronicles the farmers' movement between 1987 and 1990 that was inspired by other social movements of the early 1980s and which demanded change in state agricultural policies and in the long-running corporatist dominance over small farmers.

Hsieh Chiao-Min (1980) "Sequent occupance and place-names," pp. 107-114 in R. Knapp, *China's Island Frontier: Studies in the Historical Geography of Taiwan* (Honolulu: University of Hawaii Press), provides a brief overview of layers of placenames on Taiwan. See Lin (1937).

Hsieh, Jih-Chang C. (1973) "Irrigation and sociocultural adaptations," *Bulletin of the Institute of Ethnology, Academia Sinica* .36:57-78, describes the history of irrigation in a P'uli basin village in Lamdao Guan and proposes an ecological feedback loop to explain irrigation practices and sociocultural adaptations to an environment in which the flow of water is controlled by the government.

Hsieh, Jih-Chang C. (1979) *Structure and History of a Chinese Community in Taiwan* (Nankang: Academia Sinica), aims to explain the absence of lineage organization in Lan-ch'eng village, Lamdao Guan, where he did fieldwork in 1972-3. It is "a fully Chinese community in a rural setting having the qualities Freedman and Pasternak considered necessary for developing lineages, and yet does not have and never did have Chinese lineages" (p. 105). H contends that part of the explanation is historical: Holo men married into aboriginal households, and uxorilocal residence is incompatible with lineage organization. Irrigation, pacification of highland aborigines by the Japanese colonial government, Mazho temples, mass education, and production for world markets all facilitated regional associations rather than kinship ones. In particular, "activities and technology[ies] of production tended to draw people together into groupings that crosscut kinship and village ties... there are many kinds of social ties that drawn many different kinds of people together" in Lan-ch'eng (p. 104). Effects of governments and international marketing may be more important than frontier conditions for explaining the coalescence of lineage organization (or, as here, their lack).

Hsieh Jih-Chang C. (1982) "The impact of urbanization on Chinese family organization in Taiwan," *Bulletin of the Institute of Ethnology, Academia Sinica* 54:47-69. Based on fieldwork in a village in Bindong, H discusses the (1) the increasing frequency of higher-level (than nuclear) families which occurs despite frequent geographic separation of constituent household, (2) the increasing frequency of women working outside the home which has not been accompanied by increasing status or power within the household, and (3) the decline of meal-preparation-rotation and the concomitant lack of support for elderly parents.

Hsieh, Jih-Chang C. (1985) "Meal rotation," pp. 70-83 in J. Hsieh & Y. Chuang, *The Chinese Family and Its Ritual Behavior* (Nankang:Academia Sinica), reports data on the rotation of meal preparation for aged parents (*ja hue tou*) in four places—two in Daiba, one Lamdao and one Bindong village. "It is a high level unit that transcends the limitations of residence and cannot be strictly defined by a common economy" (p. 83). While rising life expectancy rates increase the number of elders in need of meal rotation, falling fertility reduces the number sons available for rotation. "Even though meal rotation has become something of a norm in some communities, its capability to restrain is not as strong as other norms, and probably [is] increasingly sensitive to modern change" (p. 83).

Hsu Cheng-Kuang (1976) "Ecological change and economic activities in Yen Village," *Bulletin of the Institute of Ethnology, Academia Sinica* 42:1-39 (in Chinese). "The most significant transformation in the ecological system are the change in land utilization and the reinforcing contrasts in the community structure" (p. 39). The original center of the village, less affected by industrialization has mostly retained traditional community life, while "modern" institutions have developed in the new industrial center. Considerable population shift occurred to fill new occupational niches in the industrial town.

Hsu Chia-Ming (1973) "Territorial organization of Hoklorized Hakka in the Changhua plain," *Bulletin of the Institute of Ethnology, Academia Sinica* 36:165-190, contends that ritual activities in temples delineate the territorial groupings both within and among villages. "Villages in the early days were organized on the basis of common origin and local ties of individuals or small groups of settlers who came at the same time. Village temples built after the settlements were formed, rather than the ancestral halls, became the local socio-political centers. The temples also served as symbols of unity and centers of military command between feuding villages. The 'main' deity worshipped by the people differed according to the origins of the local group.... Inter-village organization was maintained through the worship of the same deity and participation in common ritual activities....The Shan-Shan Kuo-Kwang was such an important deity for the Hakkas that even clanship ties were manifested in its temple.... Even if there is evidence of kinship organization such as the 'surname opera,' the social organization of the Chinese in Taiwan was mainly founded on a territorial basis" (p. 190).

Hsu, Chung Y., and Parris Chang (1992) *The 1991 National Assembly Election in Taiwan*. (Chicago: North American Taiwanese Professors' Association), collect observations and analyses of US monitors of the 1991 election in which KMT candidates received 71% of the votes. Most of the authors ascribe the results to the brevity of the campaign (15 days), the newness and disorganization of opposition parties, restrictions on what candidates could say (especially restriction on advocating independence for Taiwan), the government television monopoly, and dominance of other mass media and vote-buying. The chapter by John D. Martz was also published as "Taiwanese campaigning and elections, 1991: an outsider's view," *Studies in Comparative International Development* 27(1992) :84-94.

Hsu, Francis L. K. (1985) "Field work, cultural differences in interpretations," pp. 19-29 in J. Hsieh & Y. Chuang, *The Chinese Family and Its Ritual Behavior* (Nankang:Academia Sinica), challenges the interpretation of "Chinese facts" in the material from Taiwan included in Hsieh and Chuang (1985), and, particularly, the projection of Western Christian sectarianism in Michael Saso's exploration of Daoist texts and rites. "Few Chinese in history have ever started a new religion, or a new sect of an old creed, or accepted conversion to any new cult or been born-again to express their total break with the past" (p. 24). Rather religious behavior is shaped by the general values of inclusiveness, continuity and authority. The salience of these values is such that "truly voluntary associations have always been rare, and certainly a minor phenomenon among Chinese anywhere" (p. 25), although Western observers have mistaken alliances between affines and sworn brotherhoods for voluntary organizations, rather than as extensions of kinship alliances.

Hsu Jin (1976) "Counseling in the Chinese temple: a psychological study of divination by *chien* drawing," pp. 210-221 in W. Lebra, *Culture-bound Syndromes, Ethnopsychiatry and Alternative Therapies* (Honolulu: University of Hawaii Press), contends that *tiu chiam* (divination by drawing bamboo sticks and interpreting a message corresponding to the stick) is this-worldly, and therefore is a kind of psychological counseling rather than a "religious ritual." Unlike "modern psychotherapy" it "allows the therapist treating the Chinese patient to gratify the patient's need for dependency" and to circumvent "Oriental patients' strong resistance to talking about emotion and to accepting psychological interpretation" with culturally apropriate subtle, symbolic, and indirect expression (p. 219).

Hsu Mutsux (1976a) "Characteristics and adaptation of the folk religion in Yen Village," *Bulletin of the Institute of Ethnology, Academia Sinica* 42:73-95 (in Chinese), discusses the personalization of deities and situational influences on the adaptation of Taiwanese folk religion to modern, industrial society. Despite the rigid theoretical organization of the pantheon, practice is quite flexible. For instance, "Tu-ti-koing [Earth God], although located at the lowest level in the indigenous supernatural hierarchy, might be highlighted by all of the villagers as the common god. The changes of political or economic situations not only can lead the religious ceremonies to be delayed or anteceded, but also can make the natives withdraw from the original religious sphere" (p. 95). Moreover, history shows that the religious activities might be stopped completely under government pressures, but quickly revived once the pressures eased.

Hsu Mutsux (1976b) "Father absence, sons' masculinity, and behavioral adjustment: evidence from modern Taiwan," *Bulletin of the Institute of Ethnology, Academia Sinica* 48:79-88, examines the relation of long-term father absence to son's masculinity among 82 eighth grade students in a fishing harbor in northern Taiwan. Without any data on juvenile delinquency in this sample, H claims that father absence explains juvenile delinquency as a kind of male initiation.

Hsu Wen-Hsiung (1980) "Frontier social organization and social disorder in Ching Taiwan," pp. 87-105 in R. Knapp, *China's Island Frontier: Studies in the Historical Geography of Taiwan* (Honolulu: University of Hawaii Press), reviews the locales and sources of armed conflict in Qing Taiwan. "An armed population, unbalanced sex ratios, ineffective political control, weak lineage organization and supravoluntary association all were interrelated and contributed to the occurrence of social disorder" (p. 103). In particular, sworn brotherhood and secret societies launched [respectively] 27 and 10 of the total 68 revolts considered. H notes that "they offered neither ideology nor specific programs for reshuffling political power" (p. 104).

Hu Tai-Li (1979) "The surname opera of Nan' T'un: a study in the persistence and change of surname organizations," *Bulletin of the Institute of Ethnology, Academia Sinica* 48:55-78, analyzes legends and historical materials about the emergence (in 1824) and persistence (indeed revitalization) of opera performances sponsored by a surname in the oldest Hokkien village in the Daidiong valley. A comparison of 10 old and 15 new surname organizations in Nan' T'un suggests that such organizations combine characteristics of ancestor-worshipping clan organization, territorially-based religious groups, and city worship organizations (*bio*). Descent groups throughout the region are allied in maintaining the tradition, although not everyone within the region is included (especially mainlanders settling there after 1949—even with the common surname—are barred).

Hu Tai-Li (1980) "Marriage transformation in rural Taiwan," *Bulletin of the Institute of Ethnology, Academia Sinica* 50:67-89 (in Chinese). Based on the household registry for Liu Ts'o in central Taiwan, Hu calculates that of the women born before 1936 living during 1976-8 5% were pregnant at the time of marriage. The rate from 1937-71 was 35%, and from 1971-7 50%. Hu attributes this rise to rural industrialization which was accompanied by reduction in the importance of chastity, matchmakers, premarital avoidance, marriage rituals, brideprice and dowry. A lengthy fictionalized case is included.

Hu Tai-Li (1984) *My Mother-in-law's Village: Rural Industrialization and Change in Taiwan. Academia Sinica Monograph* 13. Hu lived (without her husband) in Liu Ts'o, Daidiong Guan 1976-8. 29 men from the 79 Lao Tsu families work in family owned factories located in the village. Although some of the book is personal narrative of experiences of marrying into a recently divided (1972) *ge*, there is no lack of statistical data on the village. In 1977 there were 13% joint, 34% stem, and 54% nuclear families. H (or her informants) asserts that there were fewer nuclear families during the Japanese era. Since 1962 there had been no uxorilocal or *simbua* marriages. H maintains that "the traditional family has not only adapted to but enhanced rural industrialization" (p. 188). Co-residence is too strict a criterion of family: "The parents and sons may separate residence, eating arrangements and budgets, but the fact that they live in the same marketing area allows for maintenance of a high degree of mutual dependence and interaction" (p. 118). In addition to recapitulating the data on pre-marital pregnancy from Hu (1980), she discusses rebuilding the To-De-Gong temple, the maintenance of the surname opera (*tsu-hsing-hsi*), the shortening of pilgrimages, and modification of geomancical beliefs (one of her brothers-in-law built a factory on the right side of the house). She also notices the cost in widespread pollution of decentralized industrialization ignored by most observers celebrating increasing prosperity.

Hu Tai-Li (1990) "Taros and sweet potatoes: ethnic relations and identities of 'glorious citizens," *Bulletin of the Institute of Ethnology, Academia Sinica* 69:107-132 (in Chinese), analyzes four types of mainlander ROC veteran communities on Taiwan, focusing on those of low socio-economic status and weak kin ties, who depend upon special supports and benefits to survive and defend the KMT/Chiang cult. They cannot accept a separation of Taiwan from mainland China and the loss of their identity (and special treatment) as the real "Chinese," although 90% see themselves as having settled on Taiwan.

Huang Shu-Min (1980) "The development of regionalism in Ta-chia, Taiwan," *Ethnohistory* 27:243-265, based on 1973-4 fieldwork in Daiga (in Daidiong Guan) and scrutiny of archival sources shows the prevalence of regionalism, i.e., "sociopolitical alliances among unrelated people... identifying with a region or locality where they or their ancestors live or have lived" and a shift of identification from ancestor's region to the area of current residence. H discusses elaboration of ritual organization worshipping a supreme deity for the region, and the fragility of identification with the region (in contrast to identification with a family).

Huang Shu-Min (1981) *Agricultural Degradation: Changing Community Systems in Rural Taiwan* (Lanham, MD: University Press of America), describes the dependence on remittance from (joint and stem) family members who are engaged in off-farm jobs of the Daidiong villagers of San-lin whom he observed in 1973-4 fieldwork. From around 1960, men from the village not fully employed in farming undertook industrial employment and were unavailable for the seasonal demands of labor-intensive wet rice agriculture. Capital-intensive mechanization could not make up for the loss of laborers, and marginal land stopped being planted. Although complex family forms persist, and even appear to be increasingly prevalent, integrative regional ritual has declined (pp. 168-71). Village cohesion and farmer's pride in their occupation have declined with the decline in profitability of agriculture. H provides considerable material on the worldview of "traditional peasants" in a rapidly changing social world, and sharply criticizes economic planning on Taiwan for failing to consider the effects on rural society and for promoting the interests of foreign capitalism in having satellite factories rather than local needs for balanced development. Also see H's "Peasant marketing network in Taiwan," *Bulletin of the Institute of Ethnology, Academia Sinica* 32 (1971):191-215 and "Agricultural modernization in rural Taiwan," *Journal of Asian-Pacific and World Perspectives* 7 (1983).

Huang Shun-Erh (1975) "The growth and decline of Wanhua," *Bulletin of the Institute of Ethnology, Academia Sinica* 39:1-18 (in Chinese), relates the rise and decline of a temple as the focus of a Daiba neighborhood. Other aspects of social change there were reported by Hchu (1975) and Wen (1975).

Huang Ta-Chou (1970) "The process of social differentiation in Taiwanese communities," *Cornell Journal of Social Relations* 5:1-9, validates a scale of community differentiation for Taiwan (with data from 312 communities), and demonstrates that the order in which institutions appeared over time corresponds to the order of complexity in the cross-sectional scale.

Huang Ying-Kuei (1978) "Farm mechanization in Taiwan: a village study in anthropological perspective," *Bulletin of the Institute of Ethnology, Academia Sinica* 46:31-78 (in Chinese), describes the failure of the government-sponsored joint-farming experiment in 1971 in Fu Kuei. Part of the reason for the failure was the attempt to foist an impersonal bureaucracy on the village. In contrast, mechanization undertaken by the farmers was successful, because they maintained and expanded pre-existing social relationships. This is supposed by H to have something or another to do with the "Confucian ethic."

Huang Ying-Kuei (1983) "The development of anthropological study in Taiwan, 1945-1982," *Bulletin of the Institute of Ethnology, Academia Sinica* 55:105-146 (in Chinese), presents an overview of the shift of focus on the part of anthropologists working in Taiwan from etic salvage anthropology of aboriginal populations to emic studies of functioning and changing Hakka and Hokkien communities. H criticizes the lack of cumulative knowledge, of regional and culture area comparisons, of recognition of the penetration of local life by external forces over the course of four centuries, and the avoidance of studying political life.

Huenemann, Ralph W. (1990) "Family planning in Taiwan: the conflict between ideologues and technocrats," *Modern China* 16:173-189, recalls that "the key advocates on both sides of the birth control issue were prominent mainlanders," and that the major source of opposition was military fantasies about the "reconquest" of China.

Hung, Joe (1976) "Religious activities on Taiwan," *Asian Culture Quarterly* 4:72-75, provides a superficial overview, using official statistics, of the number of religious institutions, believers, and professional personnel of Buddhist, Taoist, Confucian, Christian and Islamic religions. *Dang-gis* are not included, although H does mention "animism," "fetishism" and ancestor worship (without any numbers).

Hwang Kwang-Kuo (1988) "Taiwanese students' motives for studying abroad and returning home: the influence of the Confucian tradition," *Bulletin of the Institute of Ethnology, Academia Sinica* 66:133-167 (in Chinese), reports a survey of 449 engineers and natural scientists who had studied abroad and returned to Taiwan between 1980 and 1985. "The most important factors in the decision to return to Taiwan were" 'patriotism', 'obligations to family', 'potential contribution to one's profession', influence of family members', 'feeling of strangeness' and 'discrimination against people like me in foreign countries'" (p. 167). H believes that 'many intellectuals have transferred their *dao* to systems of knowledge originating in the West" (p. 166).

Hwang Teh-Shih (1969) "An important characteristic of Taiwan folk belief," *Journal of the China Society* 6:79-85. The characteristic is the anthropomorphizing of spirits in nature, so that they have bodies, the ability to understand human speech, five senses, a desire for food, a need for money, birthdays, honorary titles, spouses and other subordinates. In addition, they have the ability to be in two places at the same time (*huen sin*).

Ikeda Toshio (1970[1944]) *Home Life in Taiwan. Asian Folklore & Social Life Monograph* 11. Of 19 households in the Mon-ga district of Daiba in the early 1940s seven had adopted daughters, three adopted daughters-in-law.

Jacobs, J. Bruce (1976) "The cultural bases of factional alignment and division in a rural Taiwanese township," *Journal of Asian Studies* 36:79-97, discusses *guan-he* bases of organization—common native place, residence location, co-workers, affinal kin, and religion—finding a "close congruence of division among the various systems" (p. 96). J contends that class and land tenure are not important, and that politicians belonging to joint families can mobilize more economic resources and have more *guan-he* obligations than politicians living in nuclear households.

Jacobs, J. Bruce (1980) *Local Politics in a Rural Chinese Cultural Setting* (Canberra: Australian National University) examines the operation of *guan-he*, viz., locality, kin, co-workers, classmates, sworn brotherhoods, surname, and teacher-student relationships as obligations for political alliances as evident in Mazu. This research is summarized in "The concept of *guanxi* and local politics in a rural Chinese cultural setting," 209-236 in S. Greenblatt, R. Wilson & A. Wilson, *Social Interaction in Chinese Society* (New York: Praeger, 1982) and in "A preliminary model of particularistic ties in Chinese political alliances," *China Quarterly* 78 (1979):237-273.

Jacobs, J. Bruce (1981) "Chinese studies, cross-cultural studies and Taiwan," *Pacific Affairs* 54:688-698, provides a review essay of the "coming of age" of Taiwan studies, as exemplified by Meskill (1979) and Ahern and Gates (1981).

Jacobs, Norman (1965) "The phantom slasher of Taipei: mass hysteria in a non-Western society." *Social Problems* 12:318-328, describes a case of urban legend transmission that attracted "unusual interest and concentration of the political apparatus and its counterintelligence agencies," although "the razors and other cutting objects which played the key role in this incident form part of the general Chinese pattern of physical mutilation as outlet for frustration and aggression" (p. 328).

Jochim, Christian (1986) *Chinese Religion* (Toronto: Prentice-Hall), discusses the survival of organized Daoism on Taiwan (p. 58), the Mazho cult and a Bak Gong festival (pp. 150-6) and contemporary syncretism in popular Taiwanese beliefs (pp. 184-6) in a general work on Chinese religions. J stresses that industrialization has not produced secularization on Taiwan: temple activities continue to enjoy widespread support" (p. 184) and argues that the lack of sectarian intolerance is a function of an ideal of harmony rather than to superficial commitment to one of many paths to common goals.

Jochim, Christian (1990) "Flowers, fruit, and incense only: Elite vs. popular in Taiwan's religion of the yellow emperor," *Modern China* 16:3-38, discusses the attempt to forge by a mainlander legislator to forge a properly ethical Confucian religion to replace what mainlanders regarded as the "wasteful, disorderly, and superstitious excesses" of Taiwanese popular religion. Various suspect forms of "magical healing" were introduced by followers, including some near the top of the organization. J stresses the need to consider "specific agents and events at work on the 'popular' side of 'elite'/'popular'" (p. 20), and divergence between traditionalist and technocratic elites (seeing the former as an alternative status hierarchy for those who fail to achieve rank in the latter). Also see Shinohara Hisao, "New religion in Taiwan," pp. 677-694 in *Peoples and Cultures in Asiatic History: Collected Essays in Honour of Professor Tadao Sakai* (Tokyo: Kokusho Kankokai, 1982—in Japanese), and J's "'Great' and 'little,' 'grid' and 'group': defining the poles of the elite-popular continuum in Chinese religion," *Journal of Chinese Religions* 16 (1988): 18-42.

Jordan, David K. (1969) "The languages of Taiwan, *La Monda Linguo-Problemo* 1:65-76, reproduces the KMT view that Beijinghua is a neutral language, equally alien to native speakers of Hakka and Holo, and therby avoids inter-ethnic conflicts, ignoring the advantages of mainlanders in rationalizing their generally uperior position on the basis of better command of "the national language."

Jordan, David K. (1971) "Two forms of spirit marriage in rural Taiwan," *Bijdragen tot detaal-, land- en volkenkunde* 127:181-189, contrasts the recruitment of grooms for the spirits of women who died unmarried reported by Li (1968) in Jianghua with observations in a Dailam village in the mid-1960s. Li reported the would-be bride appearing in a dream, and the family finding a husband by leaving a red envelope with money in it on a path or road. Whether due to temporal or regional variation, Jordan found *dwa hsin zu* (bringing in a spirit's tablet) to follow upon a *dang-gi's* diagnosis of an illness or series of illnesses, and for the spirit to demand to be married to a sister's husband. J relates this change (if it is one) to the increasing importance of affinal relationships. He also notes the quite different dynamics of the two types: "For a ghost that appears in a dream to demand correction of her structurally anomalous position presumably is a manifestation of guilt on the part of the dreamer, while a ghost diagnosed by a medium to be causing a disaster is closer to censorship of the family by an external agency on behalf of community norms" (p. 185).

Jordan, David K. (1972) *Gods, Ghosts and Ancestors: The Folk Religion of a Taiwanese Village* (Berkeley: University of California Press). Although interpreting data on Taiwanese religion as legitimating "traditional Chinese" social structure, Jordan labels native beliefs and deities in the native language (Holo) as well as in the "national language" (Beijinghua) of the ruling ethnic group (mainlanders) in a very schematic account of the pantheon of a "particular Chinese village," Bao-An (presumably in Dailam Guan), observed in 1966-8. The predominant focus is on the medium of the spirits, viz., a Taiwanese *dang-gi* named Tian-Huah. There is also considerable attention to re-ranking of local gods as the status of the human communities (villages, factions, and ethnicities) they represent changes, and to propitiating ghosts. (Women who died unmarried are especially vengeful—unless/until someone will marry them). J claims that "chanted Hokkien is incomprehensible to native speakers as well as to me" (p. 55) in Daoist exorcisms, as well as "inessential" (cf. textual analyses by Saso and Schipper). Also see J's "The Jiaw of Shigaang (Taiwan): an essay on folk interpretation," *Asian Folklore Studies* 35(1976):81-107.

Jordan, David K. (1982a) "The recent history of the Celestial Way," *Modern China* 8:435-462, discusses factionalism within the Tian Dao religion in a narrative history of the "Lofty Splendor" branch in Shandong and Taiwan.

Jordan, David K. (1982b) "Taiwanese *poe* divination: statistical awareness and religious belief," *Journal for the Scientific Study of Religion* 21:114-118, shows that Taiwanese using *poe* (bamboo block-*bwai*) divination are aware of statistical probabilities, not credulous, though nonetheless believing that the gods determine the outcome of *poe* throws.

Jordan, David K. (1985) "Sworn brothers: a study of Chinese ritual kinship," pp. 232-262 in J. Hsieh & Y. Chuang, *The Chinese Family and Its Ritual Behavior* (Nankang: Academia Sinica), contrasts field data from Bao-An with turn-of-the-century documents from Manchuria specifying village government to conclude "that many of the objectives and understandings about sworn brotherhood which Taiwan informants express are traditional ones, and that there is ideological continuity between the institution in contemporary Taiwan and the institution as a feature of late imperial Chinese society.... [It] uses the metaphor of kinship to create a social form of great flexibility, which... allows associated families to treat selected outsiders as insiders, obviates commercial competition, and includes a provision for dispute settlement" (p. 252).

Jordan, David K. and Daniel L. Overmyer (1986) *The Flying Phoenix: Aspects of Chinese Sectarianism in Taiwan* (Princeton University Press), describe in great detail spirit writing (*fu'a*), and includes historical case studies of three sects: the defunct Hall of Wondrous Dharma, the Compassion Society worshipping Yaochi Jinmu (Golden Mother of the Jasper Pool), and the Unity Sect (Yiguan Dao) which until recently was outlawed. The major difference between sects and folk religion is the choice to participate in the former, in contrast to the kinship obligations of participation in the latter. The case studies suggest that the sects provide a context for quite diverse idiosyncratic belief systems and appeal to conventional failures who reform themselves within the fervor of the generally moralistic sects.

Ka Chih-Ming (1988) "Agrarian development, family farms, and sugar capital in colonial Taiwan," *Bulletin of the Institute of Ethnology, Academia Sinica* 66:51 4 (in Chinese) endeavors to explain why family farms were more productive than plantations for profit from sugar capitalism on Taiwan.

Kagan, Richard C. (1980) "The Chinese approach to shamanism." *Chinese Sociology and Anthropology* 12. Based on fieldwork in the Hell's Temple in Dailam, K challenges the modernization hypothesis that economic development leads to the rationalization and disenchantment of the world and a decline of salience for local ties. Revitalization of folk religion and folk medicine in Taiwan is a reaction to domination by an ethnic minority whose leaders seek to reduce "superstition" and any threat of (even covert) dissent.

Kagan, Richard C., and Anna Wasecha (1982) "The Taiwanese *dang-gi*: the shaman as community healer and protector," pp. 112-141 in S. Greenblatt, R. Wilson & A. Wilson, *Social Interaction in Chinese Society* (New York: Praeger). Distinguishing *wen* (scholar) and *wu* (warrior) types of shamans in Dailam, the K&W argue that the *dang-gis* have "traditionally been a major force in providing information, stimulating and channeling resentment and uniting different geographical communities against a common foe. Shamans have acted as prime rural arbiters of village and inter-village disputes" (p. 130). K&W suggest that folk religion/healing is an outlet for mainlander oppression on Taiwan.

Kaplan, John (1981) *The Court Martial of the Kaohsiung Defendants* (Berkeley: University of California Press), provides a general account of inquisitions with low evidentiary standards, along with a case study of the trial of alleged 1979 Go'hiong "rioters" in which no evidence of guilt other than confessions repudiated as having been obtained under duress was presented.

Katz, Paul (1990) "The Plague Festival of Tung-Kang,"*Bulletin of the Institute of Ethnology, Academia Sinica* 70:95-210, describes the tri-annual week-long processions to capture plague demons (*o'ong-iâ*) and then to send them off in burning boats and shows that there are class differences in beliefs about the deities worshipped in the Temple of Eastern Prosperity in Dong-Gan, Gohyiong, and, indeed, that differentiating *wun-hsin* from *yi-gui* is not a concern for most Taiwanese.

Kerr, George H. (1965) *Formosa Betrayed* (Boston: Houghton-Mifflin) reports the observation by a U.S. official with pre-war experience on Taiwan of the brutality and corruption of the KMT seizure of power and economy. K criticizes the refusal of "the Allies" to do anything to curb the pillage and ongoing murders of potential opponents.

Kerr, George H. (1986) *The Taiwan Confrontation Crisis* (New York: Formosan Association for Human Rights) presents a succinct political history of Taiwan, showing the lack of interest in Taiwan and the failure to exercise effective control of it by Ming and Qing dynasties, and the massive impact of Japanese colonial rule. Also see K's *Formosa: Licensed Revolution and the Home Rule Movement, 1895-1945,* (Honolulu: University Press, 1974), on sovereignty, resistance to Japanese control followed by the quest for political autonomy during the Japanese era.

Kiang, Clyde (1991) *The Hakka Search for a Homeland* (Elgin, PA: Allegheny Press). In a wide-ranging assertion of Hakka genetic and linguistic distinctiveness from Han Chinese, K outlines the history and present status of Hakka on Taiwan in the fifth chapter (pp. 76-105). This is elaborated in K's (1992) *The Hakka Odyssey and Their Taiwan Homeland* (Elgin, PA: Allegheny Press).

Kirby, E. Stuart (1960) "Rural Taiwan: Second socio-economic survey," *Current Anthropology* 1:428, summarizing his *Rural Progress in Taiwan* (Daiba: Joint Commission on Rural Reconstruction, 1960), claimed that "the traditional pattern of the rural Chinese family is disappearing," as "modernization" and urbanization supplant extended families with conjugal households, and replace elders with younger more-educated leaders. In contrast to 1952-3, males in 1959-60 marriage tended to be deferred five or six years, until military service and education were completed. Less pressure to produce grandchildren and concern about being able to support children in neo-urban patterns of expenditures also delayed marriage.

Kleinman, Arthur M. (1975 "Medical and psychiatric anthropology and the study of traditional forms of medicine in modern Chinese culture," *Bulletin of the Institute of Ethnology, Academia Sinica* .39:107-123, challenges the ethnographic description of Holbrook (1974), derides Holbrook for failing to deliver any insight into psychosocial aspects, and proposes a distinction between professional and folk healers. K's schema is elaborated in his 1980 book and challenged in a response from Holbrook (1977).

Kleinman, Arthur M. (1977a) "Comparisons of practitioner-patient interaction in Taiwan: the cultural construction of clinical reality," pp. 329-374 in Kleinman et al., *Culture and Healing in Asian Societies* (Cambridge, MA: Schenckman) prefigures the account of K's 1980 book in contrasting diagnostic and therapeutic practices of *dang-gis,*

Chinese-style and Western "scientific" doctors.

Kleinman, Arthur M. (1977b) "Commentary," *Reviews in Anthropology* 4:446-448, challenges DeGlopper's (1977:357) assertion that "anyone who wants to can set himself up as a healer by noting that some *diong-I* on Taiwan belong to a national professional organization which possesses formal bureaucratic structure, take licensing examinations, are organized into local 'medical societies,' and view themselves and are viewed by the public as 'professionals'" (p. 448). K agrees that pluralism of medical practices challenges assumptions about integrated popular belief systems—assumptions which DeGlopper specifically rejected.

Kleinman, Arthur M. (1980) *Patients and Healers in the Context of Culture* (Berkeley: University of California Press), is a very influential theoretical work on the explanatory models of disease and medical practice that draws on fieldwork in Daiba with Taiwanese, Chinese, and Western medical practitioners and their clients. Before shifting to data from mainland China, Kleinman and Tsung-Yi Lin published *Normal and Abnormal Behavior in Chinese Culture* (Dordrecht: Reidel, 1981).

Kleinman, Arthur M., and James L. Gale (1982) "Patients treated by physicians and folk healers: a comparative outcome study in Taiwan," *Culture, Medicine and Psychiatry* 6:405-423. Following-up patients treated by 188 *dang-gi* and by 112 treated by M.D.s in Daiba, K&G found that more than three-quarters of each group perceived improvements in their presenting problems. In an earlier study ("Why do indigenous practitioners successfully heal?" *Social Science and Medicine* 13B:7-26), Kleinman and L. H. Sung found that 90% of clients of *dang-gi* considered themselves cured (mostly of chronic, minor psychological problems).

Knapp, Ronald G. (1970) "Itinerant merchants in Taiwan," *Journal of Geography* 69:344-347, briefly describes peddlers (often on bicycles) as an alternative to markets for supplying consumer goods and for providing an outlet for entrepreneurs. The existence of itinerant merchants reduces the cost in time and distance of traveling to markets—even within "central places."

Knapp, Ronald G. (1971) "Marketing and social patterns in rural Taiwan," *Annals of the American Association of Geographers* 61:131-155, provides a detailed exemplification of the heuristic value of Skinner's view of marketing areas rather than villages constituting the fundamental unit of Chinese social organization, using data from Do-Hn Guan. K randomly sampled 649 households and mapped distributions of retail preference (everyday needs and special purchases), journeys to work, temple or church preferences, and don(g)*hi' ong* endogamy (varying from 7% to 100%. Both the focal points and the extent of social and economic relationships of various sorts are very similar from measure to measure.

Knapp, Ronald G. (1980) *China's Island Frontier: Studies in the Historical Geography of Taiwan* (Honolulu: University of Hawaii Press), contains chapters on spatial aspects of aboriginal-Chinese contact by Wen-Hsiung Hsu and I-Shou Wang, on the development of the Jianghua plain by Cho-Yun Hsu, on the rise and fall of Lukang as a major port city, by Donald De Glopper,p on frontier land tenure and pushcart rails by Knapp, along with chapters by T. Chiang, C. Hsieh, W. Hsu, and J. Williams abstracted in this bibliography.

Knapp, Ronald G. (1986) *China's Traditional Rural Architecture: A Cultural Geography of the Common House* (Honolulu: University of Hawaii Press), contains a chapter (pp. 88-108) on Taiwan, which concludes, "No striking structural elements separate dwellings on Taiwan from their precursors on the mainland, revealing clearly the adaptive quality of Chinese building practices that reach back to neolithic times. Even today, throughout rural Taiwan, new dwellings are being built which evoke their patrimony by preserving the basic elements of the inherited folk culture" (p. 107). The following chapter on geomancy is to some degree also based on research in Taiwan.

Ko, Mu-Shing (1969) "Social insurance in the Republic of China." *International Social Security Review* 22:258-263.

Ko Y-C, and S-J Chang (1992) "Sexual patterns and human immunodeficiency virus infection among homosexuals in Taiwan," *Sexually Transmitted Diseases* 19:335-338, reports screening for human immunodeficiency virus (HIV) of 64 homosexual men and 43 bisexual men in Go'hiong between 1988 and 1991. Five were found to carry HIV antibodies. According to a self-administered questionnaire completed before screening, the average age of the men in the study group was 27 years, and the average duration of homosexual practice was 3.8 years. 45 of 107) had some junior college or university level education. 48 reported having had only one sexual partner. The bisexual men tended to be older and were often married.

Koo, Anthony Y. (1968) *The Role of Land Reform in Economic*

Development: A Case Study of Taiwan (New York: Praeger), compiles data on increased agricultural productivity on Taiwan after 1948. Data are not disaggregated by size of landholding, nor by change in ownership, so the attribution of all changes in the agricultural sector to land reform is more an act of faith than an analysis of differential effects of various changes in agriculture on Taiwan during the 1950s and 60s (cf. Myers and Ching 1964, Yang 1970, Ho 1978).

Ku, Tun-Jou (1966) "Hsin-chuang Village: a study of a Taiwanese village in the political context of Lungchiang Township," *Chinese Culture* 7:65-106, reports on the "democratic cells" and molecules in a Daidiong sugar-cane-growing township (*sian*). K details the occupation of assemblymen, a breakdown of budgets, a description of formal organizations (the township arbitration committee, the farm tenancy committee, and the irrigation association in particular), crime, public safety, and the need for a community center (the applied conclusion of the description).

Ku, Yen-Lin (1988) "The changing status of women in Taiwan: a conscious and collective struggle toward equality," *Women's Studies International Forum* 11:179-186; and (1989) "The feminist movement in Taiwan, 1972-87," *Bulletin of Concerned Asian Scholars* 21:12-22, recounts the history of a feminist movement on Taiwan, beginning before consumer rights and environmental movements and long before advocating independence for Taiwan ceased being considered sedition by the KMT.

Kubler, Cornelius C. (1985) "The influence of Southern Min on the Mandarin of Taiwan," *Anthropological Linguistics* 27:156-176, describes Holo influences on the phonology, lexicon, and syntax of the Beijinghua spoken in Taiwan in contrast to Beijinghua in Beijing. Also see Cheng (1985a,b.) and an earlier applied linguistic paper by Kubler (1979) "Some differences between Taiwan Mandarin and 'textbook' Mandarin," *Journal of the Chinese Language Teachers Association* 14:27-39.

Kung, Lydia (1976) "Factory work and women in Taiwan: Changes in Self-Image and Status," *Signs* 2:35-58. Based on 82 informal interviews, K reports the view of women working in factories (with marked differences by generation with the older women feeling their status has improved by working, the younger ones expressing much alienation about "giving their youth to the company" (and much of their income to their natal family). They are easily replaced in labor-intensive jobs, and their high turnover is used to rationalize not training women for more skilled jobs. The young women do not claim authority based on their earnings in their natal families and don't feel liberated by joining the workforce.

Kung, Lydia (1981) "Perception of work among factory women," pp. 184-211 in E. Ahern and H. Gates, *The Anthropology of Taiwanese Society* (Stanford University Press), argues that the experience of being outside may be as important as the money young women make from factory labor. "The satisfactions that they find in work derive in large parts from the social context they themselves create.... As a largely unskilled, technologically ignorant labor force, factory women acquire some measure of economic independence only as members of a class that is economically disadvantaged.... The women are aware that their employment is largely temporary and that they are only 'factory girls'; but they are not aware of the importance of their contribution to Taiwan's economic growth" (pp. 209-11).

Kung, Lydia (1983) *Factory Women in Taiwan.* (Ann Arbor: UMI Research Press, 1983), reports 1974 fieldwork, including a survey of 450 women workers, in an electronics factory in Samgia(p)that was mostly staffed with young women from southern Taiwan. The decision to work (part of which involves a decision to migrate to the work site) is generally made by the family, not the young woman worker with the dominant ideology being that the daughter owes it to her natal family to work in order to repay it for the cost of raising her. Although her earnings are not usually demanded by the family, they are generally turned over, and often used to finance educating the worker's brothers. The women do not control their income, and working does not significantly increase their autonomy in husband selection. K discusses the pressure to work and make money before marriage conflicting with the educational needs of women in order to obtain non-dead-end jobs in the context of women belonging to their husband and his family, so that the natal family has no incentive to invest in daughters' education for future careers. Similarly, since factory work is viewed by most all concerned as only a transitory phase of the woman's life, there is little organization to improve working conditions or to ensure intra-firm mobility opportunities for woman workers. K concludes that the increase in economic importance of women's labor in Taiwan has not been matched by an increase in their social status. Although they "acquire some measure of economic independence only as members of a class that is economically disadvantaged... factory women have failed to become an informed, self-conscious proletariat" (p. 195).

Kung, Lydia (1984) "Taiwan garment workers," pp. 109-122 in M. Sheridan & J. Salaff, *Lives: Chinese Working Women* (Bloomington: Indiana University Press), presents life histories of two Do-Hn women, one an especially filial daughter, one a restless worker fleeing one unsatisfying job for another. K discusses her fieldwork in pages 95-100 in the same volume.

Kuo, Shirley W., Gustav Ranis and John C. Fei (1981) *The Taiwan Success Story* (Boulder: Westview), provides a remarkably unanalytical encomium to KMT economic policy, especially in contrast to the other analyses of economic indicators by the same authors (Fei, Ranis and Kuo 1979). Incredible assertions such as "The repair of the physical infrastructure began as soon as Taiwan was retroceded to China" (p. 49) mark this volume as government propaganda. Kuo sticks to empirical data in *The Taiwan Economy in Transition* (Boulder:Westview, 1983).

Kwan Hwa-San (1980) "Traditional houses and folk space concepts in Taiwan," *Bulletin of the Institute of Ethnology, Academia Sinica,* 49:175-215 (in Chinese), argues that Taiwanese people have three conceptions of space. The first divides the inner space of living environments into which the gods are invited from the outer space to which the ghosts are consigned; the dichotomy of god/ghost influences themes of house decoration and organizes measurement and ritual in construction. The second is the "living breath concept" in *hong-sui* (geomancy): the place where living breath accumulates is the best location for the living (the yang house) and the dead (the yin grave). Moreover, the form of yin house and yang house enable the wind to be stored rather than for it to blow away. The third space conception derives from the Confucian "ethic order concept" by which people with higher ethic order are deferred to in lefter, higher, and more central places.

Lagerwey, John (1987a) *Taoist Ritual in Chinese Society and History* (New York: Macmillan), combines extended observation of Ch'en Jung-Sheng, a Shuihu Hubei red-headed master and analysis of mainland historical material to explain Daoism.

Lagerwey, John (1987b) "'Les têtes des démonds tombent par milliers': Le fachang, rituel exorciste du nord deTaiwan," *L'Homme* 101:101-116. Based on observation of an exorcism in Shuihu Hubei in 1984, L concludes that the essence of the fachang ritual is symbolic transformation. Once the right immortal is invoked, the Taoist priest (*hua-su*) can properly execute the ritual and bring about the desired transformation.

Lamley, Harry J. (1970) "The 1895 Taiwanese war of resistance," pp. 23-77 in L. Gordon, *Taiwan and Its Place in Chinese History* (New York: Columbia University Press), shows that resistance to the establishment of Japanese control was locally-inspired, not supported from Beijing, and was wholly distinct from the preceding Sino-Japanese War.

Lamley, Harry J. (1977) "The formation of cities: initiative and motivation in building three walled cities in Taiwan," pp. 155-209 in G. W. Skinner, *The City in Late Imperial China* (Stanford University Press), describes varying official and local support of building the walled cities of Hsindi(t), Daiba, and Gilan to emulate Jianghua and other southern walled cities. "Local motives of a commercial and cultural nature, though deemed important by authorities, were accorded less weight than immediate political and strategic concerns" in building walls in the Qing era (p. 208). Cf. Chiang (1980) and Chang Sen-Dou (1963) "Historical trends of Chinese urbanization," *Annals of American Geographers* 53:140-143.

Lamley, Harry J. (1981) "Subethnic rivalry in the Ching period," pp. 282-318 in E. Ahern and H. Gates, *The Anthropology of Taiwanese Society* (Stanford University Press), shows that co-operation (and intermixture) marked the pioneering stage of Chinese settlements on Taiwan, so that inter-ethnic conflict was in no way an automatic product of cultural or linguistic differences. Holo-Hakka discord increased in the late 18th and early 19th century. Concerted efforts to readopt customs and practices (especially religious observations) native to their place of origin were key markers of difference. Almost ritualized feuding "brought about a high degree of community organization and co-operation under 'closed' conditions, factors that enabled local economic development to proceed," and boundaries between ethnic enclaves hardened. L attributes the failure to develop periodic standard markets, and also an inability to unite in rebellions and secret societies to the maintenance of Hakka/Holo conflict during the Qing era, suggesting that Qing officials encouraged ethnic boundary maintenance ("divide and conquer") on Taiwan, but not on the mainland (p. 286). Also see L's (1972) "Chinese gentral holdovers and the 'new' gentry: the case of Taiwan," pp. 187-202 in D. Buxbaum & F. Mote, *Transition and Permanence: Chinese History and Culture* (Hong Kong: Cathay Press).

Lee Yen-Ling (1981) "A study of code-switching in Taiwan," *Studies in the Linguistic Science* 11:121-136. Taiwan evidences the classical diglossic situation with a language of home differing from the official/public language. Holo is the language of family and neighborhood among the majority population on Taiwan, Beijinghua predominates in the domains of government employment and the educational system.

Lerman, Arthur J. (1977) "National elite and local politicians in Taiwan," *American Political Science Review* 71:1406-1422, presents a naive account of a modern, rational national elite deploring and claiming to be wholly distinct from the political corruption (personal favors) of local politicians in a "transition" to a democracy for which "the people are not yet mature enough." Also see L's *Taiwan's Politics: The Provincial Assemblyman's World* (Washington: American University Press, 1978) for a further account of a KMT legislator's worldview. In addition to extensive quotations from one legislator, L examines his political network and mechanically applies the Pye and Solomon model of political culture to this man and his milieu.

Lessa, William A. (1968) *Chinese Body Divination* (Daiba: Ching-Hwa Press), supplements research in documents about *kua(n)-siung* with observing Shin-Ku Chang in action in Daiba "using today the same basic principles that were so elaborately evolved during the Sung dynasty" (viii).

Li, K. T. (1988) *The Evolution of Policy Behind Taiwan's Development Success* (New Haven: Yale University Press), reports economic policy-making (specifically, unleashing market forces) on Taiwan from the inside of the process, yet appeals to an "invisible hand" rather than consistent long-range policy guiding changes. In less neoclassical economic terms, flexibility and pragmatism have been seen to be central to Taiwan's economic development (e.g., Gold 1986, Clark 1989; also see Winckler 1988b).

Li, M. C. (1985) *Sex Roles, Sex Differences, and the Relationships Between Two Sexes.* Daiba: Da Yang (in Chinese), reports an increasing trend in urban families to share households with wife's parents and for the status of daughters to rise, as evidenced by greater inheritance rights and increased educational opportunity.

Li Wen Lang (1988) "Structural correlates of emerging political pluralism in Taiwan," *Journal of African and Asian Studies* 23:305-317, uses the percentage of *donghua* (non-party) vote in the 1985 "Provincial Assembly" elections as an indicator of political pluralism. Step-wise discriminant analysis eliminates demographic variations among the 360 townships, leaving industrialization and education as the most significant explanatory variables.

Li Wen Lang (1989) "Entrepreneurial role and societal development in Taiwan," 128-148 in H. Tai, *Confucianism and Economic Development* (Washington, DC: Institute for Values in Public Policy), challenges the views of Joseph Schumpeter that entrepreneurship is uniquely characteristic of capitalism. (Long ago, this was decisively challenged by Sol Tax in *Penny Capitalism, A Guatemalan Indian Economy*, Washington, DC: Smithsonian Institution Press, 1953.) Li also challenges quasi-Weberian psychological explanations in terms of nonconformist/ non-traditional characteristics.

Li Yi-Yuan (1967) "Ethnological fieldwork in Taiwan." *Proceedings of the Seminar on Taiwan Studies*, 48-51, reports a survey of household in Chuan-Chou T'so village in Jianghua. Of 255 families, 51 had two or more sons and the family's property had already been divided. In 18 of these 51 families the parents stayed with one son (i.e., constitute a stem family). Meal rotation (*ja hue tau*) is practiced by the other 33. Li considers meal rotation a "western" innovation, or an innovation caused by individualism and declining paternal power, these both being related to industrialization. Chen Chi-Lu (1971:78-79) attested of the institution in northern China and challenged Li's view that *ja-hue-tau* is a cause rather than an effect of "modernization."

Li Yi-Yuan (1968) "Ghost marriage, shamanism and kinship behavior in a rural village in Taiwan," pp. 97-99 in N. Mabuchi, & T. Mabuchi, *Folk Religion in the Worldview in the Southwestern Pacific* (Tokyo: Keio Institute of Cultural and Linguistic Studies), describes marriages in Jianghua by men to the spirit of a woman who died unmarried, and therefore lacked any descendants to worship her. The woman appears to a member of her natal family in a dream, and they lure a groom in a trap baited by laying a red envelope with money on the road and persuading a passerby to marry the spirit. Sometimes they provide a dowry. The tablet of the woman is moved to her husband's family altar and worshipped appropriately to her status as a deceased wife.

Li Yi-Yuan (1976a) "Chinese geomancy and ancestor worship." pp. 329-338 in W. Newell, *Ancestors* (The Hague: Mouton) describes the geomancical explanations which constituted 36% of 220 problems brought to a *dang-gi* (not a *hong-sen*) in Do-Hn. Li distinguishes "the geomancy concerning the ancestor's tomb [which] reflects the more affective, supportive and rewarding-punitive relations of domestic life, while the ancestor worship in tablets falls into the realm of a more formal jural authority relationship" (p. 337).

Li Yi-Yuan (1976b) "Shamanism in Taiwan," pp. 179-188 in W.

Lebra, *Culture-bound Syndromes, Ethnopsychiatry and Alternative Therapies* (Honolulu: University of Hawaii Press), describes the *dang-gi* as a sort of systems analyst who "brings insight into the causality of the client's problem, but leaves rehabilitation up to the client himself.... The remedies he prescribes are designed to maintain harmony among the various components and to ward off the antagonistic forces that may jeopardize the functioning of the [social] system" (p. 187). Li tabulated and analyzed the diagnosis, explanations, and remedies for 220 client problems provided through one Do-Hn *dang-gi* in 1971. The major focus of the client's family was on "the reason why disaster befell a certain individual or group" (p. 185). In contrast, diagnosis was of relatively little interest. 44% of the reasons were coded as relating to relatives (living and dead), 38.5% were geomancical *(hong sui)*, and 18% related to fate *(mia)*.

Li Yi-Yuan (1985) "On conflicting interpretations of Chinese family rituals," pp. 263-283 in J. Hsieh & Y. Chuang, *The Chinese Family and Its Ritual Behavior* (Nankang:Academia Sinica), contends that most work on Chinese ancestor worship has over-emphasized authority relationships and under-emphasized sentiment (ancestors caring for their descendants), although the importance of one or the other varies from place to place.

Lin Chien (1987) "Intergenerational relationships among Chinese immigrant families from Taiwan," *Journal of Sociology* 23: 126-150, reports a survey giving problematic vignettes (dealing with job promotion, living arrangements, marriage, car use, discipline, and education) to 125 first-generation Taiwanese immigrants to Chicago and Monterey Park and to their parents. L concluded that *hauw* continues to operate in the American environment. "The child generation is generous in providing resources for the well-being of the parent, but is reluctant to be subservient to the wishes of the parent.... More child-generation respondents want to exercise control over choosing their own marriage partner and disciplining their children" (p. 145). Generally, "mothers adjust more readily to their child's new life" in America than do the fathers (p. 145).

Lin Chung-Cheng and Ramsay Leung-Hay Shu (1984) "College graduates and the jobmarket: Analysis of job search behavior." *Bulletin of the Institute of Ethnology, Academia Sinica* 58:225-250, reports what methods of finding jobs were used by 2,295 college graduates. Replying to advertisements was the method most often tried (41.4% of the attempts), but less often led to securing a job than did recommendations by friends and relatives (a 56% success rate in contrast to 48% for answering advertisements) or by schools and teachers (a 72% success rate). Women, and graduates of private universities or technical institutes relied more heavily on personal networks than did males and graduates of public (more prestigious) universities. Moreover, not relying on formal, public methods of job search was more important than sex, major, type of school or level of education in accounting for success in securing a job.

Lin Heng-Tao (1937) *A Study of Taiwan's Place Names* (Taihoku: Bon-go-ken-kyu-kai) (in Japanese), is the basic reference work on Taiwan place names and their derivation.

Lin, Jan (1989) "Beyond neoclassical shibboleths: a political economic analysis of Taiwanese economic development," *Dialectical Anthropology* 14:283-300, emphasizes colonial Japanese investment in infrastructure as the platform for subsequent development (and also for tight police surveillance and for land reform), along with heavy US aid, forcible extraction of agricultural production for industrial investment (through land reform, monopolizing fertilizer and setting rice prices), and "the traditional Chinese family system" of subordination of individual interests, particularly those of the young. L suggests that economic development in Taiwan is not a model that many other countries— authoritarian or not—can follow.

Lin Mei-Rong (1987) "The religious sphere as a form of local organization," *Bulletin of the Institute of Ethnology, Academia Sinica* 62:53-114 (in Chinese), identified "140 religious spheres in Tsaotun Township: (1) collective contributions to the construction or repair of the communal temple, (2) equal shares in the expenses or random donation for the communal rituals, (3) Touchia [Taoge] and Lotsu as representatives who take the responsibility for communal worship, (4) performing Taiwanese opera for the god with funds collected within the community, (5) inspection of the territory by the main god in a parade, (6) other communal activities associated with the worship of the god, such as feasts given to guests from outside" (p. 113), four levels (hamlet, village, supervillage, township), and five factors "to explain why people unite to form a religious sphere in a certain territory and how a religious sphere develops": needs for (1) communal worship of gods, (2) solidarity in the local community, (3) solidarity within the same surname group in the township, (4) harmonious relationships between villages that share the same irrigation system, and (5) maintenance of social order in a township in defense against the outside.

Lin Mei-Rong (1989) "Belief sphere of Chang-Hua Matsu," *Bulletin of the Institute of Ethnology, Academia Sinica* 68:41-104 (in Chinese), discusses the voluntary organization of a "ritual community" across most of central China involving the Chang-Chou and Hokkienized Hakka (but not Chuan-Chou). "The belief sphere illustrates the specific features of regional integration in Taiwanese society. Also the prolific activities and organizations maintained in this belief sphere demonstrate the great abilities of autonomic development in Taiwanese folk society" (p. 104).

Lin Mei-Rong (1990) "Ethnic relation and cultural differentiation" *Bulletin of the Institute of Ethnology, Academia Sinica* 69:93-106 (in Chinese), asserts that "all the cultural differences" between Chang-Chou and Chuan-Chou people are "confined to those persons, things, and events associated with religious rituals of folk belief" (p. 106), though recollections of past fights are the primary data.

Lin Tsung-Yi (1953) "A study of the incidence of mental disorders in Chinese and other cultures," *Psychiatry* 16:313-336, reports a census of four towns in Daiba and Dailam Guans (with a total population of 19,931) in which suspected cases of mental illness were reviewed by elders, officials, policemen, physicians and schoolteachers. Other family members were asked, and then the "suspects" were examined by L. By this procedure a rate of 10.8 per thousand was derived. L finds schizophrenia to be centered in urban areas, epilepsy and "mental deficiency" at the peripheries, and advocated mental health programs built on the cultural traditions of the family rather than impersonal mega-hospitals on the US model. L also discusses "the cultural context of drinking, which celebrates the interpersonal relationship and strengthens social communion" in contrast to individualistic Western drinking (p. 335).

Lin Tsung-Yi (1958) "Two types of delinquent youths in Chinese society," *British Journal of Delinquency* 8:244-56, reprinted, pp. 257-272 in M. K. Opler, *Culture and Mental Health: Cross-cultural Studies* (New York:Macmillan, 1959), describes youthful middle class non-conformists alienated from traditional Chinese culture, and lower-class youth, "*liu-mang* [gangsters who] follow traditional patterns of life and their group structure is intimately connected with that of the community. Their respect for or cooperation with community affairs, such as festivals, strengthens this tie. Furthermore, their lawful and illegal activities as a group contribute something to family and community in terms of economic gain" (p. 261). The specter of drug usage looms, but L provides only three case studies and no systematic inquiry—and no mention of he ethnic composition of the class-defined "delinquents.".

Lin Tsung-Yi, Hsien Rin, Eng-King Yeh, Chen-Chin Hsu, and Hung-Ming Chu (1969) "Mental disorders in Taiwan," pp. 66-91 in W. Caudill & T. Lin, *Mental Health Research in Asia and the Pacific*, (Honolulu: East-West Center Press), reports no increase in psychotic disorders and a significant increase in neuroses from a follow-up study of the locales reported in Lin (1953). Prevalence rates of neurosis per thousand for Taiwanese native to the locales studied was 6.9 in contrast to 12.1 for Taiwanese intra-national immigrants, and 16.1 for mainlanders who migrated to Taiwan.

Liu, Alan P. L. (1987) *Phoenix and the Lame Lion: Modernization in Taiwan and Mainland China, 1950-1980* (Stanford: Hoover Institution Press), dismisses structural explanations in political economy, crediting Chiang Kai-Shek and his economic advisors for the economic development of Taiwan after 1950. (For L the economic history of Taiwan began in 1950 and he entirely ignores the 1945-1949 depredations by Chiang's lieutenants and army.) L argues that Soviet aid to the People's Republic of China was as considerable as US aid to Taiwan without considering the relative sizes of territory and population of the PRC and ROC, or their relative level of development and wartime destruction in 1945, when Chiang's government took charge of Taiwan. The book includes descriptive statistics of information from the business section of a 1982 *Who's Who in the Republic of China (Chung Hua Min Kuo Hsien Tai Min Jen Lu)* and is an extended paean to the wisdom of "tutelary democracy" and of ROC planners.

Liu Chi-Wan (1979) "The rite of the plague god in southern Taiwan." *Bulletin of the Institute of Ethnology, Academia Sinica* 47:73-169 (in Chinese), describes in great detail a rite *(tzo-djo)* to keep plagues away, contrasting observations in Se-Gang village in Dailam to earlier descriptions from northern Taiwan, where a more generalized good health was sought in the rites.

Long, Howard (1960) *The People of Mushan: Life in a Taiwanese Village*. (Columbia: University of Missouri Press), provides photographs of people at work and funerals in Muksa, a Daiba Guan village, in 1957-8. Captions but no real text are included, and some of the captions are contradicted by Chinese characters in the photos.

Lu Yu-Hsia (1980) "Women's attitudes toward career role and family role through Taiwan's social change." *Bulletin of the Institute of Ethnology, Academia Sinica* 50:25-66 (in Chinese). A national sample of 293 women showed a general aspiration to participate in the labor force, along with an expectation of a career interruption to raise families.

Lu Yu-Hsia (1983) "Women's labor-force participation and family power structure in Taiwan." *Bulletin of the Institute of Ethnology, Academia Sinica* 56:111-143 (in Chinese). A national survey of 341 families indicates that husbands are the primary decision makers in most Taiwanese families. In familial task performance, however, the wife predominates. Labor force participation has no significant effect. Other characteristics which do have effects are the woman's age, education, region of residence, family type, and the family's economic status. In-depth interviews with 58 women in three rural communities "suggests that women's participation in the laborforce has not been accompanied by a significant change of their family status and role playing" (p. 143), and the sex role segregation of traditional patriarchal society continues.

Lung Kwan-Hai (1967) "A social survey of the Kuting district of Taipei City," printed in English in *Essays in Chinese Social Character. Chinese Association for Folklore and Social Life Monograph* 62:97-119, with its exhortations to community spirit and "development" within the precepts of The Father of Our Country exemplifies why sociology in Taiwan in the 1960s was not distinguished from social work akin to early 20th century settlement house/ "Social Gospel" work in North America.

Lung Kwan-Hai (1968) "The development of sociology in Taiwan, Republic of China," *Summaries of the Papers for the First International Sinological Conference* (Daiba: China Academy), reprintedpp. 89-92 in *Essays in Chinese Social Character, Chinese Association for Folklore and Social Life Monograph* 62 (1974), briefly describes the growth in numbers of sociology departments and members in the Chinese Sociological Society (CSS), and the failure of most everyone to distinguish sociology as a theoretical science from the applications of social work. Data from an intermediate point and the pre-Taiwan history of the CSS are contained in "The status and role of sociology in China," originally published in the first number of the *Journal of Sociology* (1963), and reprinted as the immediately preceding chapter in the 1974 collected English essays.

Lung Kwan-Hai (1974) "Post-war social change in Taiwan, Republic of China," pp. 120-183 in *Essays in Chinese Social Character, Chinese Association for Folklore and Social Life Monograph* 62, reviews data on changed rural social structure, the progress "from foreign rule to self-government" (p. 179), expansion of educational institutions and increased number of years of compulsory schooling, population doubling, and some social disorganization accompanying "modernization." L states, "All the changes are based on the national socio-political philosophy of Dr. Sun Yat-Sen, Father of the Republic, and are at same time with a definite threefold purpose in view which is to make Taiwan a model province of the Three Principles of the People, and to use this as the base to recover the Mainland from the hands of the Communists, and after this to utilize the constructive experience gained in Taiwan to rebuild Mainland China" (p. 180).

McBeath, Gerald A. (1986) "Youth change in Taiwan, 1975 to 1985," *Asian Survey* 26:1020-1036, contrasts results of a 1974-5 survey of 3044 middle school students with a 1985 survey of 1180, finding continued intense parental pressure to do well in school, along with increased power of adolescent peer groups and increased exposure to mass media influences. "In general, students in Taiwan are like their Western age-mates in becoming more tolerant of political differences and more cynical about political authorities the longer they sit in the schoolhouse. But unlike Western youth, they develop a lower value of their own political competence and become pessimistic about the values of political competition" (p. 1035).

McCreery, John L. (1978) "The parting of the ways: a study of innovation in ritual," *Bulletin of the Institute of Ethnology, Academia Sinica* 46:121-138, stresses that Daoist rituals serve individual expression as well as group norms in an account of a Red-head magician (*ang-tau huasu*) of the Heavenly Master sect (*Tien-su pai*). M portrays priests as "entrepreneurs competing in a market for ritual services. Masters hoard their knowledge of ritual as other businessmen hoard their own trade secrets. Disciples respond by collecting bits of information from several masters and recreating their rituals, producing rites generically similar to those their masters perform, but differing in many details. Neither professional standards nor public opinion compels priests to repeat exactly their predecessors' rituals. No professional organization with the power to enforce standards exists, despite efforts to create such organizations. Without the support of a dominant worldview and legal sanctions, all such efforts have been abortive. The public for whom Taoist priests perform rituals is pragmatically interested in whether or not a ritual is efficacious" (p. 121).

McCreery, John L. (1979) "Potential and effective meaning in therapeutic ritual," *Culture, Medicine and Psychiatry* 3:53-72, argues that rituals do not have the same meaning for everyone in a culture. M contrasts what rural Lamdao women told him about their attempts to buy their children from the parents of the children in an earlier life who are making the children chronically ill, and what a Sungshan red-head Daoist priest told him about the similar rituals he provides for the same purpose.The priest makes no effort to explain who the spirits are that he endeavors to drive off. M shows that the clients don't already know and also don't have explanations for particular ritual details. "Laymen do not expect to comprehend why an expert performs a ritual in a particular way... [and] no special steps are taken to enlighten them" (pp. 66-7). That they pay for the rituals shows that they believe in them, but the beliefs are not specific nor detailed.

McGaghy, Charles H., and Charles Hou (1990) "Female prostitution in the Republic of China (Taiwan)." To appear in Nanette Davis, ed., *International Handbook of Prostitution* (Westport, CT: Greenwood Press), survey cultural tolerance of and economic pressures to prostitution. M&H estimate that 4% of the women in Daiba and 1.5% of the women of Taiwan are engaged in prostitution. In a nonrandom sample of 209 women who had been arrested, 43% claimed they had been sold or tricked into prostitution A disproportionate number are aborigines. Since the closing of the luxurious Bak'dao brothels in 1979, prostitutes' customers have frequently been foreign "sex tourists." M&H discuss the arbitrary powers police exercise over prostitutes (while ignoring their customers) and an increasingly general sentiment that prostitution is a "social problem."

Marsh, Robert M. (1968) "The Taiwanese of Taipei: some major aspects of their social structure and attitudes," *Journal of Asian Studies* 27:578-584, reports the results of a random sample of 507 Daiba households in 1963 and compares these to surveys of cities in Denmark, Japan, and the USA. In addition to indications of economic mobility and beliefs about the possibilities of economic mobility, M found that 70% of his sample felt there were class differences (*chieh-chi ti fen-pieh*—Bei) in Taiwan. Of these 56% identified two classes. The lower one was identified as "poor" (*p'in-min*—Bei) rather than working class (in contrast to 5% of the Copenhagen sample). Twenty-five percent of the households had between 1 and 4 persons, 52% between 5 and 8 and 23% nine or more (in contrast to 46%, 50%, 4% in Tokyo and 89%, 11%, 0% in Copenhagen), but M did not distinguish joint, stem, and nuclear families. M also included data on family provision of help and attitudes about what should determine success.

Marsh, Robert M. and Robert R. O'Hara (1961) "Attitudes toward marriage and the family in Taiwan," *American Journal of Sociology* 67:1-8, contrast a survey of 651 university students in Daiba to University of Michigan students. Thirty to fifty percent maintained "traditional" attitudes about marriage and family ideal norms.

Marui, Keijiro (1974[1919]) Survey of Taiwanese Religion. *Asian Folklore & Social Life Monographs* 56/57. Not seen by authors.

Maykovich, Minako K. (1987) "Sociology in Taiwan," *International Review of Modern Sociology* 17:139-162, relates the history of sociology in post-Japanese Taiwan, emphasizing the applied focus and constraints on basic research and theorizing. (Also see Lung 1968, Chang 1983.)

Mei Wen-Li (1963) "The intellectuals on Formosa," *China Quarterly* 15:65-90, discusses the sterile and demoralized educated mainlanders trying to wrap a veneer of "national democracy" around a Leninist dictatorship, the Japanese-educated Formosans who survived the slaughter of 1947 but were cut off from Japanese publications, and "the confused outlook of youth" who were supposed to make sacrifices to "recover" a place they had never seen, and instead sought to go the other direction to study abroad.

Meisner, Maurice (1963) "The development of Formosan nationalism," *China Quarterly* 15:691-706, discusses peasant rebellions against Dutch, Manchu, and Japanese colonists, and the common identity fostered by Japanese rule, the pillage and slaughter of KMT occupation, and the continuing discrimination against Taiwanese at all levels of employment by the government and in government-dominated enterprises. "Formosans have a strong sense of common identity and believe that they belong together. Within the narrow confines of the existing totalitarian political structure they have done everything possible to prove that this is so. As with other modern nationalisms, the sense of Formosan national identity is felt most strongly by the middle-class intellectuals. But as in other nationalist movements, especially in Asia, the intelligentsia has served both to mold and articulate the feelings of much wider sections of society.... Formosans have shared a common historical experience that was and is different and separate from that of mainland China," fitting the definition of a nation as "a community of people who feel that they belong together in a double sense that they share deeply significant elements of a common heritage and that they have a common destiny for the future" (p. 105).

Mendel, Douglas (1970) *The Politics of Formosan Nationalism* (Berkeley: University of California Press). Based on necessarily clandestine interviews with more than a thousand Taiwanese between 1961 and 1964, M documents widespread disaffection with the Kuomintang dictatorship, especially with corruption, lack of real democracy and the compulsory military service devoted to preparing for the fantasy plan to "recapture the mainland." Also see Huang Mab (1976) *Internal Ferment for Political Reforms in Taiwan, 1971-1973* (Ann Arbor: Center for Chinese Studies).

Meskill, Johanna M. (1970a) "The Lins of Wufeng," pp. 19-22 in L. Gordon, *Taiwan and Its Place in Chinese History* (New York: Columbia University Press), traces the rise of a Jianghua Guan family to gentry status between 1840 and 1895. Prior to 1840, the Lins were rural strongmen (*t'u-hao*). They allied themselves with the Qing rulers and despoiled their rivals under the guise of "pacifying rebels." The following generation was involved in the camphor trade. This history is elaborated in M's *A Chinese Pioneer Family:The Lins of Wufeng, 1724-1895* (Princeton University Press, 1979). The account of the Lins' private army is a corrective of inordinate scholarly emphasis on scholar-gentry domination prior to the 20th century.

Meskill, Johanna M. (1970b) "The Chinese genealogy as a research source," pp. 139-161 in M. Freedman, *Family and Kinship in Chinese Society* (Stanford University Press). Based on close study of the Lins of Wufeng (see Meskill 1970a, 1979), M casts doubt on the reliability of written genealogies: "The data recorded may mislead the unwary scholar either by omission due to ignorance or censorship, or by imaginative reconstruction of the past.... Although genealogies cannot wholly obscure the ways the real world of families and lineages departs from the Confucian canon, they tend to record primarily what agrees with accepted standards... mask[ing] the reality [so that it] looks more uniform and conventional than it is" (pp. 139, 159). She is not convinced that written genealogies are significantly less manipulated than oral ones either.

Meyer, Jeffrey (1988a) "Teaching morality in Taiwan schools: the message of the textbook," *China Quarterly* 114:367-384, presents a content analysis of texts used in the first nine years of public education.

Meyer, Jeffrey (1988b) "Moral education in Taiwan." *Comparative Education Review* 32:20-38, reports a survey of 80 teachers in public schools on Taiwan. Their responses about needing to modernize the methods of teaching "the great moral tradition" are endorsed by M, who argues for the continued efficacy of a moral tradition stressing place, family (as the prototype authority), even while distorting the view of the place the "Republic of China" actually is (i.e., Taiwan).

Mintz, Sidney M. "Afterword," pp. 427-442 in E. Ahern and H. Gates, *The Anthropology of Taiwanese Society* (Stanford University Press), relates the papers in the volume to more general issues in anthropology, particularly comparison of sugar-growing rural proletariats in Taiwan and in the Caribbean, focus on history of non-primitive peoples, and on the political economy of villages and regions in relationship to a world economy.

Miyao Jiryo (1976) "'Pei Kau Hi': The Taiwanese Shadow Theater," *East Asian Cultural Studies* 15:61-65. Unanalytical.

Moser, M. J. (1982) *Law and Social Change in a Chinese Community: A Case Study from Rural Taiwan* (Dobbs Ferry, NY: Oceana). Based on examination of summaries of court cases involving residents of the Hsindi(t) Guan village of Beiyuan, observations of mediation and court cases in 1975-6, and interviews with litigants, M concludes that "the role of Confucian ideology in shaping traditional patterns of Chinese legal behavior has been exaggerated" (p. 182). Whatever the commitment to such values, litigation increased dramatically in the early 1900s, and again with the state penetration into community life from the early 1950s onward. Local social groups and traditional leaders declined in importance as contacts beyond the village increased in number and importance, and as social and economic complexity increased (specifically, more frequent and vital interaction in impersonal marketplaces and with the multitudinous regulations of state bureaucracies). With the creation of more predictable and efficient courts along with improved transportation, disincentives to using courts declined, and the traditional operations of mediation (often involving state officials, and required prior to litigating some classes of disputes) was subjected to government supervision and increased legalism in mediators' findings.

Mueller, Eva (1977) "The impact of demographic factors on economic development in Taiwan," *Population and Development Review* 3:1-23, uses a a neoclassical economic perspective to review data on the effects of demographic changes on economic developmente. M ignores the extent of government monopoly enterprises, as well as the drag on productive investment of supporting the world's third-highest per capita armed forces along with a government supposedly that of China. M thus overestimates the approximation to free market assumptions. Within the limits of the neoclassical perspective, she shows that the increase in the size of the workforce (1954-74) was more a function of the growth of working age population (from the postwar baby boom) than increasing labor force participation by women. Productivity increased roughly twice as much as real wages, making exports from Taiwan competitive, and profits sufficiently high to encourage continued investment (and, M stresses, a fourfold increase in savings during the 1960s, as consumption lagged behind income growth). M concludes that "the period under study was a transitional one in which Taiwan in a sense enjoyed the best of two worlds. The birth rate dropped, while the labor force growth rate still reflected earlier, much higher birth rates... [so that] the labor supply grew faster than the population" (p. 17), holding down wages while more capital-intensive industries using more skilled labor supplemented the labor-intensive enterprises of the 1960s economic boom. Although ignoring the long-range costs of widespread industrial pollution, M did recognize the faltering agricultural sector in the development strategy of rural industrialization pursued in Taiwan.

Murray, Stephen O. (1988) "The invisibility of the Taiwanese," *Taiwan Culture* 18:3-8, prints an address to Taiwanese-Americans on the importance of monitoring academic writings about Taiwan for complicity with the KMT definition of the situation that Taiwanese don't exist, and an explanation for proposed research on Taiwanese-Americans.

Murray, Stephen O., and Keelung Hong (1988) "Taiwan, China, and the 'objectivity' of dictatorial elites," *American Anthropologist* 90:976-978, defend using native Holo terms in writing about Taiwanese religion, criticizes anthropologists' complicity with the KMT in representing Taiwan as one loyal, "traditional" province of China, and reminds anthropologists of Taiwan's history of non-Chinese influences.

Murray, Stephen O., and Keelung Hong (1991) "American Anthropologists Looking Through Taiwanese Culture," *Dialectical Anthropology* 16:273-299, provide an earlier version of the critique of American anthropological literature in this volume.

Myers, Ramon H. (1987) "Political theory and political developments in the Republic of China," *Asian Survey* 27:1003-1022, questions the applicability of "authoritarian" to the ROC régime, claiming that the KMT has "deep roots in the Chinese tradition; it is one that many Chinese prefer to the PRC system; and it is one that has won majority public support in Taiwan" (p. 1021).

Myers, Ramon H., and Adrienne Ching (1964) "Agricultural development in Taiwan under Japanese colonialism," *Journal of Asian Studies* 23:555-570, question whether equality in land tenure is a prerequisite for agricultural development. "Taiwan under Japanese colonial rule achieved rapid and sustained agricultural growth despite widespread tenancy and very unequal land distribution. The Japanese successfully repeated the institutional and organizational reforms, tested during the early Meiji period, of working through the landlords and wealthy farmer class to encourage the introduction of innovations into agriculture" (p. 555). They single out improved seeds as the most important change leading to increased productivity.

Ng Mi-Yen (1988) *Thousand Year Mazho* (Daiba: Tzin Gan) (in Chinese), is a lavishly-illustrated historical account of the diferences in Mahzo worship between Taiwan and Fujien. Also see Tsuah (1989).

Niehoff, Justin D. (1987) "The villager as industrialist: ideologies of household manufacturing in rural Taiwan," *Modern China* 13:278-309, examines farming and manufacturing in Zhonge village, Daidiong. 79% of the households continued to farm, 87% of those with household factories. Most of the factories were not recorded in the Township Household Registry and were regulated less by the government than were the farms pressured to grow rice. These "postpeasants" do not work for subsistence. Rather "they are choosing to do so by following a strategy that affords them relatively great control" and autonomy (p. 303). N generalizes that "household factories in rural Taiwan have developed largely on the initiative of the villagers themselves with no formal guidance from either the government or owners of large factories" (p. 279).

Numazaki, Ichiro (1986) "Networks of Taiwanese big businessmen," *Modern China* 12:487-534, reveals intensive corporate interlock of the mainlander business elite, the ROC government and Japanese multinational corporations. N contends that there pre-World War II Japanese connections continue to be important, and that there is a "dominant class transcending immediate family consensus and forming a tightly organized corporate community" (p. 525).

O'Hara, Albert R. (1962) "Changing attitudes of university students toward marriage and the family in Taiwan," *Journal of the China Society* 2:57-79, reports a survey of 651 students at National Taiwan University and the Provincial Normal University and 238 students at the University of Michigan between 1954 and 1958. 59% of the students in the

Taiwan university sample responded that newlyweds should not live with parents, 87% reported that they wanted to choose their mate independently, whereas only 58% thought they would be able to do so (63% of mainlanders, 54% of Taiwanese, and 70% of respondents from Hong Kong and Macao).

O'Hara, Albert R. (1967a) "Comparative values of American and Chinese students in choosing a mate," *Journal of the China Society* 5:93-100, contrasts by sex samples of 600 students from Taiwan and from Wisconsin. "Dependable character" was the most important trait in both places. "Chinese girls place a much higher value on ambition in their mate than do the American girls.... American young men value a good cook and good housekeeper much more than do Chinese young men. A striking difference is the high value placed on pre-marital chastity by both Chinese boys and girls compared to the value given by American young people.... Chinese youth did not place as high a value on 'good financial situation' as many thought they would" (p. 99). Female respondents in Taiwan and Wisconsin were equivalent in rating this important. Less than a third of Wisconsin male respondents in contrast to more than half the Taiwan male students did.

O'Hara, Albert R. (1967b) "A factual survey of Taipei's temples and their functions." *Journal of Social Science* 17:323-337; reprinted pp. 91-110 in *Research on Changes of Chinese Society* (Daiba: Orient Cultural Services), reports a student survey of 91 temples. Each was independent of other temples. Although the owners and/or caretakers claimed that 44 were strictly Buddhist, 19 Taoists, 24, combined Buddhist and Taoist, two strictly Confucian, and two "admitted to including more than Buddhism and Confucianism" (p. 92), "there is no temple which is a pure Buddhist or a pure Taoist temple, but temple s in which one or the other or even a folk god may predominate and the other 'guest gods' live peacefully under the same roof" (p. 94). Most were in older portions of Daiba, and few had been started since the arrival of mainlanders. 68 had no resident monk or nun. "Only 8 Buddhist temples had resident monks.... One Taoist temple had one resident Tao Shih, but ten temples had Buddhist nuns" (p. 96). In only three temples was a "monk said to be the top authority while all others came under ownership and rule of private persons or of a committee of the faithful of the neighborhood" (p. 96). 31 supplied death services; none had fixed or required attendance at ceremonies.

O'Hara, Albert R. (1971) "Development of urbanization in Asia and in Taiwan," Reprinted, pp. 135-150 in *Research on Changes of Chinese*

Society (Daiba: Orient Cultural Services), contends that the urbanization of Daiba more closely resembles Western patterns (allegedly "pull" from the city's educational and economic opportunities, rather than "push" from the poverty of the countryside) more than the Asian colonial pattern of a single urban center "identified with foreign interests" (p. 139). O also argues that many inhabitants of the five largest cities on Taiwan "still live under essentially folk conditions, they have not become secularized... [and] have little of a cosmopolitan outlook, and have undergone but little social change" (p. 141). These dubious categorizations are accompanied by dubious 1952 and 1964 statistics on the numbers of suicide, divorces, criminals, juvenile delinquents in Daiba in contrast to numbers in the rest of Taiwan.

Okada Yuzuru (1938) "Village ritual spheres in northern Taiwan," *Minzokugaku Kenhyo* 4:1-22 (in Japanese), contends that religious organizations reinforcing territorial unities preceded the development of lineage organization among Chinese settlers on Taiwan. Early settlers developed social organization based on geographical rather than genealogical proximity, reinforced by worshipping local deities in local festivals at local temples.

Okada, Yuzuru (1949) *Kiso-shakai* (Foundation of Society) Tokyo (in Japanese). In a survey of 148 households with 1563 persons in Su-Lim, Daiba, there were sixteen adopted sons in contrast to 273 sons living with their biological parents. There were also 53 adopted daughters in contrast to 48 daughters living with their biological parents, 13 sons-in-law living uxorilocally, 152 daughters-in-law living virilocally.

Olsen, Nancy J. (1973) "Family Structure and independence training in a Taiwanese village," *Journal of Marriage and the Family* 35: 512-519, shows that in a sample of 125 families in Daiba and Lu-Shang (in Jianghua) that women who live in nuclear family households demand more independence for their children than women competing for the loyalty and affection of her children with a mother-in-law in stem family households.

Olsen, Nancy J. (1974) "Family, structure and socialization patterns in Taiwan," *American Journal of Sociology* 79:1395-1417, does not distinguish mainlanders from Taiwanese in a sample of 125 families in Daiba and Lu-Shang. Mothers directed by mothers-in-law value conformity in children more than those in autonomous nuclear family households, and the former tend to rely more on external control rather than appeals to children's feeling. "Mothers in three-generation households. ... resemble [western] working-class men in the high value they place upon conformity and obedience in children" in contrast to mothers in nuclear families, who resemble American middle-class valuation of autonomy and self-reliance (p. 1396).

Olsen, Nancy J. (1975) "Social class and rural-urban patterning of socialization in Taiwan," *Journal of Asian Studies* 34:659-667, reports a survey of 107 families with sixth graders in Daiba and Lu-Shang, in which middle-class urban mothers were more likely to use "love-oriented" than lower-class urban or rural mothers, who were more likely to use "power-assertive forms of discipline." Controlling for education eliminated the rural-urban differences (although it is difficult to regard education and class as orthogonal variables) in socialization behavior (viz., "educational level was the primary determinant of socialization values, and of affection, but that occupational position had the greater impact on punishing behaviors" - p. 674).

Olsen, Nancy J. (1976) "The role of grandmothers in Taiwanese family socialization," *Journal of Marriage and the Family* 38:363-372, contrasts mothers and grandmothers in 49 three-generation families, concluding that caretaking responsibility explains socialization attitudes: "Both grandmothers and mothers are more punitive when they have responsibility for discipline, and are more affectionate in their attitudes when they are in charge of providing nurturance. Self-reliance training is least emphasized when mother and grandmother share responsibility for child care" (p. 371).

Olsen, Nancy J. (1979) "Changing family attitudes of Taiwanese youth," pp. 171-183 in R. Wilson, A. Wilson & S. Greenblatt, Value *Change in Chinese Society* (New York: Praeger), reports a 1974 survey of 1181 urban and 211 rural youths, showing that urban youth stated a preference for extended family structure more than did rural youths, but were less likely to want three or more children, or to want parental help in mate choice. Girls were more likely than boys to prefer a conjugal family with more children.

Olsen, Stephen M. (1972) "The inculcation of economic values in Taipei business families," pp. 261-295 in W. Willmot, *Economic Organization in Chinese Society* (Stanford University Press), reports a 1967-8 survey of 643 senior middle school students (77% of whom were Taiwan-born) on occupational aspirations and economic socialization. O found a generally positive attitude towards business and belief in its social utility, although there was a "tendency for sons of very successful businessmen to reject business careers" (p. 271).

Ong Jotik (1965) "A Formosan's view of the Formosan independence movement," *China Quarterly* 15:107-114, relates the history of Formosan nationalism in Japan both during and after Japanese colonial rule (in particular, the "provisional government" of Liao Wen-Yi), as well as organizations in Hong Kong, and the League for the Reliberation of Formosa in Beijing from 1948 until purged in 1958 as "counterrevolutionaries tinged with regional nationalism" (p. 110). Also see Ong's "The literature and language of Formosa," *Formosan Quarterly* 2 (1963):9-16.

Pannell, Clifton W. (1969) "Outlanders on the island: some historical notes on form and function in the Taiwanese city," *Journal of the China Society* 6:61-78, reviews the European impetus for the first urban port centers of Taiwan, An-p'ing and Keelung, subsequent population of the western side of Taiwan not by internal migration but by continued illegal emigration from China, and Japanese effects, in particular the construction of railways and roads linking growing cities and imposition of rectangular grids in urban planning.

Pannell, Clifton W. (1971) "City and regional growth in Taiwan," *Journal of the China Society* 8:1-17, applies corridor theory to supplement central market theory for explaining historical patterns of city spacing on Taiwan's east as well as west. P sees a trend toward Daiba becoming a "primate city," despite the growth of Dai-diong as a central region core. He questioned whether the surplus labor to farm more of eastern Taiwan would be available.

Parish, William L. (1968) "Modernization and household composition in Taiwan," 283-320 in D. Buxbaum, *Chinese Family Law and Social Change* (Seattle: University of Washington Press). Based on a survey of a village in Dailam (with 18% nuclear families), the city of Dailam (with 58% nuclear families), and the city of Go'hiong (with 79% nuclear families), P presents inconclusive data on migration and differential intra-familial occupational mobility. To some extent (7%, less than in data from western societies) one brother follows another to the same city. Increased prosperity correlates with a slight decrease of the frequency of joint families. P suggests modifications of modernization theory and proposes counter-hypotheses far more complex than can be tested with the data he collected.

Pasternak, Burton (1968a) "Agnatic atrophy in a Formosan village," *American Anthropologist* 70:93-96. Based on fieldwork in a Bindong Guan Hakka village (Tatieh), P claims that a shift from a patrilateral basis occurred during Japanese rule. Local *ge* own no temples and provide little or no education subsidies.

Pasternak, Burton (1968b) "Atrophy of patrilineal bonds in a Chinese village in historical perspective," *Ethnohistory* 15:293-327. Examining historical records from Tatieh, a southern Taiwan Hakka village, suggests that, "already compromised by highly functional affiliations of a non-agnatic type, patrilineal bonds disintegrated under the pressures imposed by Japanese colonial administrators.... The loss of lineage corporation represented a further transfer of vital functions into the bonds of non-kin" (p. 322).

Pasternak, Burton (1968c) "On the social consequences of equalizing irrigation access," *Human Organization* 27:332-343. The introduction of ground pumps in the canal irrigation of Tatieh, Bindong led to "a reduction of conflict over water, a contraction of cooperative networks and an intensification of labor demand peaks.... Because water suddenly became available to most villagers at about the same time, the period of labor demand contracted and intensified.... There is a growing reliance upon hired labor... from distant places. Employer/employee relationships are consequently becoming more formal and impersonal" (p. 342). The material in this article was recycled in "On the hydraulic contribution to Chinese cultural variation," *Journal of the China Society* 6 (1969):53-60.

Pasternak, Burton (1968d) "Some social consequences of land reform in a Taiwanese village," *Eastern Anthropologist* 21:135-154, questions the generalizability of Gallin's (1963) findings to all of rural Taiwan: "There is absolutely no evidence that landlords in Tatieh either shifted their economic or social investments, or their residence from the village to town and urban centers as a response to the Land Reform Program.... There has been no evidence of either spiritual, economic, or residential flight of landlords.... While the Land Reform did contribute to the levelling of wealth differences in Tatieh village, it apparently did not produce either the 'leadership vacuum' or 'social disorganization' which Gallin describes" (pp. 146-7). Due to increased education and economic integration into the national economy, as well as to effects of land reform, the sources of leadership in Tatieh broadened, so that "wealth and land ownership no longer constitute the only source of power and influence" (p. 147).

Pasternak, Burton (1972a) *Kinship and Community in Two Chinese Villages* (Stanford University Press), contrasts a single-lineage Hokkien village in which, despite land reform, kinship remains the basis of authority (Chungshe) to a multi-lineage Hakka one where generation and sex are the major bases of authority and a village corporation pays annual dividends to most every village family (Taiteh). Village exogamy characterizes the former, whereas about half the marriages in the latter were intra-village ones. This means that affinal relationships were more separated geographically in the Hokkien village than in the Hakka one, where neighborhood and kin overlapped more. P rejects urbanization, ethnicity, and Japanese influence as explaining differences in the relative power of patrilineal ties between the villages. Instead, he argues that the need for inter-lineal co-operation in military defense occurred on a dangerous frontier at the time of settlement of Taiteh. That is, "frontier conditions," in particular competing enemy groups, inhibit the development of strong local lineages and the realization of Chinese "patrilineal ideology," although the latter presumably can account for the idiom of fictive kinship relationships and genealogical manipulations in what P calls Tatieh's "lineage fusion." Also see P's (1969) "The role of the frontier in Chinese lineage development," *Journal of Asian Studies* 28:551-561, for a shorter presentation of the theoretical model of the book.

Pasternak, Burton (1972b) "Sociology of irrigation: two Taiwanese villages," pp. 193-214 in W. Willmot, *Economic Organization in Chinese Society* (Stanford University Press) also pp. 199-220 in A. Wolf, *Studies in Chinese Society* (Stanford University Press, 1978), shows (contra Freedman) that land reclamation and irrigation construction in rice-growing southern Taiwan facilitated breakup of extended families [*huen ge hue*]. Quite to the contrary, "a more reliable water supply, the introduction of the power tiller, and the increased availability of wage labor have all served to remove obstacles to family division. [With irrigation] rice has become a reliable crop" (p. 216). Previously, Chungshe families put off division to ensure sufficient labor for crises and the annual periods of labor-intensive agriculture. These technological changes of agriculture in an area formerly dependent on rainfall for a single annual crop also led to a precipitous drop of uxorilocal marriages, which P views as another source of maximizing labor and minimizing the threat of failed crops (see Pasternak 1985a for an elaboration of the latter argument).

Pasternak, Burton (1973) "Chinese tale-telling tombs," *Ethnology* 12: 259-274, reports lineage fusion, as well as fission, recorded in the placement of graves and the composition of the groups of ancestors worshipped in the Hakka village in Meinung township studied by Myron Cohen. P takes variances from expected normative practices as evidence of lineage trusts otherwise unrecorded.

Pasternak, Burton (1976) "Seasonality in childbirth and marriage: a Chinese case," *Bulletin of the Institute of Ethnology, Academia Sinica* 41:25-45, employs data from the Japanese registries for Meinung township in southern Taiwan to suggest that reliability of food supply is more important than seasonal patterns of surviving births and marriage than temperature, rainfall, or workload, and highlight the seasonality of first births.

Pasternak, Burton (1981) "Economics and ecology," pp. 151-183 in E. Ahern and H. Gates, *The Anthropology of Taiwanese Society* (Stanford University Press), surveys village studies of types of family organization, religious behavior, and migration and calls for more systematic comparison of findings from Taiwan with those from the rest of the world.

Pasternak, Burton (1983) *Guests in the Dragon: Social Demography of a Chinese District* (New York: Columbia University Press). In the Hakka village of Lungtu in Go'hiong women traditionally worked. There was no footbinding and no female infanticide. Uxorilocal marriages were/are more fertile. Minor marriage (*simbua*) brides brought into the family before age four had fewer children and died earlier than those brought in at greater ages.

Pasternak, Burton (1985a) "On the causes and demographic consequences of uxorilocal marriage in China," pp. 309-334 in S. Hanley & A. Wolf, *Family and Population in East Asian History* (Stanford University Press), attempts to explain the very high rate of uxorilocal marriage in Chungshe in contrast to other (Hokkien and Hakka) villages on the Jianan plain (Dailam Guan) and elsewhere in Taiwan prior to 1925-30, when a dam built by the Japanese government brought irrigation. Before that, reliance on rainfall for one annual crop intensified labor demand and adding a son-in-law to the household (*jio zai*) was one accepted means of increasing the labor force. In Chungshe sons-in-law lived uxorilocally even in households with male heirs (resulting in joint households). "Uxorilocal marriages were unusually stable and fertile in Chung-she," (p. 334) and controversy over the assignment of children to lines of descent was rare (with sons taking the paternal surname, contrary to the "Chinese norms" of uxorilocal residence).

Pasternak, Burton (1985b) "The disquieting Chinese lineage and its anthropological relevance," pp. 165-191 in J. Hsieh & Y. Chuang, *The*

Chinese Family and Its Ritual Behavior (Nankang:Academia Sinica), marshals evidence from various studies, primarily of villages in Taiwan, to reconsider Freedman's model of Chinese lineages (rejecting the deductions from "frontier conditions" Freedman made—as did Pasternak (1972a)). P stresses the distinction between private property and ancestral property, and the necessity of some surplus beyond subsistence in order to endow an ancestral estate: "a lineage or lineage segment does not come into being unless a focal ancestor has been designated and the estate established in his name" (p. 178). P again contrasts the security from attack of Holo Chung-she with the perils of Hakka Tatieh. He also discusses other Taiwanese villages where temples were more important than ancestral halls, and also the aggregation (fusion) of local segments into higher-order lineages, especially (as for Hakka villages in Taiwan) "when local agnatic groups are small and the threat of external warfare great" (p. 186) and within a standard marketing area, which generally could be crossed on foot in a few hours (P notes that Hakka higher-order lineages frequently involved settlements interspersed with Holo ones).

Pasternak, Burton (1989) "Age at first marriage in a Taiwanese locality 1916-1945," *Journal of Family History* 14:91-117, uses Japanese household and land registries from the Hakka village of Lungtu in Go'hiong to show variation over time in the age of marriage with a trend towards narrowing the gap between the ages of brides and their generally older husbands, but with a parallel rise in the age of both partners between 1935 and 1940. Lungtu women married earlier than women in Hokkien locales, but later than women in south Asia in the 1920s and 30s. Men marrying uxorilocally were older (mean 26.1) than those in major or minor (patrilocal, patrilineal) marriages (mean ages 21.5 and 20.6, respectively). "Wealthier men married earlier and attracted younger wives than poorer men.... Their families were in the best position to attract the youngest, most desirable spouses, and to underwrite the costs involved" (p. 103). P challenges the hypothesis of Wolf and Huang (1980) that a shift from minor to major marriage accounted for a rising male marriage age. He also found a relationship between the productive capacity of the household, "while structural characteristics of the household [composition] exerted only an ambiguous influence on marriage age" (p. 91).

Peng Ming-Min (1971) "Political offenses on Taiwan: law and problems," *China Quarterly* 47:471-493, details the restrictions on political dissent in various edicts and the 20 May 1949 declaration of martial law, and cases showing recourse to extra-legal means in dealing with critics and opponents beyond the elaborate set of statutes and proclamations (listed in an appendix).

Pillsbury, Barbara K. (1978a) "Factionalism observed: behind the 'face' of a Chinese community," *China Quarterly* 74:241-272, generalizes observations of two Muslim (Hui) factions in Daiba (1970-2, 1975) to Chinese factionalism. According to P, "harmony is maintained out front while malicious rumour and irrelevant arguments are exchanged back stage" (p. 270), "Chinese faction leaders seek to legitimize their leadership by establishing themselves as heads of formal bodies soon after the faction forms rather than remain only an informal grouping.... A faction leader then minimizes or denies that he is a faction leader and emphasizes the formal post he occupies... argu[ing] he is working for the well-being and advancement of the whole community... and accus[ing] his opponents of being self-seeking" (p. 271). Moreover, "Chinese faction leaders try to avoid face-to-face confrontation and even all direct contact with adversaries, if possible" (p. 271).

Pillsbury, Barbara L. K. (1978b) "'Doing the month': confinement and convalescence of Chinese women after childbirth," *Social Science and Medicine* 12B:11-22, reports interviews about post-partum confinement done in Beijinghua with "over 80 Chinese" women in Taiwan, supplemented with interviews with medical practitioners from China and Taiwan. P attempts to analyze native beliefs and Western "knowledge" about the efficacy of avoiding contact with water and wind, sticking to a "hot" diet to re-equilibrate from the imbalance of giving birth, and various beliefs about the polluting powers of placental blood.

Redding, S. Gordon (1990) *The Spirit of Chinese Capitalism* (Berlin: deGruyter). On the basis of interviews with managers of businesses in Hong Kong (36), Singapore, (12) Indonesia (3), and Taiwan (21), R posits cultural bases of Chinese diaspora business success (valuing of Confucisan family-centrism, frugality, pragmatism, work ethic, personalism/networking, paternalism, flexibility to adapt to market shifts— the usual suspects) mostly differing from Max Weber's rationalizing "Protestant ethic." Beyond noting the Fujienese origins (and language retention) of Overseas Chinese in Malaysia, Indonesia, and the Philippines (p. 57), R ignores any differences within his category "Chinese," and does not report the origins of the managers he interviewed.

Rin, Hsien (1969) "Sibling rank, culture and mental disorder," pp. 105-113 in W. Caudill & T. Lin, *Mental Health Research in Asia and the Pacific* (Honolulu: East-West Center Press), reports that, in several samples of psychiatric patients in Taiwan, schizophrenia was significantly more prevalent among eldest sons. R suggests that eldest sons are overprotected in Taiwan, as in Japan, where a similar pattern was found by Caudill (1963). R also found significantly elevated rates of psycho-physiological reactions to youngest daughters, which he relates to the threat of being put up for adoption and the general rejection of a daughter by families seeking one more son.

Rin, Hsien (1975) "Suicide in Taiwan." In N. Farbershaw, *Suicide in Different Cultures* (Baltimore: University Park Press), attributes high rates of suicide among young lower class women to rising expectations of romance and lower inculcation of masochism and submissiveness in their socialization. R does not mention work experiences. Rin further discusses the stresses of social disorganization experienced by a clinical population of migrant housewives from the mainland (especially during the early 1950s in "A study of attempted suicides among psychiatric inpatients," *Journal of the Formosan Medical Association* 72((1972): 89-96. An earlier application of the social disorganization model is contained in Rin and T. Y. Lin's (1966) "Psychophysiological reactions of a rural and suburban population in Taiwan. *Acta Psychiatrica Scandinavica* 42:410-473. They wrote that people who can't "adjust" to modern life and lessen "traditional value identification" show significantly higher rates of psychophysiological disorders.

Rubinstein, Murray A. (1983) "American evangelicalism in a Chinese environment: Southern Baptist convention missionaries in Taiwan, 1949-1981," *American Baptist Quarterly* 2:269-289, recounts the involvement with and support for the KMT regime of Southern Baptist missionaries, predating their joint expulsion from mainland China, and the acquiescence with Christian evangelism of a regime repressing Taiwanese folk religion. (Contrast other denominations' involvement with Taiwanese, as discussed by Tyson 1987.)

Rubinstein, Murray A. (1987) "Taiwanese born-again: the neo-evangelical/ charismatic community on Taiwan," *American Asian Review* 5:62-83, reviews "classical" Chinese missions, the newer "bridge paradigm" and the indigenous True Jesus Church, which he argues provides a refuge from the dislocations of rapid industrialization on Taiwan. It "aspires to be both more Chinese and yet more Christian than other groups" (p. 79). Glossolalia (speaking in tongues) "provides a necessary release in an acceptable social environment" (the church) "within the confinements of a still very Confucian society" (p. 78). Further detail is contained in R's (1988) article, "Taiwan's churches of the holy spirit," *American Asian Review* 6:23-58) and (1990) book, *The Protestant Community on Modern Taiwan* (Armonk, NY: M. E. Sharpc).

Sa, Sophie (1985) "Marriage among the Taiwanese in pre-1945 Taipei," pp. 277-308 in S. Hanley & A. Wolf, *Family and Population in East Asian History* (Stanford University Press), using household registers to examine the history of 483 families, reports that—despite differences in size of household, household structure, and number of generations in the household by status groups—major marriages predominated in every group; still 11% of high-status households gave out their daughters in adoption (in contrast to 23% of low-status households), undercutting the contention that minor marriage was a desperate economically-based expedient. There were still discernable demographic consequences of difference in wealth, however.

Sangren, P[aul] Steven (1983) "Female gender in Chinese religious symbols," *Signs* 9:4-25, argues that although female deities (in Haishan) are maternal figures, they are more powerful than women in the mundane world and condense only positive attributes of women (in contrast to male gods who have negative attributes as well as positive ones). "It is not women as a social category that are symbolized in female deities, but the idea of women as they stand in a particular relationship to worshipers, that is, as mothers to children" (p. 23). Yet they are inclusive (intercessors not just for a descent group). Guanyin, Mazho and the eternal mother (Wu Sheng) are the particular objects of analysis. The last is salient only in S's imagination.

Sangren P[aul]. Steven (1984) "Traditional Chinese corporations: beyond kinship," *Journal of Asian Studies* 43:391-415, proposes a typology for variations in traditional Chinese corporate organizations with ten "representative cases" from Tach'i. S argues that "lineage" is not distinct from the range of formal associations (*hue*) and that differences in formal group-membership requirements must be complemented by attention to cultural values and norms of operations.

Sangren, P[aul]. Steven (1985) "Social space and the periodization of economic history: a case from Taiwan," *Comparative Studies of Society and History* 27:531-561, aims to spatialize [Skinnerize] Marxist political economy, showing changes in Ta-Chi-i's central place status in relation to changes in the bases of Taiwan's economy, in facilitated intra-national transportation, and in increasing integration into a world economy. S applies Skinner's hierarchy-of-market model and also follows him in arguing against application of the concept "closed corporate community," instead showing cycle of integration into national and international systems.

Sangren, P[aul] Steven (1987a) "Orthodoxy, heterodoxy and the structure of values in Chinese rituals," *Modern China* 13:63-89, claims that Guanyin is a stand-in for the Eternal Mother in heterodox sects, although sometimes spoken of as male, sometimes as female. This article largely repeats the chapter on Daqui from his 1987 book.

Sangren, P[aul] Steven (1987b) *History and Magical Power in a Chinese Community* (Stanford University Press), begins with an account of the market town of Ta Ch'i in relation to its cachement area from the 18th century onward (in the Skinner tradition of his dissertation), then describes levels of religious participation, including cross-island pilgrimages, viz. to the Mazho temple at Peikang. S criticizes overly schematic categorizations of gods, ghosts, and ancestors as well as pantheons modeled on authoritarian central governments. He substitutes equally schematic yin/yang contrasts to various phenomena and generalizes his structural analysis to all of China (using translations of Hokkien terms into Beijinghua throughout).

Sangren, P[aul] Steven (1988) "History and the rhetoric of legitimacy: the Ma Su cult of Taiwan," *Comparative Studies of Society and History* 30:674-697, purports to incorporate participants' understandings in analysis of a religion (Mazho-worship) that other ethnographers—as well as native Taiwanese devotees—see as symbolizing distinctively Taiwanese-in-opposition-to-Chinese identity. S presents no data on the content or salience of any group's beliefs, while reproducing KMT ideology that there is a progressive government of all Chinese recognized as legitimate by everyone on Taiwan, and that any native Taiwanese-mainlander conflict was transitory and had dissipated by the mid-1980s.

Sangren, P[aul] Steven (1991) "Dialects of alienation: individuals and collectivities in Chinese religion," *Man* 26:67-86, applies Marxist critique of false consciousness to Mazho pilgrims and those involved in the annual inspection of community boundaries by local deities in Taiwan. S repeats his argument about what he represents as ignorant natives mistaking the sociogenic origins of transcendence in "Power and transcendence in the Ma Tsu piligrimages of Taiwan," *American Ethnologist* 20 (1993):564-582.

Saso, Michael R. (1965) *Taiwan Feasts and Customs* (Hsinchu: Charbonel Language Institutes), provides a handbook of feasts and customs by the lunar calendar.

Saso, Michael R. (1970a) "The Taoist tradition in Taiwan," *China*

Quarterly 41:83-102, briefly describes the ceremony in Hsindi(t) that is more fully detailed in Saso (1972) and discusses the two schools (*ang-tau* and *o-tau*) of Daoism.

Saso, Michael R. (1970b) "Red-head and black-head: the classification of the Taoists of Taiwan according to the documents of the 61st Heavenly Master," *Bulletin of the Institute of Ethnology, Academia Sinica* 30:69-82, provides an emic account of the differences between *ang-tau* and *o-tau* Daoisms.

Saso, Michael R. (1972) *Taoism and the Rite of Cosmic Renewal* (Pullman: Washington State University Press), provides a brief introduction to the ritual of renewal (performed every 60 years) in Hsindi(t), with both etic and emic descriptions of the ritual and of models of dualism in "the Chinese religion." (cf. the critique by Hsu 1985). The ritual renews the temple, constitutes a rebirth for the village, releases the souls of the underworld, and renews a contract with the gods to bless the village for another generation. Each family participating in the banquet receives a copy of the contract to include above home altars.

Saso, Michael R. (1974) "Orthodoxy and heterodoxy in Taoist ceremony," pp. 325-348 in A. Wolf, *Religion and Ritual in Chinese Society* (Stanford University Press), reports the criteria Daoist priests (*hua-su*) use in Hsindi(t) Guan to evaluate each other and the intense competition between them, which include pitched battle for control of a temple and magical jousts.

Schak, David C. (1972) "Determinants of children's play in a Chinese city: the interplay of space and value," *Urban Anthropology* 1:195-204, reports observations of the "Da B'an" district of Daiba and interviews with 17 mainlander mothers, 14 of their children; 31 Taiwanese mothers, and 15 of their children. S found that for explaining play behavior and attitudes "class lines cut across ethnic lines" (p. 196). House size was also crucial: "It is the interplay between space and values which determines the play patterns of Taipei children. Working-class children, because their homes are often small and because their parents' value structure permits it, play outside. Middle-class children, on the other hand, play inside, mainly because their parents' values demand it and because their generally larger house size permits it. The pattern for the children from upwardly-mobile working-class homes. is... [that] parents try to enforce the behavior required by middle-class values, but they are hindered by an imperfect understanding of these values, by a conflict between these values and those of their neighbors, and by a lack of space for the children to play and study inside" (p. 203).

Schak, David C. (1975) *Dating and Mate Selection in Modern Taiwan. Asian Folklore & Social Life Monographs* 55, discusses the evolution of free courtship in Chinese society "as manifested in Taipei [Daiba] from *mang-hun ya-chia* (a Beijinghua locution meaning literally the marriage of a blind man and a mute woman—that is, a man who does not select a bride, and a woman who can say nothing about the choice of a husband) to *tzu-yu loan-ai* (individual choice of partners). In 1969-70 S interviewed 69 young people (30 Taiwanese, 39 mainlander) and 16 parents (9 and 7) as well as surveying 1055 students (614 and 441). He concludes, "Owing to the academic pressures most students are under, the main function of dating is mate selection rather than recreation, and the generally reserved patterns of interaction between the sexes stemming from child socialization practices and notions of propriety, dating and courtship generally begin late, at least after high school. Dating is very serious. There is little casual dating or 'playing the field.' A considerable number of people do not date until ready actively to seek a spouse, and many date only one or two persons before they marry. When seeking dates, indirect methods, such as letters and introduction through friends are often used, reducing the necessity of direct confrontation and the threat of a loss of face. Dating is generally done without the parents' knowledge, at least until the couple establishes a firm relationship. Then parents are given a chance to meet and approve or disapprove of their prospective in-law. Approval of one's parents is still important, although a small number of people indicated that they were willing to forego it if necessary.... Aside from finding one's own boy or girlfriend and being introduced, many still resort to marriage brokers or place ads in the newspaper' (pp. i-iii in the 1973 dissertation version).

Schak, David C. (1979) "Images of beggars in Chinese culture," pp. 109-133 in S. Allan & A. Cohen, *Legends, Lore and Religion in China* (San Francisco: Chinese Materials Center), presents popular conceptions of beggars in literary sources and some impressions from Daiba.

Schak, David C. (1988) *A Chinese Beggars' Den: Poverty and Mobility in an Underclass Community* (University of Pittsburgh Press), details the history, legal and social status, activities (gambling and prostitution, as well as begging), and structure of the Lion-hiat beggar community in Daiba, observed between 1973 and 1981. S argues that there is not a self-perpetuating culture of poverty in Lion-hiat, and that the people are not a permanent underclass. He shows real and fictive kinship relations within the subculture (though not large patrilineages). S describes in some detail the "pawning" of daughters (to brothels and tea shops) and a general upward mobility among the people studied.

Schak, David C. (1989) "Assistance to poor relatives: Chinese kinship reconsidered," *Journal of Oriental Studies* 27: 111-139, reports a 1983 followup study of aid to relatives from those who had resided in the Fude Sheau welfare housing in 1973 and could be traced. Only eight of 52 who had been lower-rank military personnel from mainland China had any relatives on Taiwan (of the same or older generation), whereas 35 of 38 Taiwanese families had one or more. Sisters provided 70% as much as brothers; matrilines 80% as much as patrilines. An elder sister who carried a younger brother on her back as a child was the closest of the relationships with those supposed by many to have been "lost" to their natal family by marriage. S calls attention to the concept *ga-gi-lang* (own people: *zijiren* in Beijinghua) to account for the enduring support from daughters and sisters.

Schipper, Kristofer M. (1966) "The divine jester: some remarks on the gods of the Chinese marionette theater," *Bulletin of the Institute of Ethnology, Academia Sinica* 21:81-96 describes puppet theater (*bo-de hi*) performances at weddings in Dailam Guan with puppeteers who are San-nai P'ai priests, particularly the three jesters who "open the eyes" of the puppets.

Schipper, Kristofer M. (1974) "The written memorial in Taoist ritual," pp. 309-324 in A. Wolf, *Religion and Ritual in Chinese Society* (Stanford University Press), argues that, despite the existence of a set written tradition, in the absence of an established central religious authority, Daoist priests adapt to local conditions (in particular competition with Daoists from other traditions, and fusion of some Buddhist and folk religion rites, explanations, and divinities). He analyzes a memorial written (in *ta-tzu*) for a *gau* in A-lien village in Dailam Guan in 1969, noting the use of formulae common to petitions to central governments.

Schipper, Kristofer M. (1975) *Le Fen-Teng: ritual taoiste. Publications del'École francaise d'Éxtreme-Orient* 103, contains copies and translation into French of four 17th-to-19th-century Daoist ritual texts from the village of Kouei-jen in Dailam Guan. Also see S's (1982) *Le corps detaoiste* (Paris: Fayard).

Schipper, Kristofer M. (1977) "Neighborhood cult associations in traditional Tainan." pp. 651-676 in G. W. Skinner, *The City in Late*

Imperial China (Stanford University Press) discusses the more than one hundred temples of "popular religion" in Dailam of the 1890s.

Schipper, Kristofer M. (1985) "Vernacular and classic rituals in Taoism," *Journal of Asian Studies* 45:21-57. Based on fieldwork in Dailam Guan during the 1960s and historical conjecture, S explores vernacular liturgy performed by *do-su* and argues that classical and vernacular Daoism are complementary, not just rival traditions.

Seaman, Gary (1978) Temple Organization in a Chinese Village. *Asian Folklore and Social Life Monograph* 101, provides an account of the consolidation of political power by the leaders of a spirit-writing cult in a Lamdao Guan village after land reform and the suppression of secret societies led to an impasse between rival factions. Following Weber, S argues that "the religious ideology and cosmology of the cult provide the motivation for individual villagers to undertake political action, especially those kind of political action which the cult defines as meritorious.... Persons who devoted themselves to the good of the cult or were public-spirited in their support of building roads and bridges could expect to become gods after death" (pp. 6, 161). S resided in the temple during part of his 1970-3 fieldwork, participated in nightly seances, and strongly identifies with the cult faction, going so far as to reproduce its members' ideology about its superiority to a defeated cult/faction.

Seaman, Gary (1981) "The sexual politics of karmic retribution." 381-396 in E. Ahern and H. Gates, *The Anthropology of Taiwanese Society* (Stanford University Press), argues that men (in the Lamdao Guan village in which he did fieldwork in the early 1970s) consciously use beliefs of female pollutingness to rationalize the socially inferior position of women, drawing on analysis of the "Breaking the Blood" (viz., women's need of unpolluted sons to approach the gods on their behalf, although the production of sons requires women). "Since the female body has within it the power to destroy the bone of one agnatic lineage and transform it into the bone of another [*dng-gut*], it is no wonder than men shrink from contact with such a potent substance" (p. 395).

See Chiben (1973) "Religious sphere and social organization: an exploratory model on the settlement of Changhua Plain," *Bulletin of the Institute of Ethnology, Academia Sinica* 36:191-208 (in Chinese), traces ethnic origins of Chinese settlers on the Jianghua Plain. The data on family names is not sufficient to indicate the existence of "clans" without specification of point of origin. S asserts that "the need for a psychological anchorage in an alien habitat gave rise to the predominance of village temples as nuclei of social organization and activities in the villages. The most common deity worshipped is the earth god" (p. 207). S defines a village as a ritual unit, so that the above proposition borders on tautology.

Seiwert, Hubert M. (1985) *Völksreligion und nationale Tradition in Taiwan: Studies zur regionalen Religionsgeschichte einre chinesieschen Provinz.* Stuttgart: F. Steiner.

Selya, Roger M. (1985) "Suicide in Taiwan," *American Asian Review* 3:62-84, documents a drop in the rate of female suicide around Dailam (the elevated rate was the focus of Margery Wolf's 1975 chapter on female suicide). S documents high rates of female suicide on the current "frontier" of the west coast. He argues that suicide is no longer the only escape for women from an unbearable marriage/household, and follows Diamond (1973) in seeing the isolation of middle class women as a structural pathology conducive to individual pathology, of which suicide is one example.

Shu, Ramsey Leung-Han, and Lin Chung-Cheng (1984) "Family structure and industrialization in Taiwan," *California Sociologist* 7:197-212, analyze data from a national labor force survey of 14,377 family heads conducted in May 1983. Nuclear family households accounted for 62%, single-parent for 8%, complex two- or three-generation families for 30% of the households. In rural areas 18% of the households were complex, in contrast to 28% in semi-urban areas, and 35% in urban areas. Age was positively related with living in a complex family and education was negatively related (and five times as important for explaining variance). 12% of college graduates in contrast to 38% of household heads with elementary school education and 56% of those with no formal education lived in complex family households.

Sillin, Robert H. (1976) *Leadership and Value: The Organization of Large-Scale Taiwanese Enterprises* (Cambridge, MA: Harvard University Press), contends that traditional Chinese values and interpersonal styles in regard to managing emotions and conflict, leadership, etc. lead to inordinate centralization of authority, blockage of information flow, high employee uncertainty and other economically irrational results, based on rather abstracted observations of one large industrial enterprise.

Spain, David H. (1987) "The Westmarck-Freud incest-theory debate," *Current Anthropology* 28:623-645, attempts to reconcile evidence of sexual repulsion between boys and girls raised together (in Taiwanese *simbua* arrangements reported by Wolf and Huang [1980] and in Israeli *kibbutzim*) with Freudian theory, stressing the significant decrease in fertility and increase in divorce and adultery rates between couples in which the *simbua* was adopted after the son was eight or more years old and couples in which the girl was adopted earlier. A response from Wolf reasserts support for Westmarck and rejection of Freudian theory.

Speare, Alden Jr. (1971) "A cost-benefit model of rural to urban migration in Taiwan," *Population Studies* 25:117-130. A 1966-8 survey of 321 men aged 23-41 who had moved to Daidiong from the surrounding four counties and 370 men from the same age group who had not migrated shows that cost-benefit variables identify 76% of the migrants and 84% of the non-migrants, but stressed that "many people never make any calculation at all. A great many of the non-migrants we interviewed appear to have never given any serious consideration to the thought of moving anywhere" (p. 130).

Speare, Alden Jr. (1973) "The determinants of migration to a major city in a developing country: Taichung, Taiwan," pp. 167-88 in *Population Papers* (Daiba: Academia Sinica), reports that only a very small percentage of migrants to Daidiong in a 1966-8 survey had heard of specific jobs or could estimate their chances of securing good-paying jobs prior to migrating (parts of the rational calculus attributed migrants by Todaro and others). Location of relatives was an important factor in deciding to move to the city from rural areas. 71% of those employed in tertiary industries in Daidiong had been employed in the same occupation in the rural area from which they had moved.

Speare, Alden Jr. (1974a) "Migration and family change in central Taiwan," pp. 303-330 in M. Elvin and G. Skinner, *The Chinese City Between Two Worlds* (Stanford University Press). Based on a survey of 310 migrants and 362 nonmigrants in Daidiong Guan, S reported that most men "began their married life in extended families and gradually broke away so that by the time they had reached the age of 40 or so— typically only one brother remained with the parents.... The migrants tended to break away sooner.... Most men moved with their wives and children, but few moved with their parents or other relatives" (p. 329). Within two years, 96% of the wives were also living in the city. Migrants as well as non-migrants continued to hold the traditional valuation of the extended family, but S asserts that "for most migrants, the move to the city and the resulting breakup of the extended family was more a response to the greater economic opportunities in the city than the result of absolute economic necessity. Most men were employed before moving and could have found other non-farm employment within a short distance had they desired to stay with their relatives. 16% of migrants still interacted with relatives in separate households several times a week, and another 64% at least monthly (in contrast to 46% and 37% of nonmigrants).

Speare, Alden Jr. (1974b) "Urbanization and migration in Taiwan," *Economic Development and Cultural Change* 22:302-319, combines government data with data from a 1967 Daidiong survey to show that "the higher the education, the more likely one is to seek employment away from home" and that "the number of persons leaving family work has the expected negative correlation with farm size" (p. 319). S estimates that "approximately half of all migrants from rural towns to the city return to rural towns" (p. 311), yet concludes, "On the average, for every four migrants who entered the major cities there were three migrants who left these cities, most of them probably returning to their original place of residence" (p. 319). Townships with populations greater than 50,000 generally had net in-migration; smaller ones net out-migration.

Speare, Alden Jr., Paul Liu and Ching-Lung Tsay (1988) *Urbanization and Development: The Rural-urban transition in Taiwan* (Boulder, CO: Westview), review a wide range of data on industrialization and urbanization on Taiwan and present results of a 1973 survey of 159 persons who migrated to Daiba in the previous five years, 253 who had migrated there earlier (from within Taiwan), 198 persons born in Daiba, 270 residents of other cities and 248 rural residents to contrast migrants with non-migrants. Only 9% of the latter two sub-samples had considered moving to Daiba at any time during the preceding five years. "Migration to Taipei is no longer primarily rural to urban migration. Among recent migrants and long-term migrants who moved as adults, 68.3% and 53.8%, respectively, had come from other cities or urban towns" (p. 201). Major discriminants of non-migrants from migrants included land- and home-ownership, self-employment, perceived high costs of relocation, living in the same household as parents, and being able to decide how family income was spent. Migrants anticipated more income in Daiba and were more than twice as likely to receive Daiba job information from friends and relatives than those who did not migrate. There were no significant differences between movers and stayers in satisfaction with jobs or housing outside Daiba nor in knowledge about various features of alternative locales. Controlling for education, the income of migrants to Daiba was somewhat greater than that of those native to Daiba, and substantially greater (even adjusting for variations in the cost of living) than those left behind in other locales. Migrants from rural areas were more likely to have professional or managerial jobs than those native to Daiba or migrants from other cities (25%:10%:15.9%). The contacts with mass media and "modern attitudes" of migrants was similar to patterns for Daiba natives. However, they had fewer amenities, and less space, which S attributes to less chance for migrants to accumulate assets prior to migration rather than to the greater likelihood of being tenants rather than homeowners in Daiba. Urban natives were twice as recent migrants to be homeowners (63%:31%), but more recent migrants than urban natives reported receiving money from their families (33%:23%, p>.05)

Stafford, Charles (1992) "Good sons and virtuous mothers: kinship and Chinese nationalism in Taiwan," *Man* 27:363-378. Based on fieldwork in a Bindong fishing village, S discusses contradictions between Confucian focus on preserving sons and nationalism's occasional need to sacrifice them in military actions. He finds increasingly high valuation on daughters as good investments. "Many of the grandparents I knew were as interested in the children of their daughters as of their sons, and more than one person told me they thought it was best to forget tradition and be happy with daughters, who were less trouble than unmanageable boys" (pp. 374-5).

Stites, Richard (1982) "Small-scale industry in Yingge, Taiwan," *Modern China* 8:247-279, examines the motivation for working in 471 small factories in a village 29 km southwest of Daiba, finding that no one expects to be working in the same factory in ten years and that the workers do not see themselves as part of a working class. Experience in a small factory is regarded as useful to learning how to start one for oneself, because all aspects of enterprise are more directly observable than in large factories. Workers "move out of the factory when they have family labor that can support them in other endeavors. The monetary return may not be as high in small-scale enterprise, but older men prefer it to wage labor. The work is often lighter, the return is often at least as good, and the possibility exists for striking it rich.... Setting up of a small factory is not an unattainable task for many workers, but is an alternative which depends upon experience, personal networks and family support" (p. 275). Indeed, S regards location of small factories in the countryside as stemming from dependence on local networks as much as on lower land costs.

Stites, Richard (1985) "Industrial work as an entrepreneurial strategy," *Modern China* 11:227-246, relates work in factories to learning about industrial organization in order to increase the economic security of the family and decrease dependence on non-relatives. "Lack of effective legislation on worker safety, insurance, unemployment and old age pensions, along with government laws prohibiting worker agitation, reinforces the family as the locus of security" (p. 241), so small-scale sundry shops and home factories "rather than being risk-taking behaviors, actually reflects the need of factory workers for a measure of security" (p. 243). Thus, industrialization Taiwanese style enhances rather than fragments the importance of kinship rather than leading to atomistic universalism.

Su Bing (1979) *Taiwan's 400 Year History* (San José: Paradise Cultural Association, in Chinese; an abridged English translation was published in 1986 [Washington: Taiwanese Cultural Grassroots Association]), provides an alternately Marxist and ethnic analysis of the development of capitalist agriculture on Taiwan during successive foreign dominations with detailed chronology of rebellions against those authorities.

Sugimoto, T. (1971) "Japanese in Taiwan," *Current Trends in Linguistics* 8:969-995, reviews the maintenance and loss of fluency in Japanese after the withdrawal of Japanese rule after the Second World War, suggesting that "the formation of Taiwanese was the precious byproduct of Japanese education and the spread of Japanese, and the common consciousness of the people of Taiwan has grown much in the process of forming Taiwanese" (p. 993). Other than some loan words, S predicted that "in the long run, Japanese will completely disappear from the mouth of the people of Taiwan" (p. 991).

Sung Lung-Sheng (1981) "Property and family division," pp. 361-378 in E. Ahern and H. Gates, *The Anthropology of Taiwanese Society* (Stanford University Press), provides the clearest analysis of the vexed questions of Taiwanese inheritance, the relationship between relative wealth and family structure, and the consequences of the distinction between family in the sense of descent line (*ge*) and of household (*ho*). In Chiuna (in the Daiba basin) some property (inherited from the ancestors: *zho-tsien ga-sun*) is held in trust by the male descent line, while property accumulated by the efforts of the living family (*zhu-gi ga-sun*) may be used by and for women (e.g., providing dowries in advance of inheritance). S concludes, "Wealthy families are more likely than poor families to have large amounts of inherited property: filial relationships are naturally more important than conjugal relationships when the bulk of the family's property is owned by the line, not by the family. Wealth per se, then, is not as significant in shaping the Chinese family as the principles that govern its control and distribution—principles that differ for inherited and acquired property" (p. 377). S also relates different conceptions of the power of ancestors to whether or not there is a preponderance of inherited property.

Sung Lung-Sheng (1982) "Property and lineage of the Chinese in Northern Taiwan," *Bulletin of the Institute of Ethnology, Academia Sinica* 54:25-45, argues, on the basis of examining descent in several lines from 1770-1970, that legal regulations (in particular those banning lineage property) continue to be routinely subordinated to customary practices of inheritance. S distinguishes three cooperative bases of lineage organization. A lineage emerges when a set amount of funds are collected each year from agnatically related families for the purpose of cooperative ancestral worship. A more permanent lineage involves an alternate responsibility system. The most permanent and strongest lineage organization is founded upon corporate lineage property.

Suzuki Mitsuo (1976) "The shamanistic element in Taiwanese folk religion," pp. 253-260 in A. Bharati, *The Realm of the Extra-Human: Agents and Audiences* (The Hague: Mouton), contrasts a Mazho temple in Ge-lung, a Wun-ong festival in Dailam, and a celebration of the completion of a To Di Gong temple in Hsindi(t), observing that for the Taiwanese, "the essence of a festival is not so much the elaborate ceremony performed by Taoist priests as the direct fusion of a human being with things divine; the fusion is enacted by the person of the male shaman" whose "strong inclination toward a bloody frenzy distinguishes the Taiwanese male shamans sharply from their [mostly female] counterparts in Japan and Korea" (p. 258).

Tang Mei-Chun (1971) "Parental authority and family size: a Chinese case," pp. 239-251 E. Fuchs, *Youth in a Changing World* (The Hague: Mouton). While noting "many cases in which there is a low degree of economic involvement among the members" of families in Yellow Rock, a town that has been absorbed into Daiba, that "the dispersion of family members for economic reasons is not uncommon," that no stem or joint families' domestic economy was completely intermeshed, and that "there are many cases in which there is a low degree of economic involvement among [family] member" (p. 245), T stressed that parental authority nonetheless continues. Although legal title may be transferred to sons, the latter do not possess property until the death of their fathers.

Tang Mei-Chun (1978) *Urban Chinese Families: An Anthropological Field Study in Taipei City, Taiwan* (Daiba: National Taiwan University Press), provides a community study of Yellow Rock. In addition to providing standard information about household composition and economic activity, T challenges the widespread view that "Chinese family property" is a "trust"—at least for lineal relationships (he concedes some holdings of collateral relatives are trusts). Both law and practice permit selling property and T argues that the "Chinese family is a transitory unit, not a corporate entity." Appendix 3 examines discrepancies between government registration data and data T gathered about household composition and kinship status of household members.

Tang Mei-Chun (1985) "Equal rights and domestic structure," pp. 61-69 in J. Hsieh & Y. Chuang, *The Chinese Family and Its Ritual Behavior* (Nankang: Academia Sinica), relies on a case study of a dispute over inheritance for daughters which lasted from 1969 until 1982 (at which point some claimants had died or emigrated to America) to claim that Article 1138 of the Civil Code has made daughters equal to sons in inheriting property. The failure of a quick legal resolution of the case does not seem to support this view.

Taeuber, Irene B. (1961) "Population growth in a Chinese microcosm: Taiwan," *Population Index* 27:101-126, provides a detailed account of the Japanese household registries for Taiwan. Although recognizing that "generalization from studies of specific groups is hazardous, for the historic episodes or the special conditions that led to accurate counts and vital records guarantees the atypicality of the experience that is studied" (p. 101), her goal is to estimate Chinese fertility during the Qing era despite lacking data on infant and childhood mortality from Taiwan during the Qing era and despite the distorted sex ratio of emigrants from the mainland. Data from the 1956 census are included, and contrasted to birth and death rates by Japanese administrative district from 1920, 1925, 1930, 1935, 1940.

Taeuber, Irene B. (1974) "Migrants and cities in Japan, Taiwan, and Northeastern China," pp. 359-384 in M. Elvin and G. Skinner, *The Chinese City Between Two Worlds* (Stanford University Press), contrasts demographic statistics collected by Japanese rulers of Chinese populations. For Taiwan, T shows that in 1905 the death rate and birth rate were equivalent, although by 1935 the birth rate was more than double the death rate. She also shows that between 1930 and 1935 there was only a slight net in-migration to the Daiba administrative district. Intra-island migration outside one's native district was to the sparsely populated southeastern districts of Hualien and Daidan.

Thelin, Mark (1977) *Two Taiwanese Villages* (Daidiong:Tunghai University), collects reports of Tunghai University students' fieldwork and surveys of two Daidiong villages, undertaken as comparisons to Gamble's (1954) study of Ting Hsien in China. Their census suggested that official statistics based on household registries overcounted households and undercounted the number of persons in the households. An earlier version of the chapter on religion appeared as Thelin and Li Wen-Lang (1963) "Religion in two Taiwanese villages," *Journal of the China Society* 3:44-57. This includes an example of a nativistic movement, viz., the emergence of a goddess from a girl drowned in 1957, and stress on the continued salience of pilgrimages in rural Taiwan.

Thompson, Laurence G. (1964a) "Notes on religious trends in Taiwan," *Monumenta Sinica* 23:319-349, outlines nine primary gods from among the 86 different ones worshipped in four thousand temples on Taiwan. Four are of trans-China importance: Guan-Yin (the Buddhist bodhisattva assimilated into a generalized compassionate mother figure), Fu-Teh Cheng-Sien (earth god), Guan Shengti-Chün (Emperor Guan), and Pei-Chi Yu-Sieng Chen-Chün (Protecting Lord of the Pole Star). Five are of special importance on Taiwan and/or in southeastern China: Mazho (Celestial mother), Wang-Yeh (the kings, tutelary deity of Fujien), Pao-sieng Ta-Ti (Great Emperor who Preserves Life), Shih-Chia (a Buddha popular in Taiwan only since KMT occupation), and San-Shang-Kuo Wang (King of the Three Mountain Country, i.e., Guandong from where Hakka-speakers emigrated).

Thompson, Laurence G. (1964b) "Music in Taiwan." *Claremont Quarterly* 11,3:71-78, provides an impressionistic essay about the increasing prosperity of Taiwan and what T judged to be the inevitable decline of traditional Taiwanese and Peiking operas and the irresistability of Western music.

Thompson, Laurence G. (1969) *Chinese Religion* (Belmont, CA: Dickinson), includes a recapitulation of his (1964) report on religious trends in Taiwan. (See Wei and Coutanceau 1976 for a fuller account.)

Thompson, Laurence G. (1982) "The moving finger writes: a note on revelation and renewal in Chinese religion," *Journal of Chinese Religions* 10:92-147, contains a translation of a morality tract (*shan-shu*) produced by a spirit-writing medium from Taiwan with an explication of its contents and genre.

Thompson, Stuart E. (1984) "Taiwan: rural society." *China Quarterly* 99:553-568, notes that the "burden of agricultural production falls on the shoulders of the older cohort of workers, who annually are becoming fewer in number," although "redundant labor" could become a problem with continuing integration into international economic cycles. Although rural government is "emasculated," Taiwanese folk religion and family "survive with vigor" (p. 568).

Thornton, Arland, Chang Ming-Cheng, and Sun Te-Hsiung (1984) "Social and economic change, intergenerational relationships, and family formation in Taiwan," *Demography* 21:475-498, use data from two island-wide surveys in 1973 and 1980 of married women between ages 20 and 39 to show that "social change has been accompanied by rapid changes in family structure and relationships, including the spread of schooling, the employment of young people outside the family, increasing separation of the residences of parents and children before and after marriage, growing independence of young people, and increases in pre-marital sex and pregnancies" although "farm origins tend to exert a traditional influence on the life course" (p. 475) and although the rise of a wage economy has not eliminated pooling of family resources (wages rather than labor). From birth cohort to birth cohort the percentage deciding marriage (rather than having it arranged by parents) has risen steadily (5.2% of those born 1930-4, a third of those born 1955-9). Despite the large sample size (4313 wives), cross-classified data were not used for hypothesis-testing via multivariate statistics.

Tien Hung-Mao (1989) *Political and Social Change in the Republic of China* (Stanford: Hover Institution Press), relates the transition of a Leninist dictatorship to an authoritarian one-party-dominant government comparable to Japan or México) to economic growth/prosperity, and stresses its tenuousness. In addition to describing intra-party competition, particularly generational conflict, T describes the growth of opposition politics within the constraints of censorship and KMT control of mass media.

Tong, Hollington K. (1961) *Christianity in Taiwan* (Daiba: China Post), outlines the history of Christian missions on Taiwan from the 16th century through his own tour of institutions in the late 1950s.

Tozzer, Warren (1970) "Taiwan's 'cultural renaissance,'" *China Quarterly* 43: 81-99, describes the KMT answer to the "cultural revolution" on the mainland, concluding that "the Cultural Renaissance Movement, like much of the government of Taiwan, is a façade. Behind the façade lie the realities of a movement which is neither spontaneous, democratic, nor a renaissance" (p. 98).

Ts'ai Wen-Hui (1984) "Modernization and crimes: the Taiwan case,"

Journal of Chinese Studies 1:261-279, shows an inverse relation between crime rate and economic growth rate.

Tse, John Kwock-Ping (1986) "Standardization of Chinese in Taiwan," *International Journal of the Sociology of Language* 59:25-32, recounts the history of the National Language Movement, sponsored by the KMT to promote Beijinghua. An earlier version, Robert B. Kaplan and John Tse, "The language situation in Taiwan" was published in *The Incorporated Linguist* 22:82-85.

Tseng Wen-Shing (1973) "Psychiatric study of shamanism in Taiwan," *Archives of General Psychiatry* 26:561-565, states that "a person with the ability to dissociate can be trained to utilize this talent as a shaman [*dang-gi*]. Becoming a shaman always fulfills the individual's psychological needs and solves his own personal problems such as feelings of insecurity, inferiority, etc. From the sociopsychological point of view, a successful shaman always gratifies a client's need for an 'explanation' of the misfortune he meets and to be given 'advice' on what he should do in order to cope with such a disaster" (p. 561). Two case studies are included, one male, one female.

Tseng, Wen-Shing (1975) "Traditional and modern psychiatric care in Taiwan," pp. 177-194 in A. Kleinman et al., *Medicine in Chinese Cultures* (Washington, DC: U. S. Government Printing Office), discusses the psychiatric benefits of three folk counseling practices: divination by bamboo sticks (*tiu-chiam*), fortune-telling (*sang-mia*) and examining physiognomy (*kuan-siung*). All emphasize compliance, harmonization and regulation with a strong concern for the family of the person afflicted. T interprets shamanism and divination as dealing with supernatural power, physiognomy and fortune-telling with interpreting natural causes of illness, albeit with healers' understanding of the sociopsychological situation of the ill.

Tseng Wen-Shing (1976) "Folk psychotherapy in Taiwan," pp. 168-178 in W. Lebra, *Culture-bound Syndromes, Ethnopsychiatry and Alternative Therapies* (Honolulu: University of Hawaii Press), discusses somatization of psychological problems, and the ways Taiwanese shamans, fortune-tellers and physiognomists communicate in (culturally and psychologically) acceptable terms to provide relief for "people who are used to following and being dependent on autocratic authority [and] are easily frustrated when the therapist does not take an active guiding role" (p. 176).

Tseng Wen-Shing and Jin Hsu (1969) "Chinese culture, personality formation and mental illness," *International Journal of Social Psychiatry* 16:5-14, contrasts symptoms presented by psychiatric patients in Boston and Daiba, with somatization of depressive affect and gender conflict in Daiba, and problems with homosexuality and alcohol in Boston.

Tsuah Siung-Hui (1989) *Ong-Ya and Mazho of Taiwan.* (Daiba: Dai Guan) (in Chinese), provides an accessible introduction to the Taiweanese history of two of the most important deities Taiwanese worship. Also see Ng (1989).

Tsurumi, E. Patricia (1977) *Japanese Colonial Education in Taiwan, 1895-1945* (Cambridge: Harvard University Press), provides an account of the mass primary education program of Japanese colonialism, a significant basis for increased agricultural productivity and later production of non-agricultural production for foreign markets.

Tyson, James (1987) "Christians and the Taiwanese Independence Movement," *Asian Affairs* 14:163-170, discusses the traditional Christian missionary support for the KMT (dating back to its mainland days) and the more recent support of Taiwanese demands for independence of increasingly Taiwanesized denominations (notably Presbyterians).

Tzern Ji-Ming (1986) "The new trend in religious worship as seen from biographical travels, memoirs," *Bulletin of the Institute of Ethnology, Academia Sinica* 61:105-128 (in Chinese), reviews travelogs written in didactic styles published by local temples, contending that the genre facilitates the rapid diffusion of religious novelties across Taiwan. T focuses on conjuring and cultural restoration.

Unschuld, Paul U. (1973) *Die Praxis des tradtionallen chinesichen Heilsystems - dargetellt unter Einschluß der Pharmazie an der heutigen Situation auf Taiwan.* (Wiesbaden: F. Steiner Verlag), summarized in "The social organization and ecology of medical practice in Taiwan," pp. 300-316 in C. Leslie, *Asian Medical Systems* (Berkeley: University of California Press, 1976), outlines the policy of Japanese and Nationalist occupations: the Japanese gave an "examination" in 1897 which all practitioners passed and then no further exams; the KMT permitted many mainlanders to practice "traditional Chinese medicine" who had not practiced on the mainland and were self-educated. On the basis of a survey of 250 Daiba university students and 60 workers and peasants in an unnamed rural southern area, U reported that 64% of those in the countryside and only 31% of the Daiba university students sought Western medicine first. U expressed dismay at the tendency and the unsystematic application of Western drugs by pharmacists.

Van den Berg, M. E. (1986) "Language planning and language use in Taiwan: social identity, language accommodation and language choice behavior," *International Journal of the Sociology of Language* 59:97-115, reports observation of conversations between customers and salespersons and find that the allocation of languages is not agreed-upon. Bilingual customers behaved differently in different shops.

Vander Meer, Canute (1971) "Water thievery in a rice irrigation system in Taiwan," *Annals of the Association of American Geographers* 61:156-179, reports on farmers' need to steal, awareness of opportunities to steal, and willingness to steal water from the Nan-Hung canal near Puli in Lamdao Guan. The number and distribution of thefts and conflicts are influenced by the volume of water supply, water rights customs, water control methods, the location of houses and of fields, and by the size of the irrigation system.

Wang Shih-Ching (1972) "A history of popular beliefs in villages settled by peoples from different native places," *T'ai-wan wen-hsein* 23:1-38 (in Chinese), and (1976) "History of Ha-Shan," *T'ai-wan wen-hsein* 37:49-131 (in Chinese), are based on 1969-70 fieldwork in Chiuna (Daiba Guan) and archival research. "From the time of settlement through the late Qing, the growth of a self-conscious community with clearly-defined segments have given rise to Chi'an Kung as a ritual center and the appearance of T'u Ti Gong temples as the symbolic focus of villages and neighborhoods. This process involved amalgamation of people belonging to competing ethnic groups.... Shortly after the turn of the century, place of residence became the primary criterion for defining membership in religious organizations. *Shen-ming-hui [bio]* organized by lineage or with reference to ethnicity either disappeared or were transformed into community organization" (p. 92).

Wang Shih-Ching (1974) "Religious organization in the history of a Chinese town," pp. 71-92 in A. Wolf, *Religion and Ritual in Chinese Society* (Stanford University Press), provides a historical account of ethnic differentiation of religion in Qing times. Place of residence (rather than of ancestral origin in mainland China) became central in the Japanese era. "*Shen-ming-hui [bio]* organized by lineage or with reference to ethnicity either disappeared or were transformed into community organization" (p. 92). They are continuing to expand from a purely local base.

Wang Sung-Hsing (1967) *Kwei-Shan [Guiswan] Tao: A Study of a Chinese Fishing Community in Formosa, Academia Sinica Institute of Ethnology Monograph* 13, describes family divisions where seasonal changes in the composition of fishing teams precludes large families working together as units. Sons set up separate households as soon as they marry, but still take equal shares in the father's estate and take equal part in worshipping their ancestors.

Wang Sung-Hsing (1974) "Taiwanese architecture and the supernatural," pp. 183-192 in A. Wolf, *Religion and Ritual in Chinese Society* (Stanford University Press), describes the architecture of houses in temples in Jianghua over time.

Wang Sung-Hsing (1976) "Ancestors proper and peripheral," pp. 365-372 in W. Newell, *Ancestors* (The Hague: Mouton), argues that worship of peripheral (mostly matrilineal) ancestors is not evidence of the principal of patrilinearity breaking down. Rather, this keeps a family line from ending. Han organization in the Choshui and Tatu river valleys were based on common place of origin (*tsu-chi [zho ziak in* Holo]). Lineage development occurred only in the mid-19th century after irrigation made rice-growing feasible, and while ethnic feuding was raging (thus, ethnic consciousness facilitates rather than inhibits the formation of lineage organization).

Wang Sung-Hsing (1977) "Family structure and economic development in Taiwan," *Bulletin of the Institute of Ethnology, Academia Sinica* 44:1-11, discusses increased job mobility, leverage on capital, management of industrial enterprise in relationship to traditional and changing family structure on Taiwan.

Wang Sung-Hsing (1985) "On the household and family in Chinese society," pp. 50-58 in J. Hsieh & Y. Chuang, *The Chinese Family and Its Ritual Behavior* (Nankang:Academia Sinica). Although there were only nuclear family households on Guswan island between 1950-58, villagers viewed the lineage (*ga-tszo* as an enduring unit, even if households (*bang*) split residence and meals.

Wang Sung-Hsing and Raymond Apthorpe (1974) *Rice Farming in Taiwan: Three Village Studies* (Nankang: Academia Sinica), contends that unbalanced sex ratios and high geographic mobility led early settlers to develop social organization based on propinquity, and reinforced local deities and temples instead of lineage organizations. W&A discuss one village in which villagers have long been wage laborers as well as villagers who supplement agricultural production with off-farm work.

Watson, James L. (1976) "Anthropological analyses of Chinese religion," *China Quarterly* 66:355-364, reviews Arthur Wolf's (1974) book *Religion and Ritual in Chinese Society*, most of the fieldwork for which was done on Taiwan. W follows De Glopper, Smith and Wolf (within the volume, against Maurice Freedman) in questioning whether there it is meaningful to speak of a single "Chinese religion," given the extreme heterogeneity of local-level religious traditions even within a small region. "Freedman's model does not allow for the possibility that the members of certain ethnic groups actively seek to create a separate religious tradition in order to distinguish themselves from others" (p. 360).

Watt, John R. (1985) "Medical ethnography in Taiwan: a review of English-language studies," *American Asian Review* 3:32-79, focuses on the ethnography of illness conceptions (what Kleinman calls native explanatory models), rather than on studies of practitioners.

Wei, Henry Yi-Min, and Suzanne Countanceau (1976) *Wine for the Gods: An Account of the Religious Traditions and Beliefs in Taiwan* (Daiba: Cheng-Wen), provides an overview of folk religion, in particular festivals, dream interpretation, taboos, omens, and divination methods.

Weinstein, Maxine, Te-Hsiung Sun, Ming-Chen Chang, and Ronald Freedman (1989) "Household composition, extended kinship, and reproduction in Taiwan: 1965-1985," *Population Studies* 44:217-239, reports an increase in the percentage of Taiwanese couples living in nuclear households from 43% in 1973 to 56% in 1985. Little decline (from 42% to 38%) was observed in stem households, joint households became rarer still (from 15% to 6%). Among couples with at least one living parent, 35% lived in nuclear households in 1973, 43% in 1980, and 51% in 1985.

Weller, Robert P. (1981) "Affines, ambiguity and meaning in Hokkien kin terms," *Ethnology* 20: 15-29. Based on 1976 fieldwork in Kiu Kiong Kiou, W notes that formal, respectful terms of address are employed in public interaction and/or when the referent has authority over the speaker (e.g., males, elders, and wife-givers). *Simbua*, having been raised in the family, use formal terms less than wives who marry into the family at later ages.

Weller, Robert P. (1982) "Sectarian religion and political action in China," *Modern China* 8:463-483. Analyzing contemporary Taiwanese sects (*gaumung*, especially those emphasizing spirit writing, and Buddhist vegetarian halls: *chai-tng*), W argues that sectarian ideologies can—but do not necessarily—provide an alternative worldview conflicting with official values.

Due to the inherent flexibility of religious beliefs, sectarian ideology is open to alternative, even rebellious interpretations, yet people sometimes also interpret it in politically conservative ways. W demonstrates this by examining some of the most striking aspects of Taiwanese sects—the general use of spirit mediums [*dang-gi* throwing *bwai*], the important position of Guan Gong, the worship of a consciously syncretic pantheon, the particular influence of Buddhist cosmology, and the presence of a maternal goddess (the Eternal Venerable Mother, Wusieng Laomu). Although many symbols are shared with orthodox folk, Buddhist, Daoist, and folk-religious traditions, these are given variant interpretations in sects. Dang-gi "offer greater potential flexibility than drawing lots or other forms of temple divination" (p. 467), and regime after regime has sought to suppress them, or at least to reduce their influence.

Weller, Robert P. (1984) "Social contradiction and symbolic resolution: practical and idealized affines in Taiwan," *Ethnology* 23:249-260, contrasts the usually suppressed but sometimes quite real conflict between affines with dyadic relationships to allies who are accorded idealized fictive kin terms. In places such as Kiu Kiong Kiou, where lineage ties are weak and where people are generally poor, ties through marriage become an important social resource, providing some of the assistance lineage organizations supply elsewhere. Village endogamy increases in such places. W discusses terms of address at funerals and weddings, where exaggerated deference prevails, as well as terms used in everyday interaction.

Weller, Robert P. (1985) "Bandits, beggars and ghosts: the failure of state control over religious interpretations in Taiwan," *American Ethnologist* 12:46-61, analyzes the lack of success of three subsequent régimes to redefine Universal Salvation Religion (Po Do) as supporting their rule, and the shift over time of local understanding in Samgia(p). "The move from dangerous political ghosts to pitiful kinship ghosts occurred because the marginal group in the population underwent a parallel change. The uprooted workers of the last century have become the abandoned old of today. A change in the political economy of Taiwan has changed the daily experiences that inspire specific interpretations of the Universal Salvation.... As long as the interpretation of ghosts is tied to real experiences of marginality, supported by a symbolic structure of contrasts with gods and ancestors, it cannot be countered by a new set of ideas [fostered by successive governments] that contradicts both the social and symbolic understandings of marginality" (pp. 59, 58). Indeed, interest and investment in popular religion in Taiwan has increased, especially supported by Taiwanese whose increasing prosperity has not been accompanied by participation in or influence on the mainlander-controlled government.

Weller, Robert P. (1987a) *Unities and Diversities in Chinese Religion* (Seattle: University of Washington Press). Based on 1977-9 fieldwork, W analyzes attempts of successive regimes to suppress the ghost-feeding Universal Salvation festival (Po Do), specifically the Co Su Kong temple in Samgia(p). The most recent (KMT) rationalization for suppression of these enactments of a collective ethnic consciousness—which had made generations of outside authorities uneasy—has been frugality, so it has been the expense which has been criticized overtly, rather than disorder or latent opposition to the régime. W documents mocking compliance to this goal, too (p. 141), as well as adapting politically acceptable interpretations of ghosts. Who is manipulating the beliefs of whom is a very complex question in this history: "Pragmatic and ideologized interpretations characterize everyone, and are constantly developing into and out of each other" (p. 10). The documentation of diverse styles of interpretation of popular rites by participants (as well as by external observers) means that "the popular tradition is not automatically an oppositional ideology, yet it also need not simply reinforce the structure of power. The very fact that a popular tradition is not institutionalized, which inhibits the development of oppositional ideologies, also inhibits state control of popular culture, as the state's vain attempts to manipulate the Universal Salvation festival illustrate" (p. 171).

Weller, Robert P. (1987b) "The politics of ritual disguise: repression and response in Taiwanese popular religion," *Modern China* 13:17-39, shows that the politics of ritual may outweigh symbolic structures of beliefs with accounts of rationales offered successive Japanese and KMT rulers for Universal Salvation (Po Do) rituals. W contends that the predominant motivation for performing the changing ritual was as a covert challenge to the governments' legitimacy and an assertion of local control over some part of life, although he also stresses variation in interpretation of the meaning of the parts of the ritual.

Wen Chi-Pang (1974) "Health in the midst of economic development in Taiwan," *Medical Care* 12:85-94, contrasts a number of economic, nutritional and demographic statistics (1950-70). Health expenditures, physician and hospital bed per capita were lower in Taiwan than in Japan (or the USA). W concludes that health care was not a serious concern in the economic development of Taiwan, either as a means to enhanced productivity or as an end, such as enhancing the quality of life.

Wen Chung-I (1975) "Groups and power structure in an urban community: a study of social change in Wanhua," *Bulletin of the Institute of Ethnology, Academia Sinica* 39:19-56 (in Chinese), analyzes the power structure of a Daiba precinct as it changed from a coalition during Qing times, to a pyramid under Japanese rule and early KMT rule. Two major factions developed in the late 1960s.

Wen Chung-I (1976) "Social relations and power structure in Yen Village," *Bulletin of the Institute of Ethnology, Academia Sinica* 42:41-71 (in Chinese). The status of local political leaders, e.g., *twen-diu* and *hiang-min-dai-biao*, decline as soon as they leave the political scene in an amorphous community power structure in this northern Taiwan village. Shifting of leaders did not alter the structure. W claims that "the impact of industrialization did not seem to create any anxiety and conflict. The behavioral pattern appeared to be well adapted to the industrializing community-life in a transitional society" (p. 71).

Wen Chung-I (1978) "Power elites in the changing society: a comparative analysis of four communities in Taiwan," *Bulletin of the Institute of Ethnology, Academia Sinica* 46:1-30 (in Chinese), examines the role of the economy in a commercial community, the role of kinship in an industrializing community, the role of politics in an agricultural community, and the role of religion in fishing and agricultural communities along the Do-Hn River basin in northern Taiwan, concluding that the power elites have played important innovative roles in the changing societies under the impact of industrialization.

Wen Chung-I, Chuang Ying-Chang, Chen Hsiang-Shui, and Su Yei-Fei (1980) "Farmers' traditional behavior and joint-farming operation in Taiwan," *Bulletin of the Institute of Ethnology, Academia Sinica* 49:1-114 (in Chinese). Based on interviews with 464 people in four rural communities, the authors regard the success of joint-farming operations as depending on achievement motivation, particularly that of a leader making disproportionate commitments of time or resources. Although stressing that "the behavior of farmers has a modern aspect as well as a traditional one" (p. 113), they see a strong effect of traditional lineage organizations on joint-farming behavior. See the same authors' (1975) *Social Change in Hsi-He. Academia Sinica Monograph* 6 .

bolic structure of contrasts with gods and ancestors, it cannot be countered by a new set of ideas [fostered by successive governments] that contradicts both the social and symbolic understandings of marginality" (pp. 59, 58). Indeed, interest and investment in popular religion in Taiwan has increased, especially supported by Taiwanese whose increasing prosperity has not been accompanied by participation in or influence on the mainlander-controlled government.

Weller, Robert P. (1987a) *Unities and Diversities in Chinese Religion* (Seattle: University of Washington Press). Based on 1977-9 fieldwork, W analyzes attempts of successive regimes to suppress the ghost-feeding Universal Salvation festival (Po Do), specifically the Co Su Kong temple in Samgia(p). The most recent (KMT) rationalization for suppression of these enactments of a collective ethnic consciousness— which had made generations of outside authorities uneasy—has been frugality, so it has been the expense which has been criticized overtly, rather than disorder or latent opposition to the régime. W documents mocking compliance to this goal, too (p. 141), as well as adapting politically acceptable interpretations of ghosts. Who is manipulating the beliefs of whom is a very complex question in this history: "Pragmatic and ideologized interpretations characterize everyone, and are constantly developing into and out of each other" (p. 10). The documentation of diverse styles of interpretation of popular rites by participants (as well as by external observers) means that "the popular tradition is not automatically an oppositional ideology, yet it also need not simply reinforce the structure of power. The very fact that a popular tradition is not institutionalized, which inhibits the development of oppositional ideologies, also inhibits state control of popular culture, as the state's vain attempts to manipulate the Universal Salvation festival illustrate" (p. 171).

Weller, Robert P. (1987b) "The politics of ritual disguise: repression and response in Taiwanese popular religion," *Modern China* 13:17-39, shows that the politics of ritual may outweigh symbolic structures of beliefs with accounts of rationales offered successive Japanese and KMT rulers for Universal Salvation (Po Do) rituals. W contends that the predominant motivation for performing the changing ritual was as a covert challenge to the governments' legitimacy and an assertion of local control over some part of life, although he also stresses variation in interpretation of the meaning of the parts of the ritual.

Wen Chi-Pang (1974) "Health in the midst of economic development in Taiwan," *Medical Care* 12:85-94, contrasts a number of economic, nutritional and demographic statistics (1950-70). Health expenditures, physician and hospital bed per capita were lower in Taiwan than in Japan (or the USA). W concludes that health care was not a serious concern in the economic development of Taiwan, either as a means to enhanced productivity or as an end, such as enhancing the quality of life.

Wen Chung-I (1975) "Groups and power structure in an urban community: a study of social change in Wanhua," *Bulletin of the Institute of Ethnology, Academia Sinica* 39:19-56 (in Chinese), analyzes the power structure of a Daiba precinct as it changed from a coalition during Qing times, to a pyramid under Japanese rule and early KMT rule. Two major factions developed in the late 1960s.

Wen Chung-I (1976) "Social relations and power structure in Yen Village," *Bulletin of the Institute of Ethnology, Academia Sinica* 42:41-71 (in Chinese). The status of local political leaders, e.g., *twen-diu* and *hiang-min-dai-biao*, decline as soon as they leave the political scene in an amorphous community power structure in this northern Taiwan village. Shifting of leaders did not alter the structure. W claims that "the impact of industrialization did not seem to create any anxiety and conflict. The behavioral pattern appeared to be well adapted to the industrializing community-life in a transitional society" (p. 71).

Wen Chung-I (1978) "Power elites in the changing society: a comparative analysis of four communities in Taiwan," *Bulletin of the Institute of Ethnology, Academia Sinica* 46:1-30 (in Chinese), examines the role of the economy in a commercial community, the role of kinship in an industrializing community, the role of politics in an agricultural community, and the role of religion in fishing and agricultural communities along the Do-Hn River basin in northern Taiwan, concluding that the power elites have played important innovative roles in the changing societies under the impact of industrialization.

Wen Chung-I, Chuang Ying-Chang, Chen Hsiang-Shui, and Su Yei-Fei (1980) "Farmers' traditional behavior and joint-farming operation in Taiwan," *Bulletin of the Institute of Ethnology, Academia Sinica* 49:1-114 (in Chinese). Based on interviews with 464 people in four rural communities, the authors regard the success of joint-farming operations as depending on achievement motivation, particularly that of a leader making disproportionate commitments of time or resources. Although stressing that "the behavior of farmers has a modern aspect as well as a traditional one" (p. 113), they see a strong effect of traditional lineage organizations on joint-farming behavior. See the same authors' (1975) *Social Change in Hsi-He. Academia Sinica Monograph* 6 .

Wen Jung-Kwang (1978) "Sexual attitudes of college students," *Green Apricot* 46:106-107 (in Chinese). In a survey of 147 male and 96 female students, 14% of the males and 1% of the females reported having had pleasurable homosexual experiences; 26% of the males and 21% of the females having had homosexual inclinations. A clinical sample was reported by Wen and C-C Chen "Male homosexuals in Taiwan: a clinical study of 35 cases," *Journal of the Formosan Medical Association* 79 (1980):1046-1056.

Wen Jung-Kwang (1990) "The Hall of Dragon metamorphoses: a unique, indigenous asylum for chronic mental patients in Taiwan," *Culture, Medicine and Psychiatry* 14:1-19, describes the rise of a Buddhist-tinged home for the chronically mentally ill, called Lung Hwa Tang (LHT) in rural Gohyiong. Contrasting schizophrenics in a nursing home and in an urban psychiatric hospital, W found the residents of LHT to be lower-functioning than those in the other two settings. In contrasting relatives' reports of seeking treatments, it appears that LHT was a last resort. 99% of the 112 schizophrenics had passed through psychiatric facilities, and, of the three clinical populations, they were also the most likely to have been taken to a shaman (81%). W relates the failure to continue a regimen of anti-psychotic drugs to the cost of drug treatment and the lack of public financing. Also see reports in the *Bulletin of the Chinese Society of Neurology and Psychiatry* 11,2 (1985):15-50.

Wickenberg, Edgar B. (1970) "Late nineteenth century land tenure in Northern Taiwan," pp. 78-92 in L. Gordon, *Taiwan and Its Place in Chinese History* (New York: Columbia University Press), uses 1898-1903 Japanese statistics for three northern *guans* to argue that land holdings on Taiwan were larger than in rice-growing areas of southeastern China, but that tenancy rates were equivalent. W's analysis is extended in "Continuities in land tenure, 1900-1940," pp. 212-238 in E. Ahern and H. Gates, *The Anthropology of Taiwanese Society* (Stanford University Press, 1981).

Wickenberg, Edgar (1975) "The Taiwan peasant movement, 1923-1932: Chinese rural radicalism under Japanese development programs" *Pacific Affairs* 48:558-582, contrasts tenant violence in Kwangtung under nominal KMT rule and the strikes, demonstrations and court actions against landlords in Japanese-controlled Hsindi(t) during the 1920s. Both were areas of high tenancy and high population pressure exposed to modern influences without being able to benefit from them. Land tenure is an aspect of the society the Japanese largely left alone. The difference in expression of the conflict between tenants and landlords in the two "Chinese societies" was due to the differing strengths of police control, according to W.

Wilkerson, James (1982) "A review and critique of western interpretations of Chinese folk religion in Taiwan," pp. 68-85 in *Proceedings of the Tunghai University Symposium on Folk Society and Religion* (published by the Provincial Government of Taiwan), criticizes focus on the relationship between religion and society and the conflation of analysts' and participants' interpretations of rituals and associations. "Western scholarship," according to W, has made "discoveries about folk religion in Taiwan whose [sic.] significance it is not equipped to judge" (p. 82).

Williams, Jack F. (1980) "Sugar: the sweetener in Taiwan's development," pp. 219-255 in R. Knapp, *China's Island Frontier: Studies in the Historical Geography of Taiwan* (Honolulu: University of Hawaii Press), shows the northward extension of sugar cultivation between 1913 and 1939, and subsequent shrinking back. "The Taiwan Sugar Corporation was at the forefront of agricultural mechanization, expansion of chemical fertilizer production and consumption, land reclamation, groundwater development, and promotion of cooperative farming" (p. 248), not all of which are universally regarded as beneficial in the long term.

Williams, Jack F. (1988) "Urban and regional planning in Taiwan: the quest for balanced regional development," *Tijdschrift voor economische en sociale geografie* 79:175-181, reviews attempts to plan economic development across all of Taiwan so that everyone with ambitions would not move to Daiba. Although other cities also grew, Daiba grew faster, and its suburbs fastest of all. Rural industrialization slowed rural-urban migration, but also spread pollution everywhere in Taiwan. Although regional disparities and domination by a single megapolis are considerably less in Taiwan than in other countries undergoing industrialization, and despite conscious effort to ensure regional equity in infrastructural development, there is nonetheless a concentration of medical and educational facilities in the environs of Daiba, and indicators of greater consumption there.

Williams, Jack F. (1989) "Paying the price of economic development in Taiwan: environmental degradation," *Journal of Oriental Studies* 27:58-78, suggests that the pollution in Taiwan in the late 1980s parallels that of Japan in the early 1960s, reviews various kinds of pollution (including noise and eyesores), the growth of an environmental movement (especially mobilized against building more nuclear power plants) and the development of environmental protection standards.

Wilson, Richard W. (1970) *Learning to be Chinese: The Political Socialization of Children in Taiwan* (Cambridge, MA: MIT Press), focuses on how respect for authority and loyalty to one's group are inculcated in three Daiba area schools. Observations were supplemented by survey results, although W admitted to being afraid to ask questions about Chiang Kai-Shek. Although recognizing Taiwanese alienation, he argued that hostility to mainlanders' domination was waning, and that Taiwanese support for the KMT government was increasing, at least in Daiba (p. 125).

Winckler, Edwin A. (1981a) "National, regional, and local politics," pp. 13-37 in E. Ahern and H. Gates, *The Anthropology of Taiwanese Society* (Stanford University Press), describes the long-running ideology of exogenous political elites that "the masses should defer to its broader political vision (the cadre ethnic) and that democracy should yield results convergent with technocratic analysis (the expert ethic)" (p. 23), noting that even "the substitution of Taiwanese for mainlander cadres in a Leninist party and authoritarian government—a substitution that has not gone very far or very fast in any case—is not necessarily equivalent to the concession of power to popular sovereignty" (p. 21). Some appearance of democracy was necessary to maintain U.S. aid to "Free China," so elections restricted in scope (both of issues that could be aired and of level of office) and frequency occurred. Local festivals, reinforcing community solidarity against outside rulers, and local temples have prospered, while officials have been isolated from reality both by KMT ideology and not "lowering [themselves] to personal involvement with trivial facts and tedious tasks" (Rosenhow 1973:167).

Winckler, Edwin A. (1981b) "Roles linking state and society," pp. 50-86 in E. Ahern and H. Gates, *The Anthropology of Taiwanese Society* (Stanford University Press), notes continued reliance on bureaucracy and patron-client networks characteristic of Chinese politics for millennia alongside pressure for direct exercise of popular sovereignty (from the ideology of democracy used to maintain support from the KMT's own patron, the USA—despite the reluctance of the patron to demand more than the appearances of elections). "Totalitarian control is seldom so effective that publics are unable to form opinions, politicians unable to contend, and manager unable to intervene," (p. 86) and "local politics in Taiwan offers comparative political sociology a fascinating case of an authoritarian regime sailing as close to the winds of democracy as it

dares, with no intention, however, of changing its course in any fundamental way... continu[ing] to maintain the balance between open competition and covert control that they have sustained with increasing sub-
tlety" (p. 85).

Winckler, Edwin A. (1984) "Institutionalism and participation in Taiwan: from hard to soft authoritarianism?" *China Quarterly* 99:481-499,
suggests that the Kuomintang of the mid-1980s is akin to the longtime
ruling party (PRI) in México, headed in the direction of that of Japan's
Liberal Democrats. W predicts, "Taiwan's political leadership will continue to substitute soft sell for hard measures at appropriately the rate
that new political strategies are necessary to achieve the old political
outcome—Nationalist [i.e., KMT] dominance" (p. 499).

Winckler, Edwin A. (1987) "Statism and familism on Taiwan," pp.
173-206 in G. Lodge & E. Vogel, *Ideology and National Competitive-
ness: An Analysis of Nine Countries* (Cambridge, MA: Harvard
Business School Press), provides a capsule sketch of political and
economic development on Taiwan, arguing that ideologies have little
constrained either a nationalist state that lost its nation and imposed
itself on another society (the KMT in China and then Taiwan) or family
businesses agressively competing for market edges with casual views
about accounting, research and laws (international or local)

Winckler, Edwin A. (1988a) "Mass political incorporation, 1500-
2000," pp. 41-66 in E. Winckler & S. Greenhalg, *Contending
Approaches to the Political Economy of Taiwan* (Armonk, NY: M. E.
Sharpe), reviews political restraints enforced by Dutch, Chinese, and
Japanese peripheral elites and discounts voting as measuring real politi-
cal participation (pp. 44-45).

Winckler, Edwin A. (1988b) "Elite political struggle, 1945-1985," pp.
151-171 in E. Winckler & S. Greenhalg, *Contending Approaches to the
Political Economy of Taiwan* (Armonk, NY: M. E. Sharpe), reviews
the rise to power of Chiang Ching-Kuo through military intelligence
and an increasingly indigenized "mass" party and by carefully-timed
charges of corruption against rivals. The Shanghai capitalists who fled
the mainland were dependent on the Chiangs, and Taiwanese businessmen were kept in their "place" (out of political power) by repression of
political activity, so that the KMT state has had exceptional autonomy
on Taiwan.

Winckler, Edwin A., and Susan Greenhalg (1988) *Contending*

Approaches to the Political Economy of Taiwan (Armonk, NY: M. E. Sharpe). Operating within a world system view in which Taiwan has risen to the "semiperiphery," the editors and contributors stress the inadequacy of conservative, liberal, and radical theories of development. In the postwar history of Taiwan, a politically/militarily dependent state built a niche as an economic intermediary between the core of a world system dominated by the USA, and the periphery of "the Third World," as within the Japanese-dominated region before World War II. Lacking natural resources, state capitalism developed and mobilized human resources in both instances. In the editor's contributions in particular, micro-organizations and jockeying for control of state and market share are stressed. In their view focus on micro-level processes, politics is brought back into "political economy" in danger of becoming exclusively economic.

Wolf, Arthur P. (1966) "Childhood association, sexual attraction and the incest taboo: a Chinese case," *American Anthropologist* 68:883-898. Based on fieldwork in a village near Hsulin in the Daiba basin, W argues that the early association of being raised together with a *simbua* (little bride) depresses sexual attraction when the son grows up. This aversion may explain the psychology of the incest taboo. Also see "Childhood association and sexual attraction: a further test of the Westermarck hypothesis," *American Anthropologist* 72(1970):503-515; "Marriage and adoption in northern Taiwan," pp. 128-60 in R. Smith, *Social Organization and the Application of Anthropology* (Ithaca: Cornell University Press); "Childhood association, sexual attraction and fertility in Taiwan," 227-244 in E. Zubrow, *Demographic Anthropology* (Albuquerque: University of New Mexico Press, 1976); Wolf & Huang (1980).

Wolf, Arthur P. (1968) "Adopt a daughter-in-law, marry a sister: A Chinese solution to the problem of the incest taboo," *American Anthropologist* 70:864-874. Although adopting a future daughter-in-law reduces discord between bride and mother-in-law (which is very disruptive of extended family households), a cost of this arrangement is that the future groom sees a sister rather than a wife. Sexual aversion for quasi-incest is not the best way to manufacture sons (another family goal that W argues conflicts with the goal of cross-generational concord). Also see Chen Chi-Yen (1957) "The foster daughter-in-law system in Formosa." *American Journal of Comparative Law* 6:302-314.

Wolf, Arthur P. (1970) "Chinese kinship and mourning dress," pp. 189-207 in M. Freedman, *Family and Kinship in Chinese Society* (Stanford University Press), contrasts categories of mourning dress to kinship terms used to address kinsmen in Samgia(p). "Address terms reflect daily patterns of authority; mourning dress reflects rights in property." In particular, "Anyone who comes to a funeral wearing the mourning dress of a son is understood as claiming a share of the estate" (p. 205). W emphasizes that claims are made by using certain forms (including mourning garb), not automatic, obvious, nor predictable in advance. W found considerable dissensus in the native view of what is appropriate mourning wear for daughters, and suggests that this dissensus reflects the structural contradiction of the daughter role in "Chinese society."

Wolf, Arthur P. (1974) "Gods, ghosts, and ancestors," pp. 131-182 in A. Wolf, *Religion and Ritual in Chinese Society* (Stanford University Press), discusses intra-cultural variation from Samgia(p) and Ch'i-Chou-Li within the standard trichotomy of supernatural entities. In regards to ghosts (*gui*), W notes that some are hungry and angry because they are homeless (not worshipped by any descendants), while others are hungry and homeless because they are angry.

Wolf, Arthur P. (1975) "The women of Hai-shan: a demographic portrait," pp. 88-110 in M. Wolf & R. Withe, *Women in Chinese Culture* (Stanford University Press), provides longitudinal data on adoption that is more fully presented in Wolf & Huang (1980).

Wolf, Arthur P. (1976) "Aspects of ancestor worship in Northern Taiwan," pp. 339-364 in W. Newell, *Ancestors* (The Hague: Mouton), illustrates variance in ownership of ancestral tablets and in tolerance of segmentation of the lineage in five Samgia(p) lineages. W distinguishes three types of ancestral altars: domestic altars, communal altars, and lineage shrines. Although recognizing some scope for individual choices of ancestors to worship, W challenges Ahern's (1973) contention that only inheritance creates an obligation, contending that "both descent and inheritance create an absolute obligation to the dead.... Men are obligated to worship their parents, regardless of where they take their descent" (p. 361).

Wolf, Arthur P. (1981) "Domestic organization," pp. 341-360 in E. Ahern and H. Gates, *The Anthropology of Taiwanese Society* (Stanford University Press), reviews the history of discourse about the "Chinese family" on the basis of evidence from Taiwan (especially the normatively un-Chinese frequency of *simbua* arrangements). On the basis of fertility rates of 6.51 for stem families in contrast to 6.58 for joint families in Hai-shan, W concludes that his wife was right (Maurice Freedman and Myron Cohen wrong) that conflict between wives and their mothers-in-law rather than conflict between brothers is the psychodynamic of dividing families (*huen ge hue*), and that the lower tension is exemplified by the higher fertility of elementary (nuclear) families, 7.83. W also asserts that, despite the major regional and ethnic differences observed on Taiwan (including four times the rate of *simbua* in northern in contrast to southern Taiwan, and consequent differences in fertility), and great flexibility in the application of the basic norms/rules, "the Chinese family is the same everywhere, all that varies are the conditions that make large families more or less advantageous" (p. 343), particularly whether cooperation of agnates will be mutually beneficial.

Wolf, Arthur P. (1985a) "The study of Chinese society on Taiwan," pp. 3-16 in J. Hsieh & Y. Chuang, *The Chinese Family and Its Ritual Behavior* (Nankang: Academia Sinica), aims to synthesize the papers in the volume into the Freedman paradigm of Chinese clans and lineages (defended from challenges of Fried (1970) and Wu (1985)). W stresses that common property is one kind, not a necessary criterion of corporate activity, although lineages generally emerge when corporate estates are established. He suggests a number of changes in terminology of family relations, proposes some factors to consider in analyzing changing women's status, and warns that intra-cultural diversity is so great that data from one place or time may differ from otherss.

Wolf, Arthur P. (1985b) "Chinese family size: a myth revitalized," pp. 30-49 in in J. Hsieh & Y. Chuang, *The Chinese Family and Its Ritual Behavior* (Nankang: Academia Sinica). Based on Japanese household registries of Taiwan, W concludes that "Chinese farm families were potentially large everywhere and actually large wherever material conditions were somewhat better than miserable" (p. 49, e.g., under Japanese rule). In 1935 the mean family size in the villages from which W extracted data ranged from 6.3 to 9.7 persons. According to W, "In 1906 the area under study was as typical of rural China as any other area of comparable size" (p. 36).

Wolf, Arthur P. and Huang Chieh-Shang (1980) *Marriage and Adoption in China* (Stanford University Press), discuss uxorilocal and minor marriages as chronicles in Japanese household registries from Hai-shan, Chulin, and Chung-she. W continues to marshall data on fertility of *simbua* marriages (24-30% lower than uxorilocal marriages) to support the Westermarck explanation that intimate and prolonged childhood association destroys sexual attraction, and to document considerable deviance in practice from the "Chinese [Confucian] norm" mandating major marriages in Taiwan. W notes that minor marriage and uxorilocal marriages were unknown for all practical purposes in northern China and defends the title "because we believe our argument has implication for the study of Chinese domestic organization generally, not because we believe Haishan is representative of China" (pp. ix-x). Age of adoption is an important variable both in accounting for fertility and for childhood mortality See the critique by Chun (1990).

Wolf, Diane L. (1990) "Daughters, decisions and domination: an empirical and conceptual critique of household strategies," *Development and Change* 21:43-74, Using data she gathered on Java and comparing it to what was reported by Lydia Kung and others about young women factory workers in the 1970s, W questions the tendency to attribute everything that occurs in developing economies to "household strategies." In neither place did "the household" make the decisions: the Javanese women she interviewed chose factory work, often against parental wishes; Taiwanese fathers chose to contract daughters' labor. The critique of ignoring intra-household conflict about kinds of work and control over earnings and overestimating collective economic calculations retains its force even if the contrast between Javanese and Taiwanese women is overdrawn and/or obsolete.

Wolf, Margery (1968) *The House of Lim* (London: Prentice-Hall), provides a well-known account of one Taiwanese peasant extended family over the course of three generations with constant generalizations about "Chinese" customs and beliefs. Includes cases of prostitution, adoption-minor marriage, and the division of the family (*huen ge hue*). Although the existence of a joint family permitted economic diversification, the success of the Lim family led to suspicions between the side of the family engaged in business and the side continuing to work the land. "They were too proud to divide, and the tension was too great for them to continue as they were" (p. 145). They eventually split—after the alien observers had left. W discusses her fieldwork in "Chinanotes: engendering anthropology," pp. 343-355 in Roger Sanjek (ed.), *Fieldnotes* (Ithaca, NY: Cornell University Press, 1990).

Wolf, Margery (1970) "Child family and the Chinese family," pp. 37-62 in M. Freedman, *Family and Kinship in Chinese Society* (Stanford University Press), and pp. 221-46 in A. Wolf, *Studies in Chinese Society* (Stanford University Press, 1978), discusses the importance of mothers' views of their husband in explaining the relationships between fathers and their children: "The wife who does not despise her husband is not likely to raise her children to treat him as an outsider in his own family; the husband who does not reveal an unusual attachment to his wife is not likely to motivate his mother to an anxious competition with the younger woman for the loyalty of his children" (1970: 61). Noting the indulgence of younger brothers required by older brothers in their youth, W also argues that the failure of anticipatory socialization in subordination of younger brothers makes adult relationships between brothers fragile, bluntly stating, "Had the younger brother been trained from infancy to submit to the elder, the Chinese joint family might be less of a myth" (p. 61). Not very systematically-deployed data derive from Peihotien, and are generalized to "Chinese society."

Wolf, Margery (1972) *Women and the Family in Rural Taiwan* (Stanford University Press). This account of a typical life-cycle of Chinese women in a multi-surnamed Hokkien village, enlivens the demographic analyses of her (then-) husband's work on patterns of adoption and marriage. W stresses the importance of informal neighborhood groupings of (unrelated) women and dwells extensively on prostitution, especially by adopted daughters, and on rivalry between women. In particular, W stresses the rivalry between daughters-in-law and mothers-in-law as leading to the breakup of larger family units into nuclear family households (although Wolf (1970) emphasized the fragility of fraternal relationships pre-existing sister-in-law rivalry as a centripetal force). The book was characterized as an "afterthought to fieldwork" by Norma Diamond (reviewing it in the *American Anthropologist* 77(1975): 111), who also criticized the underestimation of the extent to which women's work outside the house is important to them and to the economic well-being of their families, and complained that "there is little feel for how adult women view themselves and their lives, how they interact with the males in their lives, and how completely they accept the male evaluation of them as economically useless, ritually polluting, and of less importance" (p. 112).

Wolf, Margery (1975) "Women and suicide in China," pp. 111-141 in M. Wolf & R. Withe, *Women in Chinese Culture* (Stanford University Press), contrasts the higher rates of female suicide in Dailam to those in Hsindi(t), attributing differences to the higher status and more recognized economic role of women in the latter. Selya (1985) reports Dailam rates lowering to Hsindi(t) rates in the subsequent decade.

Wolf, Margery (1990) "The woman who didn't become a shaman," *American Ethnologist* 17:419-430, discusses a village woman who in 1960 began to move and speak like a *dang-gi* and villagers' decision that she was not one, but, instead was crazy, "because of her marginal status in the community and male ideology." This article along with two other tellings of the same misinterpretation of what occurred (and of the supposed obliteration of women's names) was published in 1992 by Stanford University Press in *A Thrice-Told Tale: Feminism, Postmodernism and Ethnographic Responsibility.*

Wong, Chun-Kit J. (1981) *The Changing Chinese Family Pattern in Taiwan.* (Daiba: Southern Materials Center), reports a national survey of 1140 households. 54% of Hakka households, 51% of Holo, and 82% of mainlander were nuclear. For stem families the ethnic rates were 24, 31, 14; and for extended 22, 18, 4. W suggests greater filial piety among Holo people to explain their greater frequency of stem families; male migration to explain the greater frequency of mainlander nuclear families; and "the Hakkas who are a minority tend to have more extended families. The extended family is an outgrowth of necessity. A minority group has more group identity and is more united than a majority group. Moreover, many Hakkas are in townships and in the rural area" (p. 234), and therefore require more agricultural labor. Mainlanders were six times as likely to have completed college, and half as likely to be unskilled laborers. 25% of Hakka respondents, 14% of Holo and 46% of mainlanders reported no religion (70, 70, and 34 percent, respectively, identified themselves as Buddhist; 6,10,0 Taoist; 2,4,16 Christian). Figure 7 (on p. 269) provides a path model of various attitudinal and demographic characteristics correlated to family type. Parent's family-type is the best predictor of son's actual family type. Ethnicity ("provincial origin") has strong direct and indirect (via religious affiliation) effects on family type. Socioeconomic status has a weak effect, and "modernity" and intermediate one.

Wu, David Y. H. (1985) "The conditions for development and decline of Chinese lineages and the formation of ethnic groups," in J. Hsieh & Y. Chuang, *The Chinese Family and Its Ritual Behavior* (Nankang:Academia Sinica). Using historical data from Taiwan and data on Chinese emigrés to elsewhere, W rejects common residence or possession of corporate property as necessary to the development of lineages, and challenges claims about the effects of national and local government on their development. The conditions for the foundation of lineages in Taiwan and of a distinct ethnic group in other places of emigration are quite similar, in particular an ideology of common descent (noting that "the further back in time Chinese genealogies are pushed, the greater the possibility that connections have been fabricated" so that "individuals can form consanguinal groups on the basis of fabricated relationships (pp. 206-7)) and common identity seeking increase the status, economic and political influence of an "us" (relative to a "them").

Wu Yuan-Li (1977) *Income Distribution in the Process of Economic Growth of the Republic of China* (College Park: University of Maryland School of Law), examines data on the distribution of money income in Kuomintang-ruled Taiwan.

Yager, Joseph (1988) *Transforming Agriculture in Taiwan* (Ithaca, NY: Cornell University Press), estimates that the outflow of capital from agriculture was 14.2% in 1951-5 and 8.6% in 1956-60, accounting in the respective periods for 74.8% and 39.7% of total capital accumulation on Taiwan.

Yang, Chung-Fang (1988) "Famialism and development: an examination of the role of family in contemporary China Mainland, Hong Kong, and Taiwan," pp. 93-123 in D. Sinha & H. Kao, *Social Values and Development: Asian Perspectives* (London: Sage), reviews surveys of values in three Chinese states, concluding that changes of cultural ideals about families are changing far more slowly than family structures, i.e., that the "Chinese family" is an adaptable institution. In regard to filial piety, Y suggests that rather than this value explaining behavior, it is the lifelong devotion of parents towards their offspring that produces the sentiment. Nonetheless, in all three locales, parents (and, even more, grandparents) have lost significant control over family economic decision-making and the selection of their children's marriage partners.

Yang, Martin M. C. (1962) "Changes in family life in rural Taiwan," *Journal of the China Society* 2:68-79, interprets widespread "modernization" of marriage with rural marriages being mostly arranged by the young people, with 65% of rural respondents (from 350 families) preferring smaller families, with wives' ties to their natal family being maintained more than in the past, and with "more democratic treatment" of wives in some semblance to egalitarian, companionate marriage. Changes in the size, structure, power distribution, internal relations, occupation, income, food consumption, clothing, housing condition, and education of rural families were all reported in Y's surveys.

Yang, Martin M. C. (1963) "Land reform and community development in Taiwan," *Journal of the China Society* 3:65-75, contends that "land reform in Taiwan was of the democratic type.... Landlords, tenants, and all of those who had any interest in the program were educated to understand and appreciate the economic and social significance involved.... [Education] had the effect of changing people's attitudes toward the economic and social securities in owning farm land and toward the traditional privileges unjustifiably enjoyed by many of the landlords. It had the effect of instilling in people an aspiration to build an equitable agrarian structure and of developing a more prosperous agricultural economy" (p. 70) and that "the change of their agrarian status from one of a tenant or a farm laborer to that of an owner-operator has encouraged them to give more support to community construction, acquire more interest in sending children to school.... [and] more concerned with environmental sanitation and public health facilities in their villages" (p. 74). No data on understandings or aspirations or involvement in local organizations are reported in this article, still less any evidence linking land reform to the asserted changes in public spirit and community involvement.

Yang, Martin M. C. (1963) "Problems resulting from developments in rural Taiwan," *Journal of the China Society* 7:18-30. After declaring that "both in principle and in practice [Taiwan's] land reform is fair and democratic for every party concerned" (p. 20) and that "there is no question that the political system in Taiwan is democratic" (p. 28), Y notes that many ex-landlords failed to prosper, and that farmholdings were so small and fragmented that they could not support a family. Y deplores the disruption of folk religions, traditional practices and established ethics, the anarchical traffic on rural and urban roads, "evil-minded people quick to take advantage of [judicial] softness" (p. 29), and the difficulties the Taiwan Sugar Corporation faced when farmers saw that "both new crops and the expansion of old crops yield greater returns than does sugarcane" (pp. 24-5).

Yang, Martin M. C. (1970) *Socio-economic Results of Land Reform in Taiwan* (Honolulu: East-West Center Press), reports the results of a 1964 survey by 30 interviewers of 1250 ex-tenant farmers, 250 current tenant farmers, 250 ex-landlords, and 100 non-farmers from five regions. Those who were still tenant farmers after land reforms provide a control group. Equivalent rates of adopting various "modern" characteristics (e.g., using Western physicians, or fertilizer, or taking an interest in community affairs, including voting) by tenant farmers and by former tenant farmers suggest that land reform was not an important cause of other changes viewed as "modernization," but a concomitant variation. Most ex-tenants considered land reform positively, and so did Yang. Nonetheless, he warned, "The land problem in Taiwan is far from being resolves.... Redistribution of landownership might later become a hindrance to the development of a modernized agriculture.... The smallness of the farms [after land reform] is such a serious deterrent to modernization and mechanization that significant advances can hardly be hope for" (pp. 258-9).

Yeh Ying-Kuin (1959) "Social psychiatry in Taiwan," *Progress in Psychotherapy* 4:306-309, describes the traditional strains of over-protection, -control, and -expectation of eldest sons and of disvalued daughters adopted-out, and also the new strains of intense competition for high school entrance exams. Y also extols the usefulness of traditional family care for psychiatric patients.

Yin, Alexander C. (1981) "Voluntary associations and rural-urban migration," pp. 319-337 in E. Ahern and H. Gates, *The Anthropology of Taiwanese Society* (Stanford University Press), describes the adaptation through regional, religious, and mutual aid associations of migrants from Pai'o islands to Go'hiong. Although migration continues, it is no longer just young, relatively uneducated men, and the Pei'o Regional Association is less important for more recent immigrants, who may also belong to diverse more narrowly-focused voluntary associations.

Yu Guang-Hong (1982) "Development of Taiwanese folk religion: analysis of government-compiled data," *Bulletin of the Institute of Ethnology, Academia Sinica* 53:67-103 (in Chinese). Y ignores any divergence of Taiwanese folk religion from mainland sources prior to 1895. During the Japanese era, he says, "the folk religion developed and was sustained in isolation from external Chinese influences. Instead, pure Buddhist elements were introduced by the Japanese and a unique religious system gradually took form" (p. 102). Increased education and prosperity have not undermined the folk religion. Although the relative importance of plague gods, such as Wang Yeh, has decreased, others have increased in popularity, and many temples have been enlarged and/or enriched.

Yu, Guang-Hong (1986) "No property, no tablet? A reanalysis of Emily Ahern's Ch'inan data," *Bulletin of the Institute of Ethnology, Academia Sinica* 62:115-177 (in Chinese), shows internal contradictions in Ahern (1973), chastising her for treating ancestors as the only supernatural agents and for reducing tablet worship exclusively to ancestor worship, questioning both the reliability and validity of her assertions, especially attributing geomancical efficacy to the ancestor rather than his grave site,

Yuan, D. Y. (1964) "The rural-urban continuum: a case study of Taiwan," *Rural Sociology* 29:247-260, uses data from the 1956 census of Taiwan to show that mainlanders were concentrated in cities of half a million inhabitants or more. 26 percent of the population of Taiwan lived in eleven cities. Y also discusses population density, occupation composition of the population, and proposed that 50,000 be used as the dividing line between rural and urban population centers (in contrast to 25,000 for the US).

Yuan, D. Y. (1968) "Marital characteristics in relation to the rural-urban continuum in Taiwan," *Demography* 5:93-103, contrasts marriage, divorce, widow rates by the size of civil divisions using census data.

Yuan, S. S. (1972) "Family authority patterns, rearing practices and children's sense of political efficacy," *Thought and Word* 10,4:35-55, reports a decline in parental, and especially in grandparental authority, especially in regards to marriage partner selection. This decline was larger in urban than in rural Taiwan.

Zito, A. R. (1987) "City gods, filiality, and hegemony in late imperial China," *Modern China* 13:333-371, recounts the Qing dynasty officials' attempts to reinforce Taiwanese folk beliefs relating the city god to the local magistrate.

American Social Science Ph.D. Dissertations Dealing with Taiwan

Discipline abbreviations:

(Anthro)	Anthropology
(Econ)	Economics
(Geog)	Geography
(Hist)	History
(Pol Sci)	Political Science
(Soc)	Sociology

Ahern, Emily M. (1971) The Cult of the Dead in Ch'inan, Taiwan. Cornell University. (Anthro)

Allee, Mark A. (1987) Law and Local Society in Late Imperial China: Tan-Shui Subprefecture in Hsin-Chu County, Taiwan, 1840-1895. University of Pennsylvania. (Hist)

Anderson, John E. (1974) Areal Variation in Fertility Trends in Taiwan, 1952-1970. University of Michigan. (Soc)

Baity, Philip C. (1974) Religion in a Chinese Town. University of California, Berkeley. (Anthro)

Barnett, William K. (1970) An Ethnographic Description of Saneli Ts'un, Taiwan with Emphasis on Women's Roles: Overcoming Research Problems Caused by the Presence of a Great Tradition. Michigan State University. (Anthro)

Barrett, Richard E. (1978) Differential Fertility in Rural Taiwan, 1905-1940. University of Michigan. (Soc)

Benton, Sylvia N. (1980) An Analysis of the Mosaic Character of a Taiwanese Clan. State University of New York, Stony Brook. (Anthro)

Bracey, Dorothy H. (1967) The Effects of Emigration on a Hakka Village. Harvard University. (Anthro)

Brockman, Rosser H. (1974) Customary Contract Law in Late Traditional Taiwan. Harvard University. (Hist)

Buxbaum, David C. (1968) Some Aspects of Substantive Family Law and Social Change in Rural China, 1896-1967 with a Case Study of a Northern Taiwan Village. University of Washington. (Pol Sci)

Casterline, John B. (1980) The Determinants of Rising Female Age at Marriage: Taiwan, 1905-1976. University of Michigan. (Soc)

Chang, Ching-Ju (1986) A Contextual Analysis of Migration and Occupational Achievement in Kaohsiung, Taiwan: Linkage between Micro- and Macro-Level Data. University of Chicago. (Soc)

Chang, Chung-Wu (1972) A Social Study of Changes in Land Tenure Status in Taiwan: A Study of Kwansi Community. Louisiana State University. (Soc)

Chang, Hsi-Chih (1968) Functional and Structural Analysis of Scientific Farm Information Development and Dissemination in Taiwan. University of Missouri. (Soc)

Chang, Jui-Shan (1990) The Transition to Sexual Experience for Women in Taiwan. University of Michigan. (Soc)

Chang, Ming-Cheng (1978) Migration and Fertility in Taiwan. University of Pennsylvania. (Soc)

Chang, Wen-Lung (1972) A Study of Political Coercion in Urban Taiwan. Northwestern University. (Soc)

Chao, Shou-Po (1972) Comparative Aspects of Conflict of Laws in Domestic Relations. University of Illinois.

Chen, Chaonan Eddie (1980) The Evaluation of Factory Educational Campaign in Taiwan with the Notion of Cognitive Structure. University of Hawaii. (Soc)

Chen, Chi-Nan (1984) Fang and Chia-Tsu: The Chinese Kinship System in Rural Taiwan. Yale University. (Anthro)

Ch'en, Ch'ing-Ch'ih (1973) Japanese Socio-political Control in Taiwan, 1894-1945. Harvard University. (Hist)

Chen, Chung-Min (1975) Ying-Ting: A Cultural-Ecological Study of a Chinese Mixed-Cropping Village in Taiwan. Michigan State University. (Soc)

Chen, Hsiao-Chang (1974) An Analysis of the Field Workers' Performance in Recruiting IUD Acceptors in Taiwan. University of Michigan. (Soc)

Chen, I-To (1968) Japanese Colonialism in Korea and Formosa: A Comparison of its Effects Upon the development of Nationalism. University of Pennsylvania. (Pol Sci)

Chen, Ching-Chih (1967) Japanese Sociopolitical Control in Taiwan, 1895-1945. Harvard University. (Hist)

Cheng, Tun-Jen (1987) Politics of Industrial Transformation. University of California, Berkeley (Pol Sci)

Chiang, Cheng-Hung (1981) Female Labor Force Participation in Sociocultural Perspective: Taiwan as a Case. University of Chicago. (Soc)

Chiu, Hei-Yuan (1979) A Test of Unidimensionality and Universality of Individual Modernity in Ten Taiwanese Communities. Indiana University. (Soc)

Chiu, Ming-Chung (1970) Two Types of Folk Piety: A Comparative Study of Two Folk Religions in Formosa. University of Chicago. (Divinity)

Chou, Lien-Pin (1963) Studies on the Registration of Births and Infant Deaths in Taiwan. Johns Hopkins University. (Public Health)

Chou, Sue-Ching (1991) Attitudes of Female Students of Teachers' Colleges Toward Women's Roles in Taiwan. University of Northern Colorado. (Soc)

Chu, Godwin C. (1964) Culture, Personality and Persuasability. Stanford University. (Anthro)

Chu, Hsien-Jen (1966) An Exploratory Study of Internal Migration in Taiwan. University of Florida. (Soc)

Chu, Solomon S. (1969) Family Structure and Extended Kinship in a Chinese Community [Daidiong]. University of Michigan. (Soc)

Chu, Yun-Han (1985) Authoritarian Regimes under Stress: The Political Economy of Adjustment in the East Asian Newly Industrializing Countries. University of Minnesota.

Cohen, Myron L. (1967) Family Economy and Development in Yen-Liao, Taiwan. Columbia University. (Anthro)

Crissman, Lawrence W. (1973) Town and Country: Central-Place Theory and Chinese Marketing Systems With Particular Reference to Southwestern Changhua Hsien, Taiwan. Stanford University. (Anthro)

Debernardi, Jean E. (1986) Heaven, Earth and Man: A Study of Chinese Spirit Medium. University of Chicago. (Anthro)

DeGlopper, Donald R. (1973) City on the Sands: Social Structure in a Nineteenth Century Chinese City. Cornell University. (Anthro)

Devoe, Pamela A. (1979) The Influence of Social Networks on Rural/Urban Orientation and Life Goals among Taiwanese Young People. University of Arizona. (Oriental Studies)

De Vos, Susan M. (1982) The Economic Old Age Security Value of Children in the Philippines and Taiwan in the Middle 1970's. University of Michigan. (Soc)

Diamond, Norma (1966) K'un Shen: A Taiwanese Fishing Village. Cornell University. (Anthro)

Fang, Jeffrey Ming-Shan (1969) Investment in Human Capital in Taiwan, 1952-1965. University of Washington (Econ.)

Feng, Yen Joyce (1988) Factors Associated with the Utilization Patterns of Prenatal and Postnatal Health Care by Chinese Women in Taiwan. University of Illinois. (Soc)

Feuchtwang, Stephan D. R. (1972) Religion and Society in Northern Taiwan. London School of Economics and Political Science. (Anthro)

Freedman, Deborah S. (1967) The Role of Consumption of Modern Durables in a Developing Economy: The Case of Taiwan. University of Michigan (Econ.)

Fu, Li-Yeh (1991) A Comparative Analysis of the Development of Social Security Systems in Taiwan and Five Industrial Democracies. University of California, Berkeley (Soc)

Gallin, Bernard (1961) Hsin Hsing: A Taiwanese Agricultural Village. Cornell University. (Anthro)

Gates [Rosenhow], Hill (1973) Prosperity Settlement: The Politics of Paipai in Taipei, Taiwan. University of Michigan. (Anthro)

Gold, Thomas B. (1981) Dependent Development on Taiwan. Harvard University. (Soc)

Gould-Martin, Katherine (1976) Women Asking Women: An Ethnography of Health Care in Rural Taiwan. Rutgers University. (Anthro)

Graff, Michael A. (1976) Changing Population Density Gradients in Taipei. Michigan State University. (Soc)

Greenhalg, Susan (1982) Demographic Differentials and the Distribution of Income: The Taiwanese Case. Columbia University. (Anthro)

Hanson, Karen J. (1984) Development and Preventive Health Behaviors: The Case of Taibei, Taiwan. Columbia University. (Anthro)

Harrell, Clyde S. (1974) Belief and Unbelief in a Taiwan Village. Stanford University. (Anthro)

Ho, Yhi-Min (1965) Agricultural Development of Taiwan, 1903-1960. Vanderbilt University. (Econ)

Hsiao, Hsin-Huang Michael (1979) Assessing and Comparing Government Agricultural Strategies in the Third World: The Cases of Taiwan and South Korea. State University of New York at Buffalo. (Soc)

Hsiao, Wey (1987) Changes in Class Structures and Reward Distribution in Postwar Taiwan. Indiana University. (Soc)

Hsieh, James Chiao-Min (1953) Successive Occupance Policies in Taiwan. University of Syracuse (Geog)

Hsieh, Jih-Chang C. (1978) Structure and History of a Chinese Community in Taiwan. Washington University. (Anthro)

Hsieh, Kao-Chiao (1976) Population Growth and Socioeconomic Development: A Case Study of Demographic Transition in Taiwan. Bowling Green University. (Soc)

Hsieh, Sann-Chung (1957) Rice and Sugarcane Competition on Paddy Land in Central Taiwan. University of Michigan. (Geog)

Hsieh, Yeu-Sheng (1985) Occupational Incongruity and Job Dissatisfaction in Taiwan. Pennsylvania State University. (Soc)

Hsieh, You-Wen (1985) Urban Deconcentration in Developing Countries: An Analysis of the Processes of Population Dispersion in Taiwan and South Korea. Rutgers University. (Soc)

Hsiung, Ping-Chun (1991) Class, Gender, and the Satellite Factory System in Taiwan. UCLA. (Soc)

Hsu, Wen-Hsiung (1975) Chinese Colonization of Taiwan. University of Chicago. (Hist)

Hu, Billy Yuh-Lin (1977) The Utilization of Nonprescribed Medication among Modern Industrial Middle-Class Families in Taiwan. University of Missouri. (Soc)

Hu, Tai-Li (1983) My Mother-in-law's Village. City University of New York. (Anthro)

Hu, Yow-Hwey (1986) Family Support Systems and Mortality Patterns: A Comparative Study of Familial Role-related Mortality Risks among Chinese in Taiwanese, Chinese-Americans and White Americans. University of Illinois, Chicago. (Soc)

Huang, Chi (1986) The State and Foreign Capital: A Case Study of Taiwan. Indiana University (Pol Sci)

Huang, Lily Chu (1973) A Cross-cultural Study of Conformity in Americans and Chinese [in Daiba]. University of New Mexico. (Soc)

Huang, Shu-Min (1977) Agricultural Degradation: Changing Community Systems in Rural Taiwan. Michigan State University. (Anthro)

Huang, Sophia Chang (1962) A Comparison of Selected Values among Formosan and American Adolescents. Ohio State University. (Soc)

Huang, Ta-Chou (1971) Rural-Urban Migration in Taiwan. Cornell University. (Soc)

Hung, Chien-Chao (1981) Taiwan under the Cheng Family, 1662-1683: Sinicization after Dutch Rule. Georgetown University. (Hist)

Hwang, Kwang-Kuo (1976) Social Stresses, Coping Styles and Psychopathological Symptom Patterns in a Formosan Urban Community. University of Hawaii.

Jacobs, J. Bruce (1975) Local Politics in Rural Taiwan: A Field Study of Kuan-Hsi, Face, and Faction in Matsu Township. Columbia University. (Pol Sci)

Jain, Anrudh K. (1968) Fecundity Components in Taiwan. University of Michigan. (Soc)

Jang, John Lun (1968) A History of Newspapers in Taiwan. Claremont Graduate School. (Hist)

Jejeebhoy, Shireen Jamsetjee (1979) Factors Affecting Fertility Transition in Taiwan, 1965-1973. University of Pennsylvania. (Soc)

Johnson, Marshall J. (1990) Classification, Markets, and the State: Constructing the Ethnic Division of Labor on Taiwan. University of Chicago. (Soc)

Jordan, David K. (1969) Supernatural Aspects of Family and Village in Rural Southwestern Taiwan. University of Chicago. (Anthro)

Kahane, Joyce D. (1984) The Role of the "Western" Pharmacist in Rural Taiwanese Medical Culture. University of Hawaii. (Anthro)

Karim, Manjur E. (1990) World System and Export Economies: A Compartive Analysis of Cuba and Taiwan. Kansas State University. (Soc)

Kindermann, Charles R. (1969) Perception and Source of Information: Their Effect on Contraceptive Use in Taiwan. University of Michigan. (Soc)

Klein, Robert E. (1978) Household Type and Extended Kinship in Taiwan. University of Michigan. (Soc)

Knapp, Ronald G. (1968) Spatial Aspects of Economic and Social Behavior in Taiwan. University of Pittsburgh. (Geog)

Koo, Helen Ping-Ching (1973) Use of Induced Abortion and Contraception in Taiwan. University of Michigan. (Public Health)

Kung, Lydia (1978) Factory Work, Women, and the Family in Taiwan. Yale University. (Anthro)

Kuo, Liangwen (1991) Capitalist Formation and Social Inequality in Taiwan. UCLA. (Soc)

Lamley, Harry J. (1964) The Taiwan Literati and Early Japanese Rule, 1895-1913. University of Washington. (Hist)

Lancaster, Robert L. (1976) Rural-to-Urban Migrants on Taiwan: Variations in Informal and Formal Groups Based on Ethnic, Marital and Religious Differences. Emory University. (Soc)

Lavely, William R. (1982) Industrialization and Household Structure in Rural Taiwan. University of Michigan. (Soc)

Lee, Chang-Kuei (1965) Major Dimensions of Non-Christian Religious Orientations in Formosa: Cultural Analysis and Interpretation of Attitudes of Non-Christian Students. University of Pittsburgh.

Lee, Fred Chwan-Hong (1983) The Recruitment of Elites in the Republic of China: A Case Study in the Social Utility of Education. University of Oregon.

Lee, Ger-Bei (1987) Values, Traditions and Social Change: A Study of School Textbooks in Taiwan and China. UCLA. (Education)

Lee, Joan (1977) Patterns of Mental Ability in Chinese Children Reared in the United States and in the Republic of China. Columbia University.

Lerman, Arthur J. (1972) Political, Traditional, and Modern Economic Groups and the Taiwan Provincial Assembly. Princeton University. (Pol Sci)

Li, Tseng-Lu J. (1977) A Study of Resident Participation in Community Development Programs in Taiwan. University of California, Berkeley. (Soc)

Li, Wen-Lang (1967) Inter-Prefectural Migration of the Native Population in Taiwan, 1905-1940. University of Pennsylvania. (Soc)

Lin, Chien-Yang (1991) The Analysis of Job-Related Attitudes of Correctional Officers in Taiwan. Sam Houston State University. (Soc)

Lin, Hui-Sheng (1988) The Determinants of the Timing of First Marriage for Women in Taiwan. University of Michigan. (Soc)

Lin, Shang-Fu (1974) The Grammar of Disjunctive Questions in Taiwanese. University of North Carolina.

Lin, Wan-I (1990) Social Welfare Development in Taiwan. University of California, Berkeley. (Soc)

Lin, Yeh-Yun (1991) Implications of management philosophy, organizational climate, and managers' learning for human resource development : a comparative study of American, Japanese, and Taiwanese firms in Taiwan. University of California, San Diego.

Liu, Suoqun (1988) The Age Patterns and Their Stability by Industry and Occupation in Taiwan during 1956-1960. University of Pennsylvania. (Soc)

Lo, Rong-Rong (1972) Marriage Patterns and Modernization in Taiwan. University of Minnesota. (Soc)

Lu, Pau-Ching (1991) Entering and Continuing Labor Force Participation: Taiwanese Women, Marriage, and Work. University of Michigan (Soc)

Lu, Yu-Hsia (1991) Family Organization and Married Women's Work Experience in a Developing Society. University of Michigan. (Soc)

Lummis, John M. III (1988) The Effects of Families and Schools on Academic Performance in Japan, Taiwan, the People's Republic of China, and the United States. University of Michigan. (Soc)

McCreery, John L. (1973) The Symbolism of Popular Taoist Magic. Cornell University. (Anthro)

McDonald, Graeme D. (1979) The Opening of Taiwan to 1860. Harvard University. (Hist)

Mark, Lindy Li (1972) Taiwanese Lineage Enterprises: A Study of Familial Entrepreneurship. University of California, Berkeley. (Anthro)

Marsh, Robert M. (1959) Mandarin and Executive Elite Mobility in Chinese and American Societies. Columbia University. (Soc)

Millman, Sara R. (1982) Breastfeeding in Taiwan: A Study of Change. University of Michigan. (Soc)

Mirzaee, Mohammed (1979) Trends and Determinants of Mortality in Taiwan, 1895-1975. University of Pennsylvania. (Soc)

Mohapatra, Partha S. (1966) The Effect of Age at Marriage and Birth Control Practices on Fertility Differentials in Taiwan. University of Michigan. (Soc)

Montgomery, Robert (1976) Rural-to-Urban Migrants on Taiwan: Variations in Informal and Formal Groups based on Ethnic, Marital and Religious Differences. Emory University. (Soc)

Moser, Michael J. (1981) Mediation and Litigation in Rural Taiwan: An Ethnographic Study of Law and Dispute Settlement in a Modern Chinese Community. Columbia University. (Anthro)

Nutting, Margaret V. G. (1973) The Fate of the Confucian Ideal in "Readings" Textbooks of Taiwan and the China Mainland. Syracuse University. (Anthro)

Olsen, Nancy J. (1971) The Effect of Household Composition on the Child Rearing Practices of Taiwanese Families. Cornell University. (Soc)

Olsen, Stephen M. (1971) Family Occupation and Values in a Chinese Urban Community. Cornell University. (Soc)

Pan, Margaret Tai-Li (1973) The Attitudes of Taiwan Businessmen toward the Entertaining Girls of the City of Taipei. New York University. (Anthro)

Pang, Chien-Kuo (1988) The State and Economic Transformation: The Taiwan Case. Brown University. (Soc)

Parish, William L. Jr. (1970) Kinship and Modernization in Taiwan. Cornell University. (Soc)

Park, Kun-Young. The Political Economy of Rapid Development: Evidence from Taiwan and South Korea. University of Colorado. (Pol Sci)

Pasternak, Burton (1967) Tatieh: A Study of Agnatic Atrophy and Village Integration. Columbia University. (Anthro)

Pillsbury, Barbara L. K. (1973) Cohesion and Cleavage in a Chinese Muslim Minority [in Daiba]. Columbia University.

Ross, Jonathan (1981) Commoditization in a Taiwanese Village. University of Michigan. (Anthro)

Sa, Sophie (1975) Family and Community in Urban Taiwan: Social Status and Demographic Strategy Among Taipei Households, 1885-1935. Harvard University. (Soc)

Sando, Ruth Ann E. (1981) The Meaning of Development for Rural Areas: Depopulation in a Taiwanese Farming Community. University of Hawaii. (Soc)

Sangren, Paul S. (1980) A Chinese Marketing Community: An Historical Ethnography of Ta-Ch'i, Taiwan. Stanford University. (Anthro)

Schack, David C. (1973) From Mang-Hun Ya-Chia to Tzu-Yu Lien-Ai: The Evolution of Dating and Free Courtship in Modern Chinas as Manifested in Taipei, Taiwan. University of California, Berkeley. (Anthro)

Seaman, Gary (1974) Temple Organization in a Chinese Village. Cornell University. (Anthro)

Selya, Robert M. (1971) The Industrialization of Taiwan: A Geographic Analysis. University of Minnesota. (Geog)

Shepherd, John R. (1981) Plains Aborigines and Chinese Settlers on the Taiwan Frontier in the Seventeenth and Eighteenth Centuries. Stanford University. (Anthro)

Shieh, Gwo-Shyong (1990) Manufacturing "Bosses": Subcontracting Networks Under Dependent Capitalism in Taiwan. University of California, Berkeley. (Soc)

Sheu, Jia-You J. (1980) Dependency Development and State Action in Hong Kong, Singapore, South Korea, and Taiwan, 1950 to 1975. Indiana University. (Soc)

Siddiqui, Mohammed K. (1979) The Initiation of Contraception in Taiwan. University of Michigan. (Soc)

Silin, Robert H. (1971) Management in Large-scale Taiwanese Industrial Enterprises. Harvard University. (Anthro)

Simon, Dennis (1980) Taiwan, Technology Transfer and Transnationals: The Political Management of Dependency. University of California, Berkeley.

Speare, Alden Jr. (1969) The Determinants of Rural-Urban Migration in Taiwan. University of Michigan. (Soc)

Speidel, W. (1968) Liu Ming-Ch'uan in Taiwan, 1884-1891. Yale University. (Hist)

Srikantan, Kodaganallur S. (1967) Effects of Neighborhood and Individual Factors on Family Planning in Taichung. University of Michigan. (Soc)

Stites, Richard W. (1982) Small-scale Industry in Yingge, Taiwan. University of Washington. (Anthro)

Sun, Te-Hsiung (1968) Sociostructural Analysis of Fertility Differentials in Taiwan. University of Michigan. (Soc)

Sung, Lung-Sheng (1975) Inheritance and Kinship in North Taiwan. Stanford University. (Anthro)

Tang, Mei-Chun (1973) Life and Family Structure in a Chinese City: Taipei, Taiwan. Columbia University. (Anthro)

Ting, Tin-Yu (1983) The Transition of Family Limitation Practice in Taiwan, 1961-1980. University of Michigan. (Soc)

Tsai, Hong-Chin (1978) The Impact of Internal Migration on Changes in Population Composition in Taiwan: 1969-1975. Brown University. (Soc)

Tsay, Ching-Lung (1980) Employment and Earnings of Cityward Migrants: A Study of Individual Outcomes of Migration to Taipei. Brown University. (Soc)

Tsung, Shiu-Kuen Fan (1978) Moms, Nuns and Hookers: Extrafamiliar Alternatives for Village Women in Taiwan. University of California, San Diego. (Anthro)

Van Alsyune, Arthur J. Jr. (1967) Urban Influence on Rural Communities: A Taiwanese Example. University of Pittsburgh. (Geog)

Van der Meer, Paul (1967) Farm Plot Dispersal: Luliao Village, Taiwan. University of Michigan.

Wang, Jenhwan (1988) Political Movements Against the State: The Transition of Taiwan's Authoritarian Rule. UCLA. (Soc)

Wang, Kuo-Yu (1991) The Initiation of the Welfare Law for the Disabled in Taiwan. Brandeis University. (Social Welfare)

Wang, Peter W. (1983) A Study of Juvenile Delinquency in Taiwan: An Application of Differential Opportunity Theory. Southern Illinois University. (Soc)

Wang, Sung-Hsing (1971) Pooling and Sharing in a Chinese Fishing Village. University of Tokyo. (Anthro)

Wei, Sou-Pen (1981) The Effect of Family Structure on Siblings' Status Achievement: The Case of Taiwan. University of Michigan. (Soc)

Weller, Robert P. (1980) Unity and Diversity in Chinese Religious Ideology. Johns Hopkins University. (Anthro)

Williams, Jack F. (1973) The Conflict Between Peasant and Public Interest in a Developing Country: A Cast Study of the Taiwan Sugar Corporation, 1950-70. (Geog)

Wilson, Richard W. (1967) Childhood Political Socialization on Taiwan. Princeton University. (Pol Sci)

Wolf, Arthur P. (1964) Marriage and Adoption in a Hokkien Village. Cornell University. (Anthro)

Wong, Chun-Kit Joseph (1980) The Changing Chinese Family Pattern in Taiwan. St. John's University. (Soc)

Wu, Ching-Lang (1978) A Study of the Role of Human Resource Development in the Economic Development of Taiwan. University of California, Berkeley. (Soc)

Wu, Jaushieh Joseph (1990) Toward Another Miracle? Impetuses and Obstacles in Taiwan's Democratization. Ohio State University. (Pol Sci)

Wu, Joseph Nin-Yuen (1989) Folk Religion in Taiwan: An Exploratory Study in the District of Wanhua. Pontificia Universitas Gregoriana. (Soc)

Wu, Raymond Raykuo (1989) Re-Interpreting the Taiwan Experience: State Planning and the Emergence of Bureaucratic-Authoritarian Pluralism. University of California, Berkeley. (Pol Sci)

Wyeth, Irving R. (1964) Status-Role Perceptions in the Taiwan Extension Organization. Michigan State University.

Yeh, Chii-Jeng (1973) Structuring Influence of Personal and Relational Attributes on Information Flow in Two Taiwan Villages. University of Missouri. (Soc)

Yen, Chen-Shen (1990) Consequences of Socioeconomic Development in Taiwan, Singapore, and South Korea: Democracy or a Continuation of Authoritarianism? Purdue University. (Pol Sci)

Yen, Han-Wen E. (1977) Knowledge Sources and Felt Needs of Family Life and Sex Education of Selected College Freshmen in Taiwan. University of Tennessee (Education)

Yi, Chin-Chun (1981) Housing Satisfaction among Residents of Taichung, Taiwan. University of Minnesota. (Soc)

Yin, Alexander Chien-Chung (1975) Migration and Voluntary Associations in Rural and Urban Taiwan: A Study of Group Adaptive Strategies in Social Change. University of Hawaii. (Anthro)

Yin, Jeo-chen Teresa (1985) Factors associated with the receipt of prenatal care in a Taiwanese community. UCLA. (Public Health)

Young, Conrad Chun-Shih (1971) The Morphology of Chinese Folk Stories Derived from Shadow Plays of Taiwan. University of California, Los Angeles. (Anthro)

Young, Russell L. (1987) Attitudinal and Sociocultural Factors Influencing Language Maintenance, Language Shift, and Language Usage among the Chinese on Taiwan. Claremont Graduate School.

Yu, Elena (1975) The Significance of Hsiao and Achievement Motivation in Taiwan. Notre Dame University. (Soc)

Yuan, D. Y. (1964) The Rural-Urban Continuum: A Demographic Case Study of Taiwan. Brown University. (Soc)

Yuan, Ju-I (1986) An Exploratory Study for the Purpose of Generating Hypotheses Concerning the Emic Aesthetic Valuing of a Group of Taiwanese Temple Participants Regarding Temple Art. University of Oregon. (Education)

Character List*

Holo term	English gloss [Beijinghua]	Characters
ang-tau-a sai-gong	red-head Daoist priest	紅頭仔師公
bang	wing of family (dwelling compound)[fang]	房
bi(n) lâng	patient [ping-ren]	病人
bio	temple (miao)	廟
bo-de-hi	glove-puppet play	布袋戲
chin-ja	relative	親戚
chong-diu	spirit striking	沖著
dang-gi	medium possessed by spirit (shaman)	童乩
jin-jia	authentic [zhen-zheng]	眞正
diong'i-sien	Chinese-style doctor [zhong'i-shi]	中醫先

* The authors would like to acknowledge the assistance of Andrew Lee in getting the characters to print.

Holo term	English gloss [Beijinghua]	Characters
dng-gut	change the bone (metaphor for male maturation)	轉骨
do su	vernacular Daoist priest	道士
dong hi'ong	fellow villager	同鄉
dong(h)ua	outside the party (1985 election non-KMT candidates) [dangwai]	黨外
dwa hsin zu	bring in a spirit's tablet	帶神主
fu-a	spirit writing	符仔
ga dieng	household	家庭
ga-gi-lang	own people [zijiren]	家己人
ga-tzo	lineage	家族
gau	religion [jiao]	教
gaumung	religious sect [jiaomen]	教門
ge	family (shared patronym) [chia/jia]	家
Guan-(y)im	goddess of mercy [Kuan-in, Kuan-ying]	觀音
gong-tsu	ancestral hall	公厝

Holo term	English gloss [Beijinghua]	Characters
guan	county/prefecture [hsien]	縣
guan-he	relationship and basis for obligation/support [kuanxi]	關係
g(/h)uan-liao wi-g(/h)uan	company representative	原料委員
gui	ghost	鬼
hauw	filial piety [hsiao]	孝
hiang-min dai-biao	district representative	鄉民代表
ho-se	proper	好適
hong sui sai/	geomancer [feng sui shi]	風水師
hong sui sien	geomancer [feng sui shi]	風水先
hsin yiong	reputability [hsinyung]	信用
hua-su	priest	法師
hue	formal association (generic)	會
huen ge hue	divide household (assets) [fen-chia]	分家夥
huen-sin	be in two places at the same time [fen shen]	分身

Holo term	English gloss [Beijinghua]	Characters
jia-e	authentic	正的
ja hue tau	meal rotation [ch'ih hue tou]	吃會頭
jio-zai	uxorilocally resident son-in-law	招婿
khi	vital essence [ch'i]	氣
kio gud sien	professional skeleton handling (prior to reburial)	拾骨先
kua(n) siung	analysis of physiognomy	看相
la sap	unclean substance	拉圾
lao tzat	old thieves	老賊
lieng huen	soul	靈魂
Mazho	goddess [Matsu]	媽祖
o-tau-sai-gong	black-head Daoist priest	黑頭師公
on bao	red envelope containing money	紅包
pua hue pun	breaking the blood bowl ceremony	破血盆
pin gim	dowry	聘金
Po Do	festival, often glossed as Universal Salvation	普渡

Holo term	English gloss [Beijinghua]	Characters
sai-k'ia	woman's property (founded on pin gim) [sufang ch'ien]	私稼
se'i-sien(g)	Western-style doctor [hsi-i-shi]	西醫先
simbua	adopted daughter-in-law	媳婦仔
sin	god [shen]	神
siun(g)-miya	fortune-telling [suau ming]	相命
Tai Di Gong	Great Pig Festival	殺豬公
tiu chiam	divination with bamboo sticks [chou-chien]	抽籤
To De Gong	earth god	土地公
tok	poison [tu]	毒
tsai-dng	Buddhist vegetarian hall [chai-tang]	菜堂
tuan diu	village leader [tzun zhang]	村長
tzo-jo	rite	做醮
tzu-yu loan-ai	individual choice of partners	自由戀愛
xia	demon (KMT view of opponent)	邪

Holo term	English gloss [Beijinghua]	Characters
Zhap-zi Un-ong	Twelve Plague Kings	十二瘟王
zho	lineage [tsu/zu]	祖
zho-sien ga-sun	inherited property	祖先家產
zho ziak	place of origin [tsuchi/zuchi]	祖籍
zho(k)-don(g)	clan organization [tzu-t'ang]	族儻
zio zi(p)	adding a son-in-law to the household	招入
zong-ch'in hue	surname meeting	宗親會
zu-gi ga-sun	property accumulated in lifetime	自己家產

Vowel Note

a is pronounced as the a's are in mama
e is pronounced as the a is in rage
i is pronounced as the ee is in sleet
o is pronounced as the o is in go where terminal in a syllable or word
o is pronounced as the o is in ox where followed by a consonant
u is pronounced as the u is in sue

Topic Index

The publication in **boldface** is a recommended starting place for someone unfamiliar with the literature on the topic relating to Taiwan.

adoption (*simbua*) - A. Wolf 1966, Eberhard 1967, Buxbaum 1968, M. Freedman 1968, M. Freedman 1968, A. Wolf 1968, Rin 1969, M. Wolf 1972, A. Wolf 1975, Cohen 1976a, **A. Wolf & C. Huang 1980**, T. Hu 1984, Sa 1985, Spain 1987, Chun 1990

aging - M-C Chang 1987, Tu et al. 1989

agricultural policy - Yang 1963, Myers & Ching 1964, Hwang 1968, Koo 1968, Yang 1970, C. Chen 1977, 1981, Cheng 1974, B. Gallin 1964, 1966a, Cohen 1976b, Ho 1976, Mao 1976, Ho 1978, Hou 1978, Y. Huang 1978, **Hsiao 1981**, S. Huang 1981, Kuo, Ranis & Fei 1981, Kuo 1983, S. Thompson 1984, Gold 1986, Ka 1988, Li 1988, Simon 1988, Yager 1988, J. Lin 1989, **Bello & Rosenfeld 1990**, Hsiao 1990; also see land reform

alcoholism - Lin 1953, Tseng & Hsu 1969, Harrell 1981a

ancestor worship - B. Gallin 1966a, C-M Chen 1967, Wang 1967, Jordan 1972, **Ahern 1973**, Y. Chang 1973, Y. Chuang 1973, Pasternak 1973, Harrell 1974, A. Wolf 1974, Harrell 1976, Wang 1976, A. Wolf 1976, Harrell 1976, Li 1976, S-H Wang 1976, Ahern 1979a, T. Hu 1979, Jordan 1979, S. Huang 1980, Harrell 1981c, S. Huang 1981, Sung 1981, Harrell 1982, Chu 1985, Y. Li 1985, Pasternak 1985b, Yu 1986, Gates 1987, Sangren 1987b

architecture - Dillingham and Dillingham 1971, S-H Wang 1974, Ahern 1979, Kwan 1980, Knapp 1986, Lin 1987

attitudes - Marsh & O'Hara 1961, O'Hara 1962, Meisner 1963, T'sai 1964, Eberhard 1965b, B. Gallin 1966a,b, O'Hara 1967a,b, B. Gallin 1967, Chu 1968, **Marsh 1968**, Appleton 1970a,b,c, Bennett 1970, Yang 1970, S. Olsen 1972, S-S Yuan 1972, Hchu 1975, Schak 1975, Appleton 1976, Chiu 1976, Thelin 1977, J-K Wen 1978, Diamond 1979, N. Olsen 1979, Lu 1980, Coombs & Sun 1981, McBeath 1986, Crittenden 1987, Lin 1987, Chiu & Tsai 1988, C-F Yang 1988, Cheng & White 1990, McGaghy & Hou 1990 beggars - Schack 1979, 1988

businessmen - Eberhard 1962a, 1964, Meskill 1970a, S. Olsen 1972, DeGlopper 1972, 1974, Silin 1976, Stites 1982, 1985, Numazaki 1986, Gold 1988a,b, Greenhalg 1988, Winckler 1988a,b, T-J Cheng 1989, Tien 1989, Bello & Rosenfeld 1990, Cheng & White 1990

capitalism - See businessmen, class, dependency, entrepreneurship

change - Yang 1962, 1963, Meisner 1963, Ong 1963, C-M Chen 1966, B. Gallin 1966a, C-C Chen 1967, Barrett 1968, Parish 1968, Buxbaum 1968, Appleton 1970c, Yang 1970, Pannell 1971, S-S Yuan 1972, Cheng 1974, Freedman et al. 1974, Lung 1974, Speare 1974a,b, D. Freedman 1975, S-M Huang 1975, Wen 1975, Wen et al. 1975, Wickenberg 1975, Hsu 1976, C-M Chen 1977, Hou 1978, Wen 1978, Chinn 1979, Coombes 1979, Gates 1979, C-M Chen 1980, Coombs & Sun 1981, Harrell 1981b,c, S. Huang, 1981, Barrett & Whyte 1982, Crane 1982, **Gallin & Gallin 1982a,b**, Moser 1982, Kuo 1983, Thornton, Chang & Sun 1984, Chao 1985, Gold 1986, McBeath 1986, Liu 1987, M.J.Cohen 1988, Gold 1988a,b, Greenhalg 1988, Li 1988, Speare, Liu & Tsay 1988, Winckler 1988a,b, Yager 1988, C-F Yang 1988, T-J Cheng 1989, Clark 1989, Faris 1989, J. Lin 1989, Tien 1989, Bello & Rosenfeld 1990, Cheng & White 1990, McGaghy & Hou 1990

Christianity - Tong 1961, Rubinstein 1983, 1988, Tyson 1987

class - Marsh 1968, Gates 1979, 1981, Su 1986, Gates 1987, 1988, T-J Cheng 1989, Bello & Rosenfeld 1990

community - H. Long 1960, B. Gallin 1963, 1966a, T. Ku 1966, Lund 1967, Vander Meer 1967, S-H Wang 1967, G. Chu 1968, B. Gallin 1968, **Diamond 1969**, Gallin & Gallin 1974, S-H Wang & Apthorpe 1974, Wen 1976, C-M Chen 1977, Thelin 1977, Tang 1978, Hsieh 1979 C. Chen 1981, Harrell 1981c, 1982, Hu 1984, M. Lin 1986, Schak 1988

Daoism - Saso 1970a,b, 1972, 1974, Schipper 1974, Baity 1975, Schipper 1977, McCreery 1978, F. Hsu 1985, Schipper 1985, Lagerwey 1987a,b

democracy (incipient) - Winckler 1981a,b, 1984, M.J.Cohen 1988, T-J Cheng 1989, Clark 1989, C. Hsu & P. Chang 1992

demography - Barclay 1954, **Taeuber 1961**, Eberhard 1963, Freedman et al. 1964, Yuan 1964, Buxbaum 1968, Chu 1968, Yuan 1968, Chang 1973, Speare 1974, Taueber 1974, D. Freedman 1975, A. Wolf 1975, Pasternak 1976, Coombs & Freedman 1979, Hu 1980, Wolf & Huang

environmental degradation - M.J.Cohen 1988, Williams 1989, Bello & Rosenfeld 1990

factionalism - **B. Gallin 1966b**, 1968b, Pasternak 1968d, Jacobs 1976, Gallin and Gallin 1977, Pillsbury 1978a, Seaman 1978, Jacobs 1980, Moser 1982, W. Li 1988, Winckler 1988b, Tien 1989, Cheng & White 1990, T-J Cheng 1990

family - C-Y Chen 1950, Kirby 1960, Marsh & O'Hara 1961, O'Hara 1962, Yang 1962, A. Wolf 1966, O'Hara 1967, Y-Y Li 1967, Barrett 1968, Buxbaum 1968, Cohen 1968a,b,c, Freedman 1968, Parish 1968, A. Wolf 1968, **M. Wolf 1968**, Tuan 1968, 1970, C-L Chen 1970, Cohen 1970, Meskill 1970a, Tang 1970, Yang 1970, C-L Chen 1971, Chuang 1972, Diamond 1973, N. Olsen 1973, Tang 1973, Gallin & Gallin 1974, N. Olsen 1974, S-S Yuan 1972, Speare 1974a, N. Olsen 1975, Schack 1975, Chuang 1976, Cohen 1976a, M. Hsu 1976b, N. Olsen 1976, Pasternak 1976, S-H Wang 1976, Chen 1977, S-H Wang 1977, Tang 1978, M. Wolf 1978, Coombs 1979, Diamond 1979, Coombs & Freedman 1979, Hsieh 1979, Hu 1979, N. Olsen 1979, Coombs & Sun 1981, Lu 1980, Wolf & Huang 1980, Sung 1981, Wang 1981, Wong 1981, Gallin & Gallin 1982a,b, Hsieh 1982, Sung 1982, Lu 1983, Hu 1984, Shu 1984, Sangren 1984, Shu & Lin 1984, Thornton, Chang & Sun 1984, Chao 1985, Chu 1985, Chuang 1985, Gallin & Gallin 1985, Hsieh 1985, Li 1985, Pasternak 1985b, Sa 1985, Tang 1985, S-H Wang 1985 , Wu 1985, M-C Chang 1987, Devoe 1987, C. Lin 1987, H. Lin & Tang 1987, Speare, Winckler 1987, Liu & Tsay 1988, C-F Yang 1988, Faris 1989, Pasternak 1989, Schack 1989, Tu et al. 1989, Chun 1990, McGaghy & Hou 1990, D. Wolf 1990; also see kinship

family planning - R. Freedman et al. 1964, Gillesipie 1966, Eberhard 1967, **R. Freedman 1969**, Cernada 1970, D. Freedman et al. 1974, R. Freedman 1975, Coombs & Sun 1978, Sun et al. 1978, 1978, Coombs 1979, Coombs & Sun 1981, Chuang 1985, Li 1988, Huenemann 1990

fertility - see demography, family planning

fieldwork - B. Gallin 1960b, **Diamond 1970, Gallin & Gallin 1974a**, B. Gallin 1975, Y. Huang1983, Wolf & Huang 1985, Gates 1988, M. Wolf 1992

folklore - Eberhard 1963, 1965, 1966, 1970a,b, 1972b, Schak 1972, Lung 1974, Pillsbury 1978b

frontier - Pasternak 1969

land reform (consequences) - C-C Cheng 1961, Yang 1962, 1963, B. Gallin 1963b, Yang 1963, Bessac 1964, B. Gallin 1966a, Bessac 1967, C-C Chen 1967, Pasternak 1968d, Koo 1968, **Yang 1970a**,b, Pasternak 1972, H-H Chen 1978, Kuo, Ranis & Fei 1981, Kuo 1983, Barrett 1988, Simon 1988, Greenhalg 1988, K. Li 1988, Yager 1988, J. Lin 1989, Bello & Rosenfeld 1990

land tenure - B. Gallin 1963c, Koo 1970, Wickenberg 1970, Yang 1970, Wickenberg 1975, H. Chen 1977, **Wickenberg 1981**, Greenhalg 1988, Ka 1988

language - Jordan 1969, Tong 1970, Sugimoto 1971, Bloom 1979, Cheng 1979, Lee 1981, **Cheng 1985a**,b, Kubler 1985, Tse 1986, van den Berg 1986, Cheng 1987, Farris 1988, 1989, 1991

law, martial or customary- C. Chen 1957, T. Lin 1959, B. Gallin 1960b, Kerr 1965, Buxbaum 1966, Gallin 1966,1967, Buxbaum 1968, K. Wang 1968, Peng 1971, Tao 1971, Kaplan 1981, **Moser 1982**, Tang 1985, Kerr 1986

lineage - Okada 1938, B. Gallin 1963c, 1966a, Cohen 1968a, Pasternak 1968b, Diamond 1969, Anderson 1970, Meskill 1970b, Pasternak 1972a, S-C Wang 1972, Ahern 1973, Y-C Chang 1973, **Y-C Chuang 1973**, Pasternak 1973, S-C Wang 1974, Wang & Apthorpe 1974, Ahern 1975, Y-C Chuang 1976, Harrell 1976, A. Wolf 1976, C-M Chen 1977, Y-C Chuang 1977, Hsieh 1979, C-N Chen 1980, W-H Hsu 1980, C-I Wen et al., 1980, Harrell 1981c, Seaman 1981, S-H Wang 1981, Gallin & Gallin 1982, Harrell 1982, Sung 1982, Sangren 1984, Weller 1984, Gallin & Gallin 1985, Y-C Chuang 1985, Pasternak 1985b, A. Wolf 1985a, D. Wu 1985, Y-C Chuang 1987, 1988

mainlanders on Taiwan - Gates 19881, 1988, Schack 1989, Hu 1990

marketplaces - Knapp 1970, **Knapp 1971**, Pannell 1971, Crissman 1972, De Glopper 1972, Crissman 1976a,b, De Glopper 1980, Crissman 1981, Sangren 1985

mediation - B. Gallin 1960b, 1966, 1967

medical - T. Lin 1953, Yeh 1959, Rin 1966, Lessa 1968, Lin et al. 1969, Rin 1969, Tseng & Hsu 1969, Tseng 1973, Unschuld 1973, Holbrook 1974, Wen 1974, Ahern 1975a,b, Gale 1975, B. Gallin 1975, Gould-Martin 1975, Holbrook 1975, Kleinman 1975, Tseng 1975, 1976, J. Hsu 1976, Unschuld 1976, De Glopper 1977, Holbrook 1977, Kleinman 1977a,b, Gould-Martin 1978, Pillsbury 1978b, Liu 1979, McCreery 1979, **Kleinman 1980, Kleinman & Gale 1982**, Koo 1982, Hansen 1984, Yu 1986, Katz 1990 migration - Lin et al. 1969, Speare 1971, Wu 1971, R. Hsieh 1972, Speare 1972, 1974, Gallin & Gallin 1974a,b, Speare 1974a,b, Taeuber 1974, Diamond 1975b, Thornton, Chang & Sun 1984, Taeuber 1977, Yin 1978, Knapp 1980, Yin 1981, Y-C Chuang 1987, Hwang 1988, **Speare, Liu & Tsay 1988**

networks - B. Gallin 1968a, Marsh 1968, Gallin & Gallin 1974a,b,c, Wen 1975, Silin 1976, Wen 1978, Yin 1981, Greenhalg 1984, Lin & Shu 1984, Numazaki 1986, Greenhalg 1988, Speare, Liu & Tsay 1988, Schack 1989

opera - see theater

physiognomy divination - Lessa 1968, Tseng 1975, 1976

placenames - Lin 1937, Chen 1960, Hsieh 1980

play - see recreation, theater

politics - B. Gallin 1960b, Mei 1963, Meisner 1963, Ong 1963, Kerr 1965, Fried 1966, B. Gallin 1966a,1968b, Y. Long 1969, Mendel 1970, Yang 1970, Peng 1971, E. Chen 1972, S-S Yuan 1972, Kerr 1974, M. Huang 1976, Jacobs 1976, Gallin & Gallin 1977, Lerman 1977, 1978, Jacobs 1979, S. Huang 1980, Gates 1981, C. Chen 1981, Winckler 1981a,b, Barrett & Whyte 1982, Crane 1982, Jacobs 1982, Winckler 1984, Gregor & Chang 1985, Kerr 1985, Gold 1986, Liu 1987, Myers 1987, Winckler 1987, Barrett 1988, S. Chan 1988, **M. J. Cohen 1988**, Gold 1988a,b, Greenhalg 1988, L. Li 1988, W. Li 1988, Simon 1988, **Winckler 1988a,b**, T-J Cheng 1989, Clark 1989, J. Lin 1989, Tien 1989, Williams 1989, Bello & Rosenfeld 1990, Cheng & White 1990, Chou, Clark & Clark 1990, Hsiao 1990, C. Hsu & P. Chang 1992

pollution - Williams 1989, Bello and Rosenfeld 1990

prostitution - M. Wolf 1968, 1972, McGaghy & Hou 1990

recreation - T. Lin 1959, Schak 1972, Winckler 1984, Wen 1985

religion - Okada 1938, Tong 1961, Thelin & Li 1963, Thompson 1964, Saso 1965, B. Gallin 1966a, Schipper 1966, O'Hara 1968, Chu 1969, Diamond 1969, T. Huang 1969, Hwang 1969, L. Thompson 1969, Saso 1970a,b, Yang 1970, Jordan 1972, Saso 1972, Ahern 1973, Y. Chang 1973, Chuang 1973, C. Hsu 1973, See 1973, Feuchtwang 1974a,b,c, Harrell 1974, Saso 1974, Schipper 1974, S. Wang 1974a,b, A. Wolf 1974, Baity 1975, Gould-Martin 1975, Aijmer 1976, Harrell 1976, M. Hsu 1976a, Hung 1976, Li 1976, Watson 1976, Wei & Coutanceau 1976, A. Wolf 1976, S. Wang 1976, Watson

1976, Harrell 1977, Keupers 1977, Schipper 1977, Feuchtwang 1977, Thelin 1977, McCreery 1978, Seaman 1978, A. Wolf 1978, Bauer 1979, DeGlopper 1979, Harrell 1979, Liu 1979, McCreery 1979, Kagan 1980, Ahern 1981a,b, Seaman 1981, Jordan 1982a,b, Kagan 1982, L. Thompson 1982, Weller 1982, Wilkerson 1982, Yu 1982, Sangren 1983, Chu 1985, F. Hsu 1985, Li 1985, Schipper 1985, Seiwert 1985, Weller 1985, Jochim 1986, Jordan & Overmyer 1986, Tzern 1986, Yu 1986, Gates 1987, Lagerwey 1987, M. Lin 1987, Sangren 1987, Tsueh 1989, Tyson 1987, **Weller 1987a,b,** Zito 1987, Ng 1988, Rubinstein 1988, Sangren 1988, Lin 1989, Jochim 1990, Katz 1990, Rubinstein 1990, Feuchtwang & Wang 1991, Feuchtwang 1992, Sangren 1993

representation (in American discourse) - Ahern & Gates 1981, Murray & Hong 1988, Hong & Murray 1989, Murray & Hong 1991

resistance - E. Chen 1972, Kerr 1974, Wickenberg 1975, Bello & Rosenfeld 1990, Hsiao 1990

shamanism - Y. Li 1968, Jordan 1972, Tseng 1973, 1975, 1976, Y. Li 1976a,b, Suzuki 1976, Ahern 1979b, Kleinman 1980, Kagan 1980, 1982, Weller 1982, K. Chang 1986, M. Wolf 1990

social insurance - Ko 1969

social science (development in Taiwan) - Lung 1968, Chang 1983, A. Wolf 1978

socialization - Scofield 1960, Appleton 1970a,b,c, Wilson 1970, N. Olsen 1971, S. Olsen 1972, Schak 1972, S-S Yuan 1972, Appleton 1976, Thornton, Chang & Sun 1984, N. Olsen 1976, Tsurumi 1977, M-C Li 1985, McBeath 1986, Spain 1987, Meyer 1988, C-F Yang 1988, Farris 1989, W. Li 1989, Farris 1991

sociology (discipline in Taiwan) Lung 1968, Maykovich 1982, Chang 1983

sojourner (mainlanders moving on to North America from Taiwan) - H-S Chen 1992

state - see politics

stratification - T. Lin 1959, Eberhard 1962b, 1964, S. Chen 1965, Chu 1968, Marsh 1968, Appleton 1970c, T. Huang 1970, Meskill 1970a, Mueller 1977, Thelin 1977, Y. Wu 1977, **Gates 1979,** Meskill 1979, Gates 1981, Barrett and Whyte 1982, Greenhalg 1985a,b, Gates 1987, Winckler 1987, Chiu & Tsai 1988, Greenhalg 1988, T-J Cheng 1989, Bello & Rosenfeld 1990, Cheng & White 1990

women - Freedman 1968, M. Wolf 1968,1972, Diamond 1973, Ahern 1974, 1975c, Diamond 1975, Rin 1975, M. Wolf 1975, Cohen 1976a, Kung 1976, Diamond 1977, Mueller 1977, Ahern 1978, Pillsbury 1978b, Coombs & Freedman 1979, Diamond 1979, Gates 1979, Arrigo 1980, DeVoe 1981, Kung 1981, S. Chang 1983, Sangren 1983, Kung 1983, 1984, Arrigo 1984, R. Gallin 1984a,b, Thornton, Chang & Sun 1984, Arrigo 1985, Greenhalg 1985b, M-C Li 1985, Selya 1985, Tang 1985, **R. Gallin 1986**, Gates 1987, 1988, Farris 1988, Ku 1988, Speare, Liu & Tsay 1988, Farris 1989, Ku 1989, Schack 1989, Bello & Rosenfeld 1990, Chou, Clark & Clark 1990, McGaghy & Hou 1990, D. Wolf 1990, M. Wolf 1990

work - Diamond 1969, Tsai 1969, Yang 1970, DeGlopper 1972, Kung 1976, 1978, Hou 1978, DeGlopper 1979, Diamond 1979, Arrigo 1980, Kung 1981, Gallin & Gallin 1982a, Harrell 1982, **Kung 1983**, Lu 1983, R. Gallin 1984, Kung 1984, Arrigo 1984, Thornton, Chang & Sun 1984, Arrigo 1985, M. J. Cohen 1988, Gates 1988, Speare, Liu & Tsay 1988, Bello & Rosenfeld 1990, McGaghy & Hou 1990, D. Wolf 1990, Redding 1990

work ethic - Gallin 1966a, Yang 1970, S. Olsen 1972, Harrell 1985, 1987, Gates 1988, Winckler & Greenhalg 1988, D. Wolf 1990